**Kamala Elizabeth Nayar** was born in Montreal, Quebec of parents of South Asian and American origin. She is Chair, Asian Studies at Kwantlen Polytechnic University, British Columbia, and author of, among other books, *The Sikh Diaspora in Vancouver* and *Hayagriva in South India*.

**Jaswinder Singh Sandhu** is a psychotherapist and clinical counsellor in British Columbia. He specializes in mental health.

# Guru Nānak's
# *Discourse to the Nāth Yogis*

KAMALA ELIZABETH NAYAR
and
JASWINDER SINGH SANDHU

SPEAKING
TIGER

SPEAKING TIGER BOOKS LLP
125-A, Ground Floor, Shahpur Jat
New Delhi – 110049

First published by State University of New York Press, Albany
This edition first published in India by Speaking Tiger Books, 2023



ISBN: 978-93-5447-568-9
eISBN: 978-93-5447-569-6

10 9 8 7 6 5 4 3 2 1

Printed at Chaman Enterprises, New Delhi

*For our daughters,*
*Shardha and Sangeeta*

# Contents

## PART 4: *SIDDH GOṢṬ*

# Illustrations

FIGURES



TABLES

# Preface

The world religions of India are continuous in their belief in the cycle of birth, death, and rebirth (*saṃsāra*). The more ancient religious traditions (Hinduism, Buddhism, and Jainism) emphasize renunciation from mundane existence as the valid means to achieve release from *saṃsāra*. Unlike the earlier traditions of India, Sikhism—the youngest world religion born out of Indian soil—holds a strong position against renunciation of the world as a means to liberation. Along with its rejection of world renunciation, Sikhism embraces the spiritual path while "living-in-this-world," which is most effectively described in the eminent Sikh philosophical text called *Siddh Goṣṭ*.

*Siddh Goṣṭ, Discourse to the Nāth Yogis,* is a discourse between Guru Nānak and the Nāth yogis associated with the Himalayan region of the Indian subcontinent. In this dialogue, Guru Nānak—both the first human Sikh guru and the revered founder of Sikhism—expounds his religious worldview and elaborates the spiritual path toward liberation. Guru Nānak teaches his life approach to the Nāth yogis, who had contrarily been pursuing a rigorous path of mental and physical discipline as renunciates from the material world. In sum, *Siddh Goṣṭ* is a religious text meant to inculcate a certain set of religious and ethical values along with a specific perception of the world and an understanding of how one should live in the world. While *Siddh Goṣṭ* is regarded as one of the fundamental philosophical texts composed by Guru Nānak, the stories about Guru Nānak's encounters with the Nāth yogis are also very much cherished and celebrated in the Sikh tradition.

Along with an original English translation of the text, this work provides an analysis of *Siddh Goṣṭ*. First, the work provides an original conceptual framework for a sharper understanding of the *Siddh Goṣṭ* message regarding world renunciation in the light of the various perspectives on the matter found among the major religions of India. Second, it examines the context of *Siddh Goṣṭ* in order to come to a more accurate understanding and interpretation of the text. Third, it highlights the main theological and ethical teachings expounded in *Siddh Goṣṭ*. Fourth, the analysis uniquely demonstrates how the Sikh scriptural teachings are actually put into practice. Last, it demonstrates the Nāth yogic presence in Sikh religious literature. Unlike the importance given to the role of Indian Bhakti (devotion) and Islamic Sufism, the "impact" of the Nāth yogic tradition on the development of Sikhism is rarely touched on. More broadly, the introductory analysis seeks to contribute to a greater understanding of the evolution of the Sikh philosophical system.

*Siddh Goṣṭ* is not only a fundamental religious text that outlines the Sikh philosophical system or worldview, but it also makes a very fitting counterpart to the Hindu *Bhagavad Gītā* and Buddhist *Dhammapada* for introductory courses on Indian religions. In fact, this work on *Siddh Goṣṭ* emerged out of necessity in teaching a course on the religions of India. While there are introductory textual sources for Hinduism and Buddhism, there is no suitable single text for Sikhism. More important, given the minimal available literature on Sikh theology, and in contrast to the substantial amount of work on Sikh history, this work should also prove useful to college and undergraduate university students studying Sikhism or Indian religions in general. Moreover, the textual analysis and translation of *Siddh Goṣṭ* should be of interest to the many diasporan Sikhs who find learning about the meaning of their scripture a challenge, given the language barrier and limited resources available on Sikh theology. Last, although this work specifically focuses on the Sikh tradition, it is also relevant for those personally interested in Eastern spirituality, especially the Indian traditions of devotion and yoga.

In the research and writing of this study, I have benefited from the help of many. First and foremost, I would like to acknowledge my coauthor, Jaswinder Singh Sandhu, who collaborated on the translations and aided me with his expertise in Sikh spirituality. I am also thankful to the students enrolled over the years in the Religions of India class that I teach at Kwantlen University College. Many students have given their time and interest to share both their thoughts about learning the main concepts of Sikhism by means of *Siddh Goṣṭ*, and their frustration at reading the available colonial-style English translation of the text. The class discussions have been an inspiration to me in terms both of undertaking and conceptualizing the project. I would also like to express my sincere appreciation to Roger Elmes, former Dean of Arts at KUC, for taking a genuine interest in my research endeavors.

My coauthor, Jaswinder Singh Sandhu, would like to thank Harvinder Singh for his ongoing support and encouragement. Thanks are also owed to the British Columbia Foundation for the Study of Sikhism, especially Gurhimat Singh Gill, who went out of his way to provide materials that would have been otherwise difficult to obtain. State University of New York Press editors Nancy Ellegate, Diane Ganeles, and Anne Valentine provided excellent support.

I would also like to express my deepest gratitude to various friends who have enriched my life in one way or another, including Linda Friedland, Harjeet Grewal, Yogesh Kyal, Kalwarn (Michael) Mann, Tazim Mawji, Ryan Minihan, Susan Motyka, and last, Aditya Bery, who tragically died over the Irish Sea on the way to Mumbai 27 January 1985.

I am thankful to my parents who have read this study and offered many useful comments and suggestions. I am also indebted to my husband who is a continuing source of support, especially in terms of helping me balance both my family life and academic career. Finally, I would like to express all my love for my two daughters, Shardha and Sangeeta, who have both opened a door to a whole new realm of life experience.

Although indebted to many, we alone bear the responsibility for the final analysis.

# Note on Translation

This study includes terms drawn from Sanskrit, Pali, Hindi, and Punjabi sources. In order to be clear and consistent in the transliteration of the foreign concepts, we have provided it in the predominant language of the specific subject matter for each of the six chapters: In chapters 1 and 2, the standard transliteration of Sanskrit (*devanāgarī* script) is used for all italicized words. However, rather than use the Sanskrit term *Nātha* in chapters 1 and 2, we consider it appropriate to use the Punjabi term *Nāth* throughout the manuscript in order to be consistent with the title of the work. Moreover, in the brief discussion on Buddhism in chapter 1, the Pali forms are also given in parentheses. In the remaining chapters (3 to 6), the standard transliteration of Punjabi (*gurmukhī* script) is used for all italicized words. However, in the latter four chapters, the transliteration of the Sanskrit form is also occasionally provided in parentheses in order to demonstrate the continuity of many Sikh religious concepts with those derived from the pan-Indian Sanskrit tradition. Last, the standard transliteration of Punjabi (*gurmukhī* script) is given for all italicized words in the original English translation of *Siddh Goṣṭ* and other verses taken from the Sikh scripture. Words that have come into use in English are not italicized or given diacritical marks (such as yogi, guru, hath-yoga, and karma).

The original translation of *Siddh Goṣṭ*—along with the additional verses by Guru Nānak used in the analysis—is translated from an archaic or medieval form of Punjabi to the English language. The nontechnical language of this genre of hymns from the *Gurū Granth Sāhib* can be problematic. In order to avoid awkward constructions, in some places we have provided a loose translation, not always following the literal pattern of Punjabi grammar. We have split the verses into small units in order to facilitate readability. Furthermore, although the verses of *Siddh Goṣṭ* have been left in their original order, we have divided the text into sections according to the themes of the verses.

We have also been particularly concerned with capturing the meaning of the verses in English. Previous translations of portions of, or the *Gurū Granth Sāhib* proper, have, for the most part, been based on colonial or Christian templates that have at times changed the connotative meaning of the Sikh teachings. An example of a translation using a Christian template is:

> Thou, my Eternal Lord, hast staged Thy own Play:
> It is through the Guru that one Knoweth.
> Thou Thyself Pervadest all ages, O God, for, without
> Thee there is not another. (*Siddh Goṣṭ* 73)[1]

Whereas, the present translation is as follows:

> The Eternal Sovereign One
> has staged this play,
> and the *gurmukh* understands it.
> Nānak says: You existed,
> throughout the ages,
> and never was there another. (*Siddh Goṣṭ* 73)

In this instance, the use of "Lord" connotes a personal God often associated with the Judeo-Christian tradition, when, in fact, the Sikh image of God or Guru is quite different from the former (as will be discussed in chapters 5 and 6). For that reason, we have been particularly attentive to the specific phraseology and imagery of the Sikh tradition. While the aim of these translations has been to capture the meaning in modern English idiom, we have kept the key Sikh terms in their original form in order to most accurately convey the meaning of the Sikh teachings. These key concepts are explained in both the analysis and the glossary. Finally, the following abbreviations for citations of the scriptural texts of the translated verses are used:

*SG: Siddh Goṣṭ*
*GGS: Gurū Granth Sāhib*

# Part 1

# Introduction

# Chapter One

# The Quest for Liberation in Indian Religions

*Siddh Goṣṭ* is comprised of a discourse between Guru Nānak (1469–1539 CE)—the first of the ten human gurus[1] of the Sikh religion—and a group of Nāth yogis or ascetics (*siddhas*)[2] associated with Śaiva heterodoxy in the northern region of the Indian subcontinent. The *Siddh Goṣṭ* discourse addresses the popular yet contentious issue of whether or not renouncing mundane existence is necessary for the attainment of liberation (*mokṣa*). The question on renunciation as a prerequisite to escape from the cycle of birth, death, and rebirth (*saṃsāra*) is a prominent theme within the four major religions originating in the Indian subcontinent—Hinduism, Buddhism, Jainism, and Sikhism.

There are disparate religious paths toward liberation in the development of Indian religions. Even though the unifying concept among the four Indian religions is *saṃsāra* and liberation is viewed as some form of escape from this cycle, the manner in which it is to be sought is variously defined. The different religious paths advocated by the Indian religions reflect contradictory perspectives on "living-in-this-world" and "renouncing-this-world" in the pursuit of the ultimate religious goal of *mokṣa*.

Within the Śaiva stream of Hinduism, the tension between "living-in-this-world" and "renouncing-this-world" is vividly expressed through the ambivalent mythological and iconographical depictions of the Hindu god Śiva. The myths surrounding Śiva portray him sometimes as a householder accompanied by his consort Pārvatī and at other times as an ascetic. According to Wendy Doniger, the erotic and ascetic depictions of Śiva are not diametrically in opposition to each other. In actuality, the images reflect the tension between the householder and the renunciate lifestyle models, with Śiva being the mediating principle: "among ascetics Śiva is a libertine and among libertines he is an ascetic."[3] The disparate depictions of Śiva, no doubt, reflect the tension that exists between the domestic and ascetic ideals in the pursuit of the ultimate religious goal of liberation from *saṃsāra*.

In contrast to the common religious traditions of asceticism and renunciation found in Hinduism,[4] Buddhism and Jainism, Sikhism (the most recent of the four) holds a definite and uniform position against the path of renunciation as a valid means to liberation. Sikh literature, such as *Siddh Goṣṭ*, advocates the path of devotion while "living-in-this-world." Not only does *Siddh Goṣṭ* teach that one should live in the world, but it does so in the specific context of Guru Nānak's disapproval of asceticism as practiced by the Nāth yogis.

Before analyzing the *Siddh Goṣṭ* text and its attitude toward renunciation, it is necessary to look first at the divergent Indian religious perspectives on the paths advocated in pursuit of the common goal of liberation. An examination of these disparate perspectives on domesticity and renunciation among the Indian religions will not only provide the background from which Sikhism emerged and evolved but also, more specifically, contextualize the discourse Guru Nānak had with the Nāth yogis.

## DOMESTICITY OR ASCETICISM?

Scholarship on Indian religions often discusses the issue surrounding the prerequisites for attaining liberation (*mokṣa*) from the cycle of rebirth in terms of two polarities, the religious paths of: (1) "living-in-this-world" and (2) "renouncing-this-world."[5] The issue surrounding domesticity and asceticism is manifest in all four of the major Indian religions (Hinduism, Buddhism, Jainism, and Sikhism). While the more ancient traditions tend to embrace asceticism, the later traditions seem to place greater importance on devotionalism meant for the layperson.

From the standpoint of the development of Indian religions, four main categories can be delineated in order to highlight the nuances of the religious lifestyles pertaining to the various traditions' particular theological orientation and practical pursuit of liberation. The four categories of the ideal religious lifestyle types (see fig. 1) are: (1) a householder living in society, (2) a renunciate living outside society, (3) a householder living in the larger context of eventual withdrawal from society, and (4) a renunciate living in the larger context of involvement in society.

The four religious lifestyle types can be understood along two axes. The first axis is concerned with the type of religious persons, which is directly related to the religious goals being pursued. The two types of religious person are (1) the householder oriented toward the acquisition of worldly or material goals, and (2) the renunciate oriented toward spiritual realization. The second axis pertains to the religious person's living situation or dwelling place, which is closely linked to eligibility for the attainment of spiritual goals. The two types of environments for religious pursuits are: (1) living in society whereby religious goals are attainable by all, and (2) living outside society, whereby liberation is achievable only by a certain elite group based on status, whether by ascription or achievement.

RELIGIOUS PERSON TYPE:

HOUSEHOLDER

| DWELLING PLACE: IN SOCIETY | | | DWELLING PLACE: OUTSIDE SOCIETY |
|---|---|---|---|
| | A HOUSEHOLDER LIVING IN SOCIETY (Brāhmaṇism) | A HOUSEHOLDER LIVING IN THE LARGER CONTEXT OF EVENTUAL WITHDRAWAL FROM SOCIETY (Classical Hinduism) | |
| | A RENUNCIATE LIVING IN THE LARGER CONTEXT OF INVOLVEMENT IN SOCIETY (Mahāyāna Buddhism, Bhakti, Sikhism) | A RENUNCIATE LIVING OUTSIDE SOCIETY (Upaniṣad tradition, Theravāda Buddhism, Jainism) | |

RELIGIOUS PERSON TYPE:

RENUNCIATE

Figure 1. Ideal Religious Lifestyles Among the Indian Religions

These four types not only broadly distinguish the nuances of the various religious lifestyles evident in Indian religions at large, but they can also be used as an aid to understand the development of Indian religions. That is, in the evolution of Indian religions, there has been a move away from the more traditional or ancient polarities of the domestic and ascetic ideals toward more integrative ones, like the categories of the "householder living in the larger context of eventual withdrawal from society" and the "renunciate living in the larger context of involvement in society."

This typology of the four ideal religious lifestyles emerged in the process of research for the present work on *Siddh Goṣṭ*, in order to demonstrate Guru Nānak's precise stance, theological orientation and arguments concerning the attainment of liberation. Sikhism is often described as a "householder religion"[6] because of its explicit rejection of renunciation and asceticism. However, as this work demonstrates, Guru Nānak actually denounces the first three types of religious lifestyles—including the traditional householder path—even as he uses Nāth "ascetic" or "yogic" terminology to illustrate his devotional path while "living-in-this-world." An elaboration of the four types of religious lifestyles in the light of the development of the four major Indian religions is essential to understanding Guru Nānak's Sikh philosophy.

### *The Householder Living in Society*

The *householder living in society* represents the one "living-in-this-world," whose path entails the fulfillment of social duty and the performance of rituals for the attainment of material goals both for the present life and the afterlife in heaven. The foremost and earliest example of domesticity as a religious path is the one promulgated by the Vedas (ca. 1500 BCE), often referred to as Brāhmaṇism.[7] Action is of primary importance because it results in the accumulation of merit. The boons that are sought, many of which are materialistic, pertain to good fortune, enjoyment, longevity, and the like for those who are very much living in the mundane world:

> Whoso, for righteous life, pours offerings to you, O Heaven and Earth, Ye Hemispheres that man succeeds; He in his seed is born again and spreads by Law: from you flow things diverse in form, but ruled alike . . .
>
> May Heaven and Earth make food swell plenteously for us, all-knowing father, mother, wondrous in their works. Pour-

ing out bounties, may in union, both the worlds all beneficial, send us gain, and power and wealth. (*ṚgVeda* 6.70.3, 6)[8]

Vedic rituals (*dharma*) are to be performed in the presence of the married couple of the household seeking boons in this life, in heaven (*svarga*), or both.

Even though the Vedas are venerated as "Hindu scripture" in terms of the development of Hindu religion, many scholars have debated on the actual influence of the Vedas.[9] Vedic practices and mythology are considered to have been influential on later Hindu ritualism. In fact, the Vedic path of religious and social action toward materialistic goals became an integral part of the classical Hindu orientation of the *householder living in the larger context of eventual withdrawal from society.*

*The Renunciate Living Outside Society*

The category of the *renunciate living outside society* represents the one who, "renouncing-this-world," is either a wandering hermit or lives in a monastic community in order to subdue or conquer desire and thus attain spiritual wisdom and, ultimately, liberation. In doing so, it is common practice for a renunciate to take a vow of celibacy (that is, not to engage in sexual activity, which also means not to get married nor have any progeny), pursue a life of asceticism, study rigorously, and perform meditation. The prime examples of the *renunciate living outside society* are found in the late Vedic period (900–500 BCE), during which there emerged three important religious streams that regard total renunciation as the sole means toward liberation—the Upaniṣadic, the Buddhist, and the Jain traditions.

In reaction to Vedic ritualism and the futility of the materialistic goal-orientation of Vedic practice, including the pursuit of heaven (*svarga*), the Upaniṣadic, the Buddhist, and the Jain traditions ideally upheld the new and distinct worldview of *saṃsāra*, wherein one ought to renounce worldly affairs in the pursuit of liberation from the web of rebirth. Attachment and the desire to accumulate good "action" or "merit" (*karma*) attained both in one's previous and present life are taken to condition the circumstances of one's future life. Attachment is viewed as the underlying source of all suffering, including attachment to the notion of a better rebirth.

The Upaniṣadic challenge (ca. 900–500 BCE) to Vedic ritualism (even though there are also mythic and ritual passages in the Upaniṣads)[10] calls for a new quest for spiritual knowledge *jñāna*—the metaphysical understanding of the true nature of Reality—necessary for escape from the cycle of rebirth. This new metaphysical orientation views Vedic rituals and their materialistic goals as both an inferior and an ineffective means to liberation:

> Thinking sacrifice and merit is the chiefest thing, naught better do they know—deluded! Having had enjoyment on the top of heaven won by good works, they re-enter this world, or a lower. (*Muṇḍaka Upaniṣad* 1.2.10)[11]

Rather, the Upaniṣadic path calls for the renunciation of the material world in the pursuit of "higher" wisdom:

> The one who practice austerity (*tapas*) and faith (*śraddhā*) in the forest, the peaceful (*śānta*) knowers who live on alms, depart passionless (*vi-rāga*) through the door of the sun, to where is that immortal Person (*puruṣa*), e'en the imperishable Spirit (*ātman*).
>
> For the sake of knowledge . . . let him go, full in hand, to a spiritual teacher (guru) who is learned in the scriptures and established on Brahman. (*Muṇḍaka Upaniṣad* 1.2.11–12)

The escape from the cycle of rebirth is ultimately achievable only by a rigorous and austere path of study and meditation. In the pursuit of knowledge (*jñāna*) of the true nature of Reality, one must take on a path of renunciation in order to eliminate all passion and desire. This wisdom ultimately leads to the realization of the equation of the Supreme Essence (referred to as Brahman) with *ātman*. The goal of liberation, however, is attainable only by the privileged males belonging to the three upper classes (*dvija*), based on the strict rule that Vedic learning and the attainment of wisdom is accessible only to them. Indeed, *mokṣa* is achievable only by a small elite group, based on the ascriptive status of male gender among the three higher Hindu classes (*brahmin*, *kṣatriya*, and *vaiśya*).

In a similar fashion, the founder of Buddhism, Gautama Buddha (ca. 624–544 BCE), is said to have renounced his royal family life and taken on ascetic practices in the pursuit of enlightenment on seeing the "four" miseries—an old person, a sick person, a corpse, and an ascetic.[12] In his challenge to Vedic ritualism and in his recognition of the Four Noble Truths,[13] the Buddha advocated the Eightfold Path as the renunciate path to liberation from the cycle of rebirth.[14] Through the controlling of all of one's desires and the perfecting of one's actions, one becomes aware of impermanence, including the experience of the insubstantiality of the personal self (*anatta* in Pali for *anātman*).

The *arhant* ("noble one"; Buddha-like) is the enlightened one, who will have no rebirth as he or she no longer desires anything, not even the pleasures of meditation. However, according to the Buddha, it does not suffice to simply wander as an ascetic in the forest in quest of liberation:

> Many for refuge go
> To mountains and to forests,
> To shrines that are groves or trees—
> Humans who are threatened by fear.
>
> This is not a refuge secure,
> This refuge is not the highest.
> Having come to this refuge,
> One is not released from all misery.
> (*Dhammapada* 14. 188–89)[15]

Rather, the act of taking refuge in the three jewels (*triratna*)—Buddha, *dharma* (*dhamma* in Pali), and *saṃgha* ("community"; *saṅgha* in Pali)—is the only valid means to the ultimate goal of escape from the cycle of rebirth:

> But who to the Buddha, Dhamma,
> And Sangha as refuge has gone,
> Sees with full insight
> The Four Noble Truths . . .
>
> This, indeed, is a refuge secure.
> This is the highest refuge.
> Having come to this refuge,
> One is released from all misery.
> (*Dhammapada* 14. 190, 192)

The *saṃgha* of *bhikṣus* ("monks," literally "beggars"; *bhikkhu* in Pali) and *bhikṣuṇīs* ("female monks"; *bhikkhunī* in Pali) is the community of renunciates, who have relinquished worldly affairs, including family, in the pursuit of liberation. To become a realized person (*arhant*) is the goal, and it is achievable only by formally ordained monks and nuns who have renounced worldly life, symbolized by shaved heads, loose clothing and a begging bowl:

> A monk chooses a remote lodging in a forest, at the foot of a tree, on a mountain slope, in a wilderness, in a hill-cave, in a cemetery, in a forest haunt, in open or a heap of straw. Returning from alms-gathering after the meal he sits down cross-legged, holding the back erect, having made mindfulness rise up in front of him. He, by getting rid of covering, he purifies the mind of coveting. (*Majjhima-nikāya*, pp. 328–29)[16]

Notwithstanding the superior status and the greater privilege that the monks have as compared to the nuns in the Theravāda tradition, the *saṃgha* path outlined by the Buddha is open to all, regardless of caste, class, or gender. As against the renunciates, the laypeople, those who do not take to the path of renunciation, are believed to suffer through future rebirths until they become an *arhant*.

Like the Buddha, Mahāvīra (540–468 BCE),[17] the revered founder of Jainism, also taught that one has to completely renounce domestic life for spiritual attainment. Indeed, only through renunciation from mundane existence can liberation be attained:

> ... What you acknowledge as sagedom, that you acknowledge as righteousness. It is inconsistent with weak, sinning sensual, ill-conducted house-inhabiting men. 'A sage, acquiring sagedom, should subdue his body.' 'The heroes who look at everything with indifference, use mean and rough' ... Such a man is said to have crossed the flood (of *saṃsāra*), to be a sage, to have passed over (*saṃsāra*) to be liberated, to have ceased. Thus I say. (*Ācārāṅga Sūtra* 47)[18]

Renunciation is seen as a prerequisite for liberation of the soul, because worldly affairs are viewed as binding one to the cycle of rebirth. Furthermore, renunciation decreases external stimulation, making for a suitable tranquil environment for the soul. For that reason, there is great emphasis on cutting oneself off from the everyday world by living in the wilderness in small groups or in relative solitude in order to meditate and contemplate on the nature of the world.

The Jain path of renunciation is a gradual one, as is Buddhism and the Upaniṣadic tradition, because it can take many lifetimes before one actually attains *nirvāṇa*. The path is one of absolute self-discipline, during which the three jewels (right insight, right knowledge, and right conduct) and five practices (nonviolence, truthfulness, nonstealing, sexual purity, and nonpossession) lead one toward perfection. One is asked to attain self-control (in contrast to the utterances of the Vedic priests) through rigorous study and meditation in order to achieve liberation. There are also more extreme practices to cultivate self-reliance and self-discipline that require Jain monks and nuns to undertake acts of self-deprivation (such as starving oneself) and self-mortification (such as beating oneself). Although there is great emphasis on formal monastic renunciation for the devout, there also exist at the same time the mass of Jain laypeople, who venerate the twenty-four perfected beings (*jinas*) and accept the three jewels, but follow the five practices in varying measure in the belief that liberation will eventually occur after many rebirths.[19]

There are likewise various yogic traditions like the Nāth sect that flourished later during the twelfth to thirteenth century CE, which have been influenced by the more ancient Indian traditions of asceticism. The Nāth tradition will be specifically discussed in chapter 2.

### *The Householder Living in the Larger Context of Eventual Withdrawal from Society*

The category of the *householder living in the larger context of eventual withdrawal from society* refers to the path that synthesizes domesticity and asceticism. It includes the fulfillment of one's social and religious duty for material goals, but places these goals within the larger context of eventual "renunciation-of-this-world" for liberation. However, such liberation is attainable only by a certain elite group based on ascriptive status. The paramount example of this category is Classical Hindu belief and practice,[20] wherein there is an earnest attempt to synthesize the earlier Vedic path of religious and social action with the opposing austere Upaniṣadic path of renunciation open only to the privileged males belonging to the three upper-Hindu classes (*dvija*).

In the *Bhagavad Gītā* (ca. 100 BCE–100 CE),[21] Kṛṣṇa outlines three different religious paths: *jñāna-yoga* (discipline of wisdom), *karma-yoga* (discipline of action), and *bhakti-yoga* (discipline of devotion). Although Kṛṣṇa discusses these three paths, his teaching of the renunciation of the fruits of one's actions (*niṣ-kāmā-karma-yoga*) is of central importance.

> The man who acts, having rendered his actions to Brahman and abandoned attachment is untainted by evil, in the same way that a lotus leaf is untainted by (muddy-) water.
>
> The disciplined man, having abandoned the result of action, attains complete peace; the undisciplined man, whose action is impelled by desire, and who is attached to the result, is bound. (*Bhagavad Gītā* 5.10.12)[22]

The *Bhagavad Gītā* teaches that one has to fulfill social and religious duty at the personal level for the sake of attaining *mokṣa* and for the maintenance of the social order at the community level. While one may live in the world as a householder, it is with the ultimate goal or aim of renouncing the fruits of one's actions.

At first blush *niṣ-kāma-karma-yoga* would seemingly fall into the fourth category *"renunciate living in the larger context of involvement in society."* In the case of the medieval Bhakti and modern interpretations of the *Bhagavad Gītā* it could.[23] However, during the period of classical Hinduism, the pan-Indian socioreligious law books outlined schemas that differentiated four stages of life with distinct goals. That is, it prescribes different stages in life for the action-oriented path of "living-in-this-world" with the fulfillment of material goals and the path of "renouncing-this-world" for self-realization. During the second quarter of one's life, one has prescribed social or religious obligations to fulfill materialistic goals, while during the last quarter of life one ought to renounce the material world in order to pursue the ultimate goal of *mokṣa* (*saṃnyāsa-āśrama*).

According to the socioreligious law books—like the *Dharmaśāstras* (ca. 200 BCE) and *Manusmṛti* (ca. 200 BCE–100 CE)—there are four aims of life corresponding to one's stage in life (*āśrama*),[24] that is, in turn, determined by one's class (*varṇa*)[25] and gender. The four aims of life include the performance of social and religious duty (*dharma*), the acquisition of wealth and prosperity (*artha*), the experience of sensual-pleasures (*kāma*), and the attainment of liberation (*mokṣa*). While there are four aims of life, it is the first three (*dharma, artha,* and *kāma*) that are to be fulfilled during the second quarter of life or the householder stage (*gṛhastha-āśrama*).

> A twice-born one shall reside for the first quarter of his life in the residence of his preceptor, and the second quarter (thereof) in his own house as a married man. (*Manusmṛti* 4.1)[26]

Meanwhile the fourth aim—*mokṣa*—is meant to be pursued in the last stage of life called the *saṃnyāsa-āśrama*. The males of the three higher classes, referred to as "twice-born" (*dvija*), having received Vedic learning during the first quarter of life (*brāhmaṇa-asrama*), ought to renounce mundane existence in the pursuit of liberation during the *saṃnyāsa-āśrama*. However, non-*dvija* (women and males belonging to the *śūdra* class) have to be reborn as a male in one of the higher three classes in order to attain liberation. Therefore, while there is an important orientation to pursue material goals as a householder, there is nevertheless the notion that the ultimate goal of liberation is attainable only by those with the ascriptive status of *dvija*, who are in a position to take on the traditional renunciate lifestyle of withdrawal from society during the last stage of life.

*The Renunciate Living in the Larger Context of Involvement in Society*

The last category, the *renunciate living in the larger context of social involvement*, refers to the path that consists of renouncing one's desires within the context of "living-in-this-world" in order to attain the ultimate goal of liberation. Various devotional movements began emerging around the first to sixth century CE for the masses throughout the Indian subcontinent. The devotional streams—including Mahāyāna Buddhism, Hindu Bhakti, the Sant tradition, and Sikhism—challenged the earlier and more socially conservative forms of religion, which had contended that renunciation is a prerequisite for liberation. Rather, the new devotional movements emphasized a path while living very much in the world, and it was open to both women and men of all castes. Renunciation now came to mean the renunciation of one's ego in the larger context of social involvement and responsibility.

Mahāyāna Buddhism (first century CE)[27] explicitly rejects the conservative Theravāda tradition of monasticism as the necessary means to liberation. The rejection of withdrawal from society is based on the premise that, while monks lead a life of purity to extinguish desire, they inevitably become preoccupied with it. Furthermore, renunciation often becomes a source of spiritual pride because Theravāda Buddhists view it as the only valid means to liberation, thus making it the "superior" choice or way to live.

Mahāyāna Buddhism teaches that the elimination of ignorance, desire, hatred, and anger can be achieved through acts of devotion and pure faith. Indeed, any devotee, who, with a pure heart and mind, remembers the name of a blessed Buddha, will be liberated:

> Now what do you think, O Sariputa, for what reason is that repetition (treatise) of the Law called the favour of all Buddhas? Every son or daughter of a family who shall hear the name of that repetition of the law and retain in their memory the names of the blessed Buddhas, will be favoured by the Buddhas, and will never return again, being once in possession of the transcendent true knowledge. Therefore, then, O Sariputa, believe, accept, and do not doubt of me and those blessed Buddhas! (*The Smaller Sukhavati-vyūha* 17)[28]

The premise that anyone is able to attain liberation is based on the belief that everyone has the potential of becoming a Buddha through the compassion of the *bodhisattvas*—mythical beings who postpone their own *nirvāṇa* in order to help others attain liberation.[29] Compassion and grace are the key means for laypeople to attain liberation.[30] The notion that all humans possess the potential of buddhahood and that liberation is dependent on the devotee's faith and the *bodhisattva*'s compassion, no doubt, improves the religious or spiritual status of females and the laity in general.

Unlike the mythical orientation of Mahāyāna Buddhism (with concepts like the *bodhisattva*), Hindu devotionalism—referred to as Bhakti ("devotion")—is of an earthly nature, using human relations as the prototype for the relation between God and devotee.[31] Liberation was now attainable by all because the key elements in Bhakti are a simple faith and love directed to a personal God. The devotee is required to renounce his or her "ego," and completely surrender to God with the single-minded desire of blissful union with Him. Liberation does not depend on renunciation of mundane existence (unlike the *varṇa-āśrama-dharma* schema described in the classical Hindu law books) because Bhakti calls for the renunciation of one's ego and total surrender to God. Here we see the theological break with the notion that liberation is achievable by only *dvijas*, because *mokṣa* is no longer dependent on Vedic education. There was, furthermore, a break—at least theoretically—with the strict rules surrounding brahminical rituals and the concepts of purity and pollution, thus also making temple religious practice and *mokṣa* accessible to all.

Another stream of Hindu devotion, called the Sant tradition, flourished from the fifteenth to the seventeenth century CE. The Sant tradition consists of Hindi speaking poet-saints in Northern India (such as Rajasthan and the Punjab) who taught a more "radical" path to liberation in which the realization of God is to be attained through devotional meditation on the Divine Name (*nāma*). In the Sant tradition, God is represented as a deity without form (*nirguṇa*).[32]

More radical than the Bhakti poet-saints, the Sants explicitly rejected all institutional forms of religion. In doing so, they denounced the notion of revelation (as in the *Vedas* or *Qur'an*), places of worship (*maṇḍira, masjid*), temple rituals, yogic practices, pilgrimage places, religious texts, and the need for clergy. Kabīr (ca. 15th century CE), a Sant, rejected all institutional forms of religion, even as he taught the simple yet difficult path of devotion to the Divine Name:

> Pandit, do some research
> And let me know

How to destroy transiency.
Money, religion, pleasure, liberation—
Which way do they stay brother?
North, South, East or West?
In heaven or the underworld?
If Gopal is everywhere, where is hell?
Heaven and hell are for the ignorant,
Not for those who know Hari.
The fearful thing that everyone fears,
I do not fear.
I am not confused about sin and purity, heaven and hell.

Kabīr says, seekers listen!
Wherever you are
Is the entry point. (Kabīr, *Bījak śabda* 42)[33]

According to the Sants, one need not be preoccupied with religious customs or beliefs, since liberation or the realization of the true nature of one's soul is attainable through the mere recitation of the Divine Name. And, since liberation is achievable through the mere recitation of the Divine Name, giving up household life is not a requirement. In fact, renouncing this world is frowned on as it is viewed as a religious practice that only distracts devotees from self-realization.

According to McLeod, it is through the Sant tradition that Vaiṣṇava Bhakti, the Nāth yogic tradition, and Sufism have influenced Sikhism.[34] Although the Sikh tradition shares continuities with the Sant tradition, especially during its inception, it nevertheless has its own specific interpretation and integration of various beliefs and practices. The foundations of Sikhism were laid by Guru Nānak (1469–1539 CE), the first of a succession of ten Sikh gurus, who together established the Sikh religion.

The Sikh gurus, like the Sants, taught a radical rejection of all external forms of religion. Likewise, they also rejected the notion of renouncing the world and the taking to ascetic practices in order to attain *mokṣa*. The third Sikh guru, Amar Dās (1479–1574 CE) explains the futility of renunciation thus:

Some sit in the forest realms,
and do not answer any calls.
Some break ice in the cold [winter],
and bathe in freezing water.
Some rub ashes on their bodies,
and do not wash off the dirt.

With their hair matted,
 some look wild,
 and bring dishonour to their family lineage.
Some wander naked,
 during the day and night,
 and do not sleep.
Some burn their limbs with fire,
 and damage themselves.
Without *nām*,
 the body is reduced to ashes. . . .
(Vār Malār, M.3, *GGS*, pp. 1284–85)[35]

In their religious and social dissent, the Sikh gurus taught that the mere recitation of the Divine Name is the sufficient means to spiritual attainment. This inner devotion to *nāma* is open to all, irrespective of gender or caste. The Sikh theological and social stance on equality is similar to that of the Sant tradition; it opposes the classical Hindu belief that liberation is open only to males belonging to the three higher classes (*dvija*)—*brahmin*, *kṣatriya*, and *vaiśya*; as well it opposes the necessity of monastic or ascetic life advocated by Buddhism and Jainism.

In contrast with the opposing perspectives on renunciation as a prerequisite for liberation found in Hinduism and Buddhism, Sikhism offers a distinct stance against individuals withdrawing from society in the pursuit of liberation from *saṃsāra*. And it is in *Siddh Goṣṭ* that the founder of Sikhism, Guru Nānak, explicitly expounds on the question of why renunciation of the material world is not necessary for, or even useful in, the pursuit of *mokṣa*. Consequently, *Siddh Goṣṭ* is a fundamental philosophical text in the understanding of the Sikh position on renunciation and liberation. This brief but important text is essential to a better understanding of the unique evolution of the Sikh philosophical system. The present analysis of the text is addressed precisely to that aim.

## METHODOLOGY

In the academic field, Sikh studies have, for the most part, been extremely polarized:[36] the "traditional historians" (for example, Trilochan Singh, Gurdarshan Singh Dhillon, Daljeet Singh)[37] versus the "critical [skeptical] historians" (e.g., W. H. McLeod, Harjot Singh Oberoi, Pashaura Singh).[38] While the "traditional historians" have as their aim to preserve or protect what Sikhs hold as the Truth, the "critical historians" have as their primary goal the determination of historical facts concerning the development of Sikhism, such as the authenticity of texts and their authorship, and the historical accuracy in the interpretation of texts. In actual fact, the "traditional historians" have come to perceive the "critical historians" as attacking the Sikh faith and identity, whereas the latter view the former as being insensitive to the canons of scholarly research and the quest for historical truth.

It is noteworthy that, in addition to these two types of scholars, there has also been the tradition of the *giānī* (literally "possessors of knowledge"), Sikh philosopher-preacher. Although the term *giānī* has come to be used loosely to refer to anyone who may talk authoritatively about religion in the *gurdwārā* (Sikh temple) setting, traditionally there are teacher-student lineages involving rigorous training in learning about the religion and its practices (equivalent to the Hindu *ācārya*) for the purpose of propagation and teaching about the religion to the community. In acknowledging the *giānī* as an important traditional resource for learning about the Sikh tradition, the religious discourse has nevertheless to be viewed in the light of the *giāni*'s audience:

> There is always the possibility of several interpretations in this process [*kathā*] of religious discourse, since each individual *giānī* maybe offering his or her own interpretation specific to the situation of a particular audience.[39]

Indeed, for the *giānī*, the nature of any particular religious discourse is necessarily contextual, that is, influenced by his audience. Although *giānīs* are very learned in Sikh (and Hindu) literature and the beliefs and customs of the common folk, they do not, for the most part, engage in intellectual dialogue with the "traditional historians."

Scholarship on Sikhism can be traced back to the mid-nineteenth century, when the British began their rule in the Punjab. The early European scholars were interested in both Sikh religion (Trumpp, Macauliffe)[40] and Sikh history (Cunningham).[41] Their work was soon followed by the emergence of Sikh scholars (such as Teja Singh and Sahib Singh),[42] who entered into dialogue with the "Orientalists" during the period of the Singh Sabha movement, which had as its focus the creation of a distinct Sikh identity. This Orientalist-Sikh dialogue can be viewed as the embryonic stage of the more contemporary contentious debate on issues that have divided the traditional and critical historians in relation to academic work on Sikhism. Much controversy surrounds Sikh studies regarding a number of issues[43] most often rooted in the scholar's particular methodology. It centers primarily on the employment by the "critical historians" of the textual-criticism method to Sikh scripture and religious literature as well as the use of historical methodology that involves deconstruction of events, followed by a new reconstruction.

As between the positions of the two opposed groups, this analysis adopts an approach that takes the middle ground. Related to the field of Indology, the analysis certainly recognizes and incorporates the relevant issues surrounding historical authenticity and accuracy. However, while the analysis looks at historical context and consistency, it does so without losing sight of that which is viewed as important to Sikh theology/tradition even as it deals with the religious significance of particular phenomena. An example from the study of another tradition is certainly enlightening here. In the work on Christianity, it is regarded as useful to reconstruct the "historical Jesus," yet it is done without losing sight of the religious significance of the "Christ of faith."[44] Similarly, it is important to keep in mind both the "Guru Nānak of faith" and the "Faith of Guru Nānak."[45]

This work, indeed, includes an inquiry into the historical accuracy and consistency of the corpus of Sikh literature, including the *janam-sākhīs* (hagiographies about Guru Nānak); yet it also takes into serious consideration that which does not strictly emerge as historical fact. Surely, "improbable" events described in the hagiographies may well have some religious significance beyond the domain of history. And, while historical context is undoubtedly important in looking at religious development, a mere historical reconstruction may well fall far short in understanding matters relating to religious beliefs and practices. Indeed, one needs to shed light on religious phenomena that matter and make sense to the believer.[46]

This work on *Siddh Goṣṭ* is a textual analysis of the hymn in the context of the Sikh literature concerning Guru Nānak and his meetings with the Nāth yogis. It aims not only to take into consideration the historical context of the hymn, but also seeks to explore the hymn's religious significance beyond historical fact and inconsistency. That is, this work attempts to look at the metaphorical meanings and theological significance of the seemingly illogical events in the hagiographies surrounding Guru Nānak and the Nāth yogis. In doing so, the study draws on information that is communicated by *giānīs*, who are familiar with the oral tradition surrounding *Siddh Goṣṭ*.

## AIMS OF THE STUDY

The chief aims of this work are: (1) to provide an understanding of *Siddh Goṣṭ* (and Sikhism in general) in the larger framework of the typology of the four different religious lifestyles manifest among the four main Indian religions, (2) to provide an analysis of the key theological beliefs of Guru Nānak that are expounded in *Siddh Goṣṭ*, (3) to demonstrate how Guru Nānak's philosophical system is actually put into practice, (4) to establish how Nāth yogic terminology has been appropriated in Sikh scripture even as the latter rejects Nāth belief and practice, and, last, (5) to provide an original English translation of *Siddh Goṣṭ*.

The textual analysis of *Siddh Goṣṭ* (or for that matter, any text, regardless of its size) involves knowledge about three aspects concerning the context of the text to be interpreted. These three aspects are: (1) the historical life-situation of the author of the text (chapter 3), (2) the function of the text, including the audience for whom, and the purpose for which, the text was written (chapter 4), and (3) the theological or philosophical orientation of the text (chapter 5). Since the *Siddh Goṣṭ* consists of a discourse between the author and a second party, there is an additional aspect that requires attention, and that is familiarity with the second party—the Nāth yogis—the people with whom the author is engaged in discussion (chapter 2). Further, adequately grasping the meaning of the text involves special focus on how Guru Nānak rejects the traditional householder and ascetic religious lifestyles even as he uses ascetic terminology to teach the path of "True" yoga while "living-in-this-world" (chapter 6). All four aspects of textual analysis require attention, and are therefore explored in the chapters that follow.

Before commencing the analysis of Guru Nānak's teachings on "True" yoga as expounded in *Siddh Goṣṭ*, it is necessary to first provide background material on the Nāth yogis and Guru Nānak, the two participants in the *Siddh Goṣṭ* discourse. Therefore, an analysis of the Nāth yogic tradition as well as information on the life of Guru Nānak and the sources regarding his encounters and discourses with the Nāth yogis are the topics of the next two chapters, respectively.

# Part 2

# Setting the Stage for *Siddh Goṣṭ*

## Chapter Two

# The Nāth Tradition and Hath-Yoga

A yogi (*jogī* in Punjabi) is technically a practitioner of yoga. That is, a person committed to a certain set of mental and physical exercises for the sake of acquiring occult powers (*siddhis*) and for the attainment of liberation or immortality (*jīvan-mukti*). Traditionally, a yogi renounces the material world, with renunciation often consisting of an ascetic lifestyle, the taking of a vow of celibacy, rigorous study, and the practice of meditation. However, the word "yogi" came to acquire the negative connation of (especially Śaiva) sectarianism, which, in orthodox circles, has been viewed as heretical since it was based on its non-Vedic beliefs and practices.

Closely related to the term "yogi" is the appellation *siddha*, which literally means a "realized, accomplished or perfected" one. *Siddha* is a broad word for an ascetic who has through specific practices realized (1) superhuman powers (*siddhis*) and (2) immortality (*jīvan-mukti*). In first century CE, there existed a cult that believed in a blessed abode where there are divine *siddhas*. It was not until the medieval period (ca. twelfth century CE) that there was an emergence of both Hindu and Buddhist *siddha* cults following a common body of mystic dogma and practices.[1]

There are many different groups of *siddhas* across the Indian subcontinent, including Maheśvara Siddhas in the Deccan region, Sittars in Tamil Nadu, Mahāsiddhas or Siddhācāryas in Bengal, Nāth Siddhas in northern India, and Rasa Siddhas, who were alchemists in medieval India.[2] Although many groups of yogis or *siddhas* existed during ca. twelfth to thirteenth century CE in medieval India, the Nāth sect is, in fact, the sole surviving group of yogis in the Indian subcontinent.[3] Moreover, the Nāth sect is regarded as one of the higher classes of yogis in India.[4] It is important to note that, while the term *siddha* includes both Hindus and Buddhists, the Nāths are exclusively Hindu[5] (albeit the Nāth tradition itself evidences Mahāyāna and Tantric Buddhist influence).[6]

Though Nāth is the name used in reference to a specific class of yogis/*siddhas*, Guru Nānak uses it interchangeably with the umbrella term *siddha*. *Siddh Goṣṭ*, "*siddh*" (in Punjabi) refers specifically to those associated with the Nāth tradition. That is, the "*siddhs*" here are members of the Nāth tradition that pioneered hath-yoga (*haṭha-yoga* in Sanskrit). In this chapter, therefore, only Nāth yogis/*siddhas* will be examined since it is with them that Guru Nānak had his discourse in *Siddh Goṣṭ*. Besides the fact that the text is a dialogue between some Nāth yogis and Guru Nānak, *Siddh Goṣṭ* also contains various references to Nāth beliefs and practices. Hence, it is important to understand the Nāth tradition in order to fully grasp the meaning of the *Siddh Goṣṭ* text. It is noteworthy to mention here that Nāth presence has been significant in the Punjab. Indeed, Sikh literature—like Guru Nānak's *Siddh Goṣṭ* and in the legendary accounts about Guru Nānak's life (discussed in chapter 3)—makes references to the Nāth yogis. Significantly, popular Punjabi folk songs also make reference to the Nāth yogis.[7]

This chapter examines the specific religious orientation of the Nāth tradition. First, the chapter discusses the Nāth lifestyle of renunciation, and provides a general overview of Nāth religious beliefs and rituals. Second, it analyses the Nāth practice of hath-yoga in the larger context of the classical Indian tradition of yoga. The chapter contextualizes and interprets the several references to Nāth yogic belief and practice in *Siddh Goṣṭ*. Besides, it demonstrates how the Nāth yogis definitely fall into the category of *renunciates withdrawn from society* even as they engage in practices that have been branded as Hindu heterodoxy.

## THE NĀTH LIFESTYLE OF RENUNCIATION

The word *Nāth* literally means "master." It is the suffix given to the names of the most fully initiated, accomplished, and revered members of the Nāth order. The Nāth sect is an ascetic tradition associated with northern India, which recognizes its founder to be the North Indian figure by the name of Gorakhnātha or Gorakṣanātha, who may have lived during the eleventh century CE. Having its roots in heterodox Śaivism associated with Kashmir,[8] the Nāth yogis worship the Hindu god Śiva as Ādi Nātha, the "original master." The tradition flourished during the twelth to thirteenth centuries in many regions of the Indian subcontinent, including Bengal, Punjab, Rajasthan, and Sind.

Various other names are used to refer to the Nāth yogis, reflecting their distinctive characteristics. First, they are referred to as Gorakhnāthis, following their celebrated founder Gorakhnātha. Second, Nāth yogis are also simply called Yogis because of their practice of hath-yoga and their adherence to an ascetic lifestyle. Third, they are popularly known as Kānphaṭas, which refers to the fact of them having split their ear cartilage for the placing of earrings, a distinctive practice and feature of the Nāth tradition. Last, they are also known by the name Darṣanīs ("huge earrings") because of their distinctive mark of wearing huge earrings.[9]

The Nath tradition—like many other medieval Indian religious traditions—has been influenced by Tantra.[10] The Tantra tradition has been looked down on—and often completely dismissed—in orthodox circles because of its unsystematic heterodox or non-Vedic beliefs and practices, including sorcery, shamanism, and erotic rituals. As a result, there is great variance in Tantric practices, with some sects having actually tried to distance themselves from the sexual or magical orientation of some of the earlier Tantric practices. In fact, some Tantric sects have incorporated "orthodox" concepts to reinvigorate the tradition as also for the purpose of legitimation or Vedicization. In the same manner, around the eleventh century (and later), Tantric beliefs and practices began to also have an influence on "mainstream" Hinduism.[11]

Tantric culture, according to Bhattacharya, presupposes *raja-yoga* and hath-yoga,[12] indicating that the culture surrounding and influencing the Nāth tradition is more ancient than that tradition's particular pioneering practice of hath-yoga. Moreover, David White contends that the *siddhas* appropriated traditions that existed prior to those of Tantrism.[13] The Nāth tradition in terms of both its religious beliefs and practices, in fact, evidences strong features of the ancient Indian tradition of asceticism and Tantrism even as it includes some elements associated with "mainstream" Vedic and classical Hinduism. The convergence of the various religious streams are evident in some important features of the Nāth tradition: (1) the lineage of gurus (Indian asceticism, mainstream Hinduism, Tantra); (2) renunciation for the purpose of acquiring occult powers and immortality (Tantra); (3) the nature of its esoteric teachings (Indian asceticism, Tantra); (4) its religious orientation to shamanism, magic, and exorcism in order to ward off evil omens or spirits (Vedic, Tantra); as well as (5) its sexual practices, including accumulating spiritual heat (*tapas*), for spiritual advancement (Upaniṣadic, Tantra).

The Nāth yogis follow the tradition of guru-disciple lineages. The Nāth tradition reveres nine immortal teachers (yogis) and eighty-four ascetics (*siddhas*). The nine immortal teachers are viewed as the immortal religious leaders or gurus of the tradition, whereas the eighty-four ascetics (*siddhas*) are celebrated for having become perfected ones or semidivine beings through their rigorous yogic practices. There is much confusion surrounding the various *siddha* lists because it is a broad term that came to refer to divine beings and legendary figures as well as historical people.[14]

There are also many versions of the lineage of the "nine" revered Nāth immortal teachers that had come to be recognized around the twelfth or thirteenth centuries.[15] One of the more fundamental lineages of the nine immortal Nāth teachers, according to Briggs, begins with Gorakhnātha as the disciple of Śiva: (1) Gorakhnātha, (2) Matsyendranātha, (3) Carpaṭnātha, (4) Mangalnātha, (5) Ghugonātha, (6) Gopīnātha, (7) Prāṇnātha, (8) Sūratnātha, and (9) Cambanātha.[16] In contrast, according to White the most common names in the Nāth list of "nine" immortal teachers include: (1) Matsyendranātha, (2) Gorakhnātha, (3) Carpaṭnātha, (4) Jālandhara, (5) Kaṇerī, (6) Cauraṅgi, (7) Nāgārjuna, (8) Bhartṛhari, and (9) Gopīchand. Indeed, Matsyendranātha is frequently placed before Gorakhnātha because he is often revered as Gorakh's guru.

Besides the disparate lineages of the nine immortal Nāth teachers, there exist many subsects of the Nāth cult throughout the Indian subcontinent. Traditionally, there have been "twelve" recognized subsects of the Nāth Order,[17] most of which are said to have been established by the disciples of Gorakhnātha or Matsyendranātha (e.g., Gopīchand, Bhartṛhari, Nāgārjuna, Cauraṅgi). There is much variation in the listings, primarily because the tradition spread throughout the Indian subcontinent. That is, the many master-disciple lineages belonging to the various subsects reflect the expansion of the Nāth religious order around the fifteenth to sixteenth century across many regions, especially in western India.[18] For example, in the Punjab during the sixteenth century, one list of the "nine" Nāth teachers differs from the common names listed above. The Punjabi list of the nine immortal teachers includes: (1) Śiva, (2) Ude (Udaya), (3) Matsyendranātha, (4) Jālandharī-pā, (5) Gorakhnāth, (6) Arjan Nāga, (7) Nīm-/Pāras-nātha, (8) Bārtrinātha, and (9) Kāṇipā.[19]

The various Nāth lineages are often traced back to the religious figure Gorakhnātha (whose guru, as aforementioned, is often said to have been the highly revered Matsyendranātha), associated with the Gurkha region of Nepal. There is dispute surrounding the meaning of the name Gorakhnātha. Some scholars contend that Gorakhnātha refers to the "malevolent" or "fearful" (*ghor*) lord (*nātha*), while others take Gorakṣanātha to mean "Lord of Cattle" or "Lord of Gorakṣa" or as referring to the deity of Gorkha (Nepal).[20]

Along with ambiguity regarding the name Gorakhnātha, there is also a lot of vagueness surrounding this religious figure. Gorakhnātha seems to be a composite of history and the earlier legendary literature. It is important to note that he is connected with the earlier legendary figure called Gorakh in the *siddha* divine abode. Moreover, Gorakh has also been portrayed as guru or disciple in other Śaiva or Siddha sects.[21]

Along with his various guru-disciple roles, Gorakhnātha became deified and revered as the embodiment of Śiva or Ādinātha.[22] Although Gorakhnātha is associated with the northern Himalayan region of the Indian subcontinent, Nāth yogis can be found throughout India, including the regions of the Punjab, Rajputana, Deccan, and Bengal.[23] In other parts of India, historical figures like Gorakhnātha and Matsyendranātha have become revered as demigods:

> Gorakhnātha who having discovered the shrine of the godling *gorkha* (divinity of the Gurkhas of the Himalayan region of Gurkha in Nepal) took the name Gorakhnātha "he whose Lord is Gorakh." There has been a conceptual shift from "shrine served by a holy man" himself was effected in the Indian popular imagination and in the generation of legends that grew up around this composite figure.[24]

The many narrative accounts about Gorakhnātha predominantly describe him as possessing great divine stature based on his occult powers evident in his saving people from evil and the like.[25]

Following the ancient Indian tradition of asceticism, the Nāth yogis renounce worldly life; that is, they remove themselves from mundane existence in order to pursue their ascetic and yogic discipline. Indeed, they fall into the category of *renunciates living outside society*. Although the Nāth yogis are required to renounce worldly affairs, they are not supposed to do it in isolation, such as wandering alone or living as hermits. Rather, Nāth yogis are to live in the company of their fellow yogis—either by residing in monasteries or by traveling together in groups even as they remove themselves from worldly affairs. *Siddh Goṣṭ* makes reference to the Nāth practice of renunciation, describing it both in terms of living in the forests as well as visiting pilgrimage places:

*Siddhas:*
Away from the stores and highways,
  we abide in the woods among the plants and trees.
Our food is fruit and roots;
  [To live like this] is the wisdom spoken of by the wise ones.
We bathe at sacred pools and attain fruits of peace,
  so that our minds are free from filth.

Gorakh's disciple Loharipā says:
this is the way of yoga. (*SG* 7)

The practice of renunciation from mundane existence is viewed as the practical way of creating an environment suitable for the Nāth yogic pursuits of acquiring occult powers and attaining immortality.

Not engaging oneself with the world includes not earning a living, celibacy, and not having progeny. One is not to work in the world, but rather to sustain oneself by begging for food. *Siddh Goṣṭ* describes the dress of the *siddhas* as carrying a "begging bag," along with the wearing of a "patched coat," and the bearing of "huge earrings":

Nānak:
O yogi! Let your vision be
the patched coat, ear-rings, and [begging] bag. . . . (*SG* 9)

The vow of celibacy removes the yogis from the social responsibilities of marriage and having a family, especially progeny, which is regarded as a distraction from the yogic way of life.

Theoretically, only twice-born (*dvija*) people are allowed to enter the Nāth sect, even though the order itself does not uphold caste stratification.[26] There are two stages to becoming a Nāth yogi: (1) novice (Āughar), during the probationary period; and (2) a full-fledged or accomplished yogi.[27] When one becomes a novice (Āughar) the individual's head is shaved. On initiation as a full-fledged yogi, the practitioner's ears are split by a chosen guru or religious teacher with a double-edged razor. The ears are then plugged with *nīm* wood in order to hang huge earrings. These earrings are referred to as *munḍrā*, the symbol of the yogi's faith.[28] The practice of ear-splitting and the custom of wearing huge earrings symbolize the yogi's spiritual status as an immortal. These symbols are the distinctive marks of a Nāth yogi.

Besides the ear-splitting and wearing of huge earrings, the Nāth yogis have other distinguishing characteristics indicating their status as a Nāth yogi, including (1) a thread tied on the wrist for protection; (2) ashes on the body in order to protect one from the evil spirits, as well as to signify death to the world;[29] (3) *tripuṇḍ* mark on the forehead, three horizontal lines made of ashes or sandal paste, a universal Śaivite mark; (4) brand mark of a *liṅga-yoni*[30] on their right forearm received at Koteśwar (in western India[31]) when yogis take pilgrimage to Hiṅg Lāj,[32] a center to be visited in order to become a "perfected one"; (5) saffron robe, which is believed to provide protection from the demons; (6) headdress, which varies from turban to nothing; and (7) rosaries even though they are not standardized.[33]

The Nāth tradition includes many esoteric practices. In their effort to acquire occult power—especially over the evil spirits—they resort to exorcism, shamanism, alchemy and more important hath-yoga, even as they engage in some "mainstream" Hindu forms of worship. The statues of the various divine Nāth figures are to be worshiped, including the nine revered Nāth immortal teachers and the eighty-four celebrated *siddhas*. These statues are to be worshipped at various Nāth centers and temples.[34] Along with the Nāth religious figures, Nāth yogis also worship many gods of the Hindu pantheon, especially Śiva. The primary deity for the Nāths is Bhairava (a malevolent and horrific manifestation of Śiva), even though other Hindu gods like Hanumān are also worshiped. Offerings are made in worship (*pūjā*) to the gods and Nāth religious figures in temples, with *bulva* leaves, *dhatura*, water, uncooked rice, sweets and camphor, coconuts, and cooked food. Blood offerings are also made to Bhāirava from the yogi's little finger or tip of his tongue.[35]

Pilgrimages to sacred places (*tīrtha* in Sanskrit) are also important. Nāth yogis make pilgrimages to both mainstream Hindu places like Ayodhyā,[36] Vārāṇasī,[37] and Hardwār,[38] as well as important Nāth centers or monasteries such as Ṭilla[39], and Hiṅg Lāj. The monastery at Hiṅg Lāj is the center that a novice must visit in order to become a "perfected one" since it is the place where Gorakhnātha is said to have split Bhartṛhari's ears.[40] There are also other sites to visit like the cave temple of Gorakhnātha, a sacred hearth of the Gurkhas located in western Nepal.[41]

Among the many Hindu sacred feasts and festivals (*ustava*), Śivrātri is the most important one for the Nāths. Śivrātri occurs on the thirteenth of the light half of each lunar month. During the sacred time of Śivrātri, devotees worship Śiva at sunset and fast until the stars appear on the night of the thirteenth of each month.[42] The fast lasts twenty-four hours long, during which one is to abstain from food and drink. During Śivrātri, the Nāth yogis worship the malevolent form of Śiva. The *liṅga*—the aniconic form of Śiva—is also worshiped every third hour of the day and throughout the night. The Nāths remain awake all night long in order to sing songs in devotion and honor of Gorakhnātha. According to the Nāth tradition, upholding the Śivrātri rituals actually expiates all sin, helps in the attainment of one's desires during this life, as well as brings one toward union with Śiva or final release after death (*mukti*).[43] The worship is open to all people, including untouchables and women. The use of the *Auṃ*[44] mantra is, however, only accessible to *dvija*, the men belonging to the three higher Hindu classes.[45]

Along with the practice of Hindu worship (*pūjā*) and the celebration of the sacred festivals (*ustava*), there is also a great deal of emphasis placed on acquiring control over evil spirits. In fact, breathing is used to detect good and bad omens; exorcism is used for the cure of diseases;[46] charms are used as devices to ward off evil spirits. Similarly, the yogis use box-shaped or cylindrical-shaped amulets made out of gold, copper, or silver, worn on the arm or hung from the neck for protection from evil spirits. The Nāth earrings also carry with them a special protection, as does the black thread (*kaṅgan*) worn on the wrist.[47]

Following common Hindu belief and practice, the Nāths, too, regard animals like the cow as sacred. Higher regard is, however, given to black animals, including the rhinoceros, black buck, dogs, and snakes. The rhinoceros is particularly important. As part of animal sacrifice, the rhinoceros' body and legs are offered to Gorakhnātha. Moreover, the Nāth rings and earrings are made from the rhinoceros horns. Even though different species of snakes and serpents are worshiped, the cobra is the most popular snake because it represents Śiva.[48]

In combination with its practice of hath-yoga, the Nāth tradition also recognizes the power of semen (*bindu*) or "procreative fluids" for spiritual realization. The *Gorakṣa Śataka*[49] describes the power of semen:

> But the *bindu* is the cause of the body. In it arise all the channels which together constitute the body, from head to foot. . . . his *bindu*, even (though he be) embraced by a woman, does not fall. While the *bindu* remains in the body, there is no fear of death. As long as the *khecarīmudrā* is continued, so long the *bindu* does not go down. (*Gorakṣa Śataka* 68–70)

The yogic practices aimed at the conservation of, and control over, *bindu* is central. The tradition transmits to the disciples esoteric teachings about the practices surrounding the control over *bindu* and the transformation of sexual desire or heat into spiritual or thermal heat (*tapas*).[50] This spiritual heat travels through the six *cakras* up to the head for the experience of illumination. The act of masturbation without the release of semen (ejaculation) is regarded as a means to control desire and to turn sexual heat into spiritual energy and hence eventual immortality or illumination.

The esoteric teachings are intended to guide practitioners, especially for the purpose of attaining union with Śiva. Similar to Śaiva

Tantra practitioners (*tantrikas*), the Nāths view Śiva as supreme consciousness and Śakti as his consort. The practitioner is required to approach Śiva through various yogic and esoteric practices with the ultimate aim of union.[51] While Śiva is god, there are two manifestations of *śakti*: vibration (*nāda*) and illumination (*jñāna*). Vibration leads to, and awakens, illumination. The path of controlling the breath (*prāṇayama*), in fact, awakens the mind for illumination to occur. A mystical sound (mantra)[52] is experienced at the height of the practice of channeling energy.[53]

The emphasis on mantra is built on three concepts: (1) life-support (*nāda*), which supports all things of the universe, also referred to as the universal soul; (2) word (*śabda*),[54] which has fifty radical elements of vibrations connected to the fifty letters of the Sanskrit alphabet; and (3) breath (*prāṇa*), which internally harmonizes the gross body. These three concepts altogether constitute cosmic energy. *Śabda* and *prāṇa* generate the vibrations of *nāda*. The higher cerebral centers are regulated by meditation with *śabda* through which *nāda* resonates. *Nāda* is powerful and causes the *kundalinī* to rise up to the head. In turn, one experiences the unstruck sound (*anāhata nāda*), also described as mystical union (*sahaj*), during which duality is destroyed.

In light of the foregoing discussion, Nāth yogis belong to the category of the *renunciate living outside society* based on the fact that (1) they are oriented toward esoteric practices leading to spiritual realization, and (2) they "renounce-this-world" and take on the ascetic lifestyle, which is viewed as the prerequisite for liberation. While immortality is the ultimate goal, the Nāths also pay a lot of attention to attaining occult powers through practices such as hath-yoga. The Nāth yogis are revered as the pioneers of hath-yoga, one of the several types of yoga. The following section examines the Nāth practice of hath-yoga.

## THE INDIAN TRADITION OF HATH-YOGA

The word "yoga" is derived from the Sanskrit verb root *yuj* "to join, unite, harness, yoke, fasten, prepare," and has a variety of meanings, including "union, conjunction, discipline." The term "yoga" connotes some sort of experience of union with the universal soul or attainment of wisdom achieved through the path of disciplined mental and physical exercises. While yoga literally means "union," it is important to note that the emphasis of the Indian traditions of yoga is actually on the *disciplined path toward union* rather than on union itself.[55]

Yoga is simply one among many paths meant to be pursued in the context of a broader religious worldview, with the larger purpose of self-realization. The physical benefits of yoga are less significant than the primary goal of liberation. As stated by B. K. S. Iyenger: "The original idea of yoga is freedom and beatitude, and the by-products which come along the way, including physical health, are secondary for the practitioner."[56]

The classical tradition of yoga (also referred to as *rāja-yoga*) has had a vital impact on the development of Hindu belief and practice. Yogic practice, however, preceded Patañjali's formalization of classical yoga. There had prevailed different Vedic and Tantric practices for controlling the bodily and mental processes, even as some practices may have emerged from non-Aryan sources.[57] The practices associated with yoga, like celibacy, study, and asceticism, can be traced as far back as the Brāhmaṇas (ca. 700 BCE), which form part of the Vedic corpus of literature.[58]

There are many references to yogic discipline in the *Upaniṣads*, including *Kaṭha Upaniṣad*, *Kena Upaniṣad*, and *Śvetāśvatara Upaniṣad*.[59] Yogic practice is primarily described as the controlling of the senses in order to attain discriminative wisdom:

> When cease the five
> knowledge, together with mind (*manas*),
> and the intellect (*buddhi*) stirs not—
> That, they say, is the highest course.
>
> This they consider as Yoga—
> the firm holding back of the senses.
> Then one becomes undistracted.
> Yoga, truly, is the origin and the end. (*Kaṭha Upaniṣad* 6.10–11)

The essence of yoga is the path of controlling the senses for the purpose of acquiring discriminative wisdom.

In a later ritual text that employs the Upaniṣadic literary genre (in order to legitimize or "Brahmanize" Tantric ritual hymns), the *Yogatattva Upaniṣad* (ca. posterior to tenth century CE)[60] describes four main types of yoga: (1) *rāja-yoga*, the path of mental discipline, (2) *mantra-yoga*, the path of mantra,[61] (3) hath-yoga, the path of breath control, and (4) *laya-yoga*, the path of quieting the senses.[62] While this text is late, it nevertheless refers to four main types of yoga. Significantly, among the four is hath-yoga, the particular practice associated with the Nāth yogis.

Before discussing hath-yoga as the chief Nāth practice, one needs to first look at classical *rāja-yoga* because: (1) *rāja-yoga* provides the philosophical foundation to the general understanding of yoga, and, more important, (2) although hath-yoga specifically concentrates on breath control, it is to be done in conjunction with the mental exercises of *rāja-yoga*.

*Classical Rāja-yoga*

The classical tradition of yoga is often referred to as *rāja-yoga*, the "royal way" of discipline that focuses on controlling the intellectual faculties.[63] Yoga as outlined by Patañjali in his *Yoga-sūtras* (ca. 100 BCE) can be regarded as the formalization of classical yoga in the Indian subcontinent; thereafter, yoga came to be considered as one of the six Hindu orthodox philosophical schools.[64] The classical Yoga school is often grouped with the Sāṃkhya philosophical system because of the interconnectedness between the two. Indeed, the Sāṃkhya school is regarded as the theoretical foundation of the Yoga school's practical orientation in respect of spiritual attainment.[65] The Sāṃkhya-Yoga schools can thus be viewed as constituting the classical philosophical foundation of Hindu yogic traditions and practices.

The Sāṃkhya school is considered to be the most ancient of the orthodox Hindu philosophical schools. Kapila, although a mythical figure, is the celebrated founder of the Sāṃkhya school. Those who recognize Kapila as a historical figure consider him to have lived during the sixth century BCE. Kapila, as a religious figure and the son of the Hindu god Brahmā, expounds the Sāṃkhya system of thought in the much later text, *Bhāgavata Purāṇa* (ca. 900 CE).[66] The earliest Sāṃkhya text, the *Sāṃkhya-kārikās* (ca. 300 CE), was, however, written by the historical figure Īśvarakṛṣṇa.

Sāṃkhya metaphysics is based on a dualistic realism: there are two eternal realities (1) the self or pure consciousness (*puruṣa*) and (2) matter (*prakṛti*). The two eternal realities are under the influence of the three constituents or attributes (*guṇas*) that are considered to make up the material world.[67] Bondage occurs when *puruṣa* forgets its true nature and its actual relationship with *prakṛti*; that is, *puruṣa* as pure consciousness misidentifies itself with *prakṛti*, including the physical body, the senses, and the ego. This results in *puruṣa* losing awareness of its true nature as pure consciousness.

The classical Yoga school accepts the Sāṃkhya school of thought based on the fact that the latter provides the theoretical foundation for the Yoga system of practice or discipline of spiritual exercises for the attainment of discriminating wisdom. There is, however, one critical difference between the Sāṃkhya and Yoga schools. In addition to the twenty-five elements of reality that are delineated in the Sāṃkhya system, the Yoga school recognizes a twenty-sixth essential one—a distinct *puruṣa*—that is, the omnipresence of God. Unlike the Sāṃkhya schema of reality, the Yoga school allows for the belief in God (*Yoga-sūtras* 1.23–29). Hence, the Yoga school can be considered more theistic than the Sāṃkhya one.

Patañjali, both the revered founder of the classical Yoga system and the author of the *Yoga-sūtras* (ca. 100 BCE), delineates a practical system of spiritual exercises for the sole purpose of conquering the senses in order to attain discriminating knowledge about the true nature of pure consciousness. It is an intellectual process that entails the controlling of the mind: "They [mental modifications] are restrained by practice and desirelessness" (*Yoga-sūtra* 1.12).[68]

The commentary by Vyāsa on the above-cited aphorism on the yogic practice of controlling the mind for the acquisition of discriminating knowledge is:

> The stream of mind flows both ways: it flows towards good and it flows towards evil. That which flows on to perfect independence (*kaivalya*) down the plane of discriminative knowledge is named the stream of happiness. That which leads to rebirth and flows down the plane of indiscriminative ignorance is the stream of sin.
>
> Among those, the flow of the desirables is thinned by desirelessness; the flow of discrimination is rendered visible by habituating the mind to the experience of knowledge.
>
> Hence suppression of the mental modification is dependent upon both. (*Yoga bhāṣya* 1.12)

Yogic practice that leads one "down the plane of discriminative knowledge" is eightfold, with the ultimate goal of the experience of freedom:

1. physical ethical action (*yama*), such as nonviolence, truth, sexual abstinence, and generosity);
2. ritual ethical action (*niyama*), such as religious observances, purification;
3. posture (*āsana*);
4. breath control (*prāṇayama*);
5. the withdrawal of the senses (*pratyahāra*);
6. fixed attention on God (Īśvara) or unlimited space (*dhāraṇa*);
7. concentration or meditation (*dhyāna*); and
8. union or illumination (*samādhi*).

Union or illumination is the discriminative wisdom of the self (subject) and its relationship with matter (object).

It is important to note that Patañjali's *Yoga-sūtras* discuss the issue surrounding the experience of occult powers (*siddhis*) when practicing *rāja-yoga*.[69] The *sūtras*, however, emphasize that occult powers are incidental and should be regarded only as subsidiary. Unlike the Nāth yogic tradition, these occult powers, in actuality, should not be given too much or any attention at all, because they are a distraction from the ultimate experience of discriminative wisdom or freedom.

### *Hath-Yoga*

Hath-yoga literally means the "yoga of force," referring to the forceful physical exercises. Hath-yoga is a rigorous discipline of physical practices, consisting of posturing (*āsana*), hand gesturing (*mudrā*), and breathing (*prāṇayama*) exercises.[70] This physical discipline has as its purpose the reversing of natural tendencies like the aging process.[71] According to the hath-yoga tradition, natural processes are associated with the imbalance of the sun and moon principles; that is, there is too much buildup of solar heat. In fact, the term hath-yoga can also be interpreted metaphorically as the "union of the sun (*ha*) and moon (*tha*),"[72] reflecting the Nāth yogic belief that its practice should lead to a balance between the sun (arousal energy) and the moon (calming energy) for the practitioner's physical and mental well-being.[73]

This tradition's rigorous practices are for physical purification and strengthening of individuals. For instance, postures (*āsana*) restore or maintain flexibility, vitality, and overall well-being for the aspirants. Moreover, the aim of the yogic practice of breath control (*prāṇayama*) is for the freeing of the subtle body from the web of the gross body through gaining control over the physical body, including the senses. The channeling and controlling of the vital breath (*prāṇayama*)[74]—the most popular form of yoga in the West—causes the *kundalinī-śakti* to move from the base through the psychospiritual centers of energy (*cakra*) to higher states of consciousness, and ultimately illumination.

Transformation begins when the yogi concentrates on all of his vital breaths at the base of his central or medial channel. The concentration of breath opens the medial channel and cleanses the peripheral pathways (*nāḍīs*):

> If the air be inhaled through the left nostril, it should be expelled again through the other, and filling it through the right nostril, confining it there, it should be expelled through the

> left nostril. By practicing in this way, through the right and left nostrils alternately, the whole of the collection of the *nāḍīs* of the *yamis* (practitioner) becomes clean, i.e., free from impurities, after three months and over. (*Haṭha-yoga Pradīpikā* 2.10)[75]

According to Indian yogic traditions, there are 72,000 pathways (*nāḍīs*), which are the arteries of the subtle body. There are three crucial pathways: The first is the central or medial pathway called *suṣumanā-nāḍī*, which runs along the axis of the body from the base of the spine to the top of the head. Along this central pathway, the six major *cakras* are located. Twisting around the central pathway and crossing over at each *cakra* is the *iḍā-nāḍī* and *piṅgalā-nāḍī*, which also originate at the base of the spine.[76] On the one hand, when the subtle energy flows through the *iḍā* pathway, the result is an overall cooling or calming effect. On the other hand, the subtle energy flowing through the *piṅgalā* pathway results in arousal activity.[77] The *Gorakṣa Śataka* describes these three primary energy channels:

> Below the navel and above the male organ (is) the *kandayoni*, shaped like the egg of a bird. There (are) the origins of the seventy-two thousand *nāḍīs*. Among these thousands of *nāḍīs*, seventy-two have been specially noted. Again, among these ten carriers of the *prāṇa* are designated as the most important. *Iḍā* and *piṅgalā* and also the third *suṣumanā*, *gāndhārī*, *hastijihvā*, *pūṣā* and also *yaśasvinī*. *Almabuṣā*, *kuhūś*, and also *śaṃkhinī* the tenth are taught. The centres containing these *nāḍīs* should be known always by the Yogīs. *Iḍā* (is) situated on the left side, *piṅgalā* on the right, and *suṣumanā* in the mid region (e.g., between them); and *gāndhārī* in the left eye . . . (*Gorakṣa Śataka* 25–29)

The awakening of the *cakras* proceeds from the lowest center (pelvic) to the highest (head), during which physical cleansing and the stabilization of the body's energies occurs.[78] This process consists of the *kundalinī-śakti* energy piercing through the six *cakras* along the spinal column in the subtle body starting from the (1) anus (*mūlādhāra*), and proceeding through the (2) genitals (*svādhiṣṭhāna*), (3) navel (*maṇipura*), (4) heart (*anāhata*), and (5) throat (*viśuddhi*), to (6) between the eyebrows (*ājṭā*). When breath is stable so is the mind. This energy is forced upward to the head, causing yogic integration (*samādhi*):

> As one might open a door by force with a key, so the Yogī may break open the door of release by means of *kundalinī*. (*Gorakṣa Śataka* 51)

> As salt being dissolved in water becomes one with it, so when *ātma* and mind become one, it is called *samādhi.* (*Haṭha-yoga Pradīpikā* 4.5)

Yogic integration (*samādhi*) is the reversal of the aging process and death: "By cleansing the *nāḍīs* the *prāṇa* (is) restrained as desired, the digestive fire (is) kindled, internal sound is heard (becomes manifest), (and) one becomes diseaseless" (*Gorakṣa Śataka* 101). This process is sometimes referred to as the "seventh *cakra*" (*sahasrāra*) represented by a thousand-petal lotus crown.[79]

The yogic practices make the aspirants insensitive to pain, which, in turn, endows them with supernatural powers. Ultimately, the body needs to be trained so as to overcome obstacles—like the aging process—that lie in the path to immortality. Although the deeper spiritual or philosophical foundations are not often understood or are overlooked, the larger goal is to move toward self-realization or transformation. Traditionally, the physical exercises are meant to lead aspirants to the experience of freedom and immortality. Illumination consists of the merging of *śakti* with Śiva consciousness in the crown *cakra*. That is, the goal is to bring about the union of the polar eternals: energy (*śakti*) and consciousness (*cit*), the giver of ecstasy and bliss.

In sum, the Nāth yogis renounce worldly affairs for the purpose of acquiring occult powers and, ultimately, immortality. This puts them in our category of the *renunciates living outside society*. The tradition requires renunciation—including begging for food and celibacy—as the prerequisite to liberation. Amid their shamanistic, magical, and mystical practices to overcome evil spirits, they are also the pioneers of hath-yoga. Nāth yogis place great importance on the strenuous exercises of breath control in order to awaken the *kundalinī-śakti* so that it ascends to the highest *cakra*, where union occurs between *śakti* and Siva-consciousness. Unlike the *rāja-yogi*, who discourages giving any attention to occult powers, the Nāth yogis place much importance on acquiring occult powers in order to conquer the evil spirits and omens even as they simultaneously strive for immortality.

The Nāth yogis are the *siddhas* that participate in the *Siddh Goṣṭ* discourse, but it is Guru Nānak who is the central figure of the text. Guru Nānak is the author of *Siddh Goṣṭ* and the main speaker in the text. As such, it is important to analyze his life and the sources regarding his encounters and discourses with the Nāth yogis, all of which is discussed in the next chapter.

# Chapter Three

# Guru Nānak: Doctrine, Hagiography, and History

Guru Nānak, the first Sikh guru, is frequently revered as a mystic, based on his many spiritual compositions. Guru Nānak however also denounced the contemporaneous religious, socioeconomic and political beliefs and practices of northern India. Popularly known and revered for his protests against social injustice, Guru Nānak explicitly critiqued the caste system and the hypocrisy associated with it. His sociopolitical orientation, in a sense, can be viewed as mirroring his theological and moral stance as expressed through his hymns.[1] For instance, the value of equality and universality as expressed in his hymns provides the theological context for his rejection of the caste system:

> Acknowledge that everyone is high.
> No one should be seen as low.
> The One has made the vessels (humans),
>     and the One light pervades the three worlds.
> (Srī Rāg, M. 1, *GGS*, p. 62)

Guru Nānak notes in this hymn that the notions of superiority and inferiority are false; that is, no one should be viewed as superior (*uttam*) or inferior (*niche*) to another person because everyone is but a creation of *EkOaṅkār*, a vessel that contains the Divine Name (*nām*).

Like Guru Nānak, the classical Hindu philosophers or theologians also contend that everyone is equal in terms of the *ātma*. However, it is important to note that, in contrast to Guru Nānak, the classical philosophers accept the caste system at the social level.[2] For this reason, Guru Nānak's devotional hymns should be viewed in the light of his social and religious orientation as described in the Sikh traditional hagiographies on his life (*janam-sākhīs*).[3] Indeed, "tradition complements scripture,"[4] in that tradition provides a holistic or more complete understanding of Guru Nānak and his philosophical perspective.

Tradition as per the hagiographies about Guru Nānak provides a context for understanding his scriptural hymns because these accounts shed light on Guru Nānak's character as well as his existential situation. Guru Nānak's hymns—like *Siddh Goṣṭ*—should therefore be read with an understanding of his life story, including his disciplined way of "living-in-this-world," spiritual travels, and the events surrounding his religious discourses, all of which can be drawn from the Sikh hagiographies.

While ambiguity and historical inconsistency may exist in the various hagiographies about Guru Nānak, they, at the very least, reflect his spiritual orientation and message. Furthermore, the hagiographies reveal the reverence in which he is held by Sikh devotees. In the case of *Siddh Goṣṭ*, the hagiographies surrounding his spiritual journeys, and more specifically his encounters with the Nāth yogis, are relevant in that they provide some understanding of the context of Guru Nānak's meetings with them. Moreover, the narratives concerning Guru Nānak's encounters with the Nāth yogis are very much cherished and celebrated in the Sikh tradition evident in religious sermons (*kathā*).

This chapter provides a general overview of Guru Nānak's life based on both Sikh scriptural sources (*Gurū Granth Sāhib* and Bhāī Gurdās's *Vārāṅ*) and the *janam-sākhīs*. More specifically, it critically examines the scriptural references to Guru Nānak's encounters with the Nāth yogis, and also the hagiographies surrounding these encounters. The chapter highlights the importance of Guru Nānak's travels in his larger spiritual journey and attempts to situate *Siddh Goṣṭ* in relation to the hagiographies about him, in particular their descriptions of his encounters with the Nāth yogis.

## THE LIFE OF GURU NĀNAK

There are three main sources from which Guru Nānak's life can be drawn from: (1) *Gurū Granth Sāhib*, (2) Bhāī Gurdās's *Vārāṅ*, and (3) *janam-sākhīs* "life [hagiographical] stories [of Guru Nānak]." The first source, *Gurū Granth Sāhib* (*Ādi Granth*), the primary Sikh scripture, includes nine hundred and seventy-six hymns attributed to him. These hymns refer to various religious figures, teachers, and beliefs, reflecting his knowledge of many religious traditions. However, by no means are the hymns an historical account of Guru Nānak's life; rather, they primarily reveal Guru Nānak's philosophical thought. Having said that, there are several hymns about Bābar's invasion of the Indian subcontinent, referred to as "Bābar-bāṇī,"[5] from which one can delineate some very limited information about Guru Nānak's life. These hymns would nevertheless not suffice for an adequate biographical account of Guru Nānak.

The second source for the reconstruction of Guru Nānak's life is Bhāī Gurdās's commentary on the *Gurū Granth Sāhib* called the *Vārāṅ*.[6] The *Vārāṅ* provides some references to Guru Nānak's life and activities (I.23–45 and XI.13–14), including his spiritual journeys and meetings with the Nāth yogis. Like the *Gurū Granth Sāhib*, Bhāī Gurdās's *Vārāṅ* is also not a historical account of the first five Sikh gurus; rather, it primarily focuses on their spiritual teachings. According to W. H. McLeod, the references in the *Vārāṅ* can be accepted as valid, given the brevity of the life account of Guru Nānak. In fact, the selection of Guru Nānak's life events in Bhāī Gurdās coincide with the two main "life-stories" (*janam-sākhīs*) (see below the discussion on Guru Nānak's life for more elaboration).[7]

While both the *Gurū Granth Sāhib* and the *Vārāṅ* provide minimal information regarding Guru Nānak's life, the third and final main source for the reconstruction of Guru Nānak's life story is the genre of hagiographical literature known as the *janam-sākhīs* (literally "life-stories"), including (1) *Purātan Janam-sākhī*, (2) *Miharbān Janam-sākhī*, (3) *Bālā* or *Bhāī Bālā Janam-sākhī*, and (4) *Gyān-ratanāvalī* or *Manī Siṅgh Janam-sākhī*. The pan-Indian genre of hagiography (also referred to as "sacred biography") consists of stories about historical figures that mix fact with legend. Hagiographies relate historical events, even as they intertwine them with stories of supernatural births, miracles and the like. Although a story's kernel may be historical, the hagiographical accounts often reflect religious or societal concerns of the times. The purpose may more often than not be to transmit the kernel of truth contained in the stories.[8]

There are many pan-Indian hagiographical motifs that are common to stories about religious figures, leaders, philosophers, and mystics. First, religious figures or gurus of a lineage are frequently linked back to divine figures or even God. Second, the religious figure written about is often described in relation to other religious people in order to demonstrate his or her superiority. Last, stories contain miraculous birth and death accounts, in order to establish the spiritual status of the person along with a particular theological perspective.[9]

The Sikh hagiographies of Guru Nānak are most likely based on an oral tradition that began during the sixteenth century and was only later put into written form. The *janam-sākhī* corpus is believed to have emerged during the middle of the seventeenth and early eighteenth century (around one and a half centuries after Guru Nānak), continuing in to the nineteenth century.[10] That is, the extant *janam-sākhīs* can be traced back only to as early as the middle of the seventeenth century CE.

For Sikhs, the *janam-sākhīs* are highly revered stories reflecting Guru Nānak's spiritual stature, and are indeed a testimony of faith. Hagiographies convey a supernatural message in concrete terms, but they are often perceived as illogical to Sikhs who have acquired a critical and analytical orientation.[11] The stories are nevertheless central to Sikh belief and practice. One of the most renowned stories about Guru Nānak is "His immersion in the river for three days":

> One day they saw him [Nānak] going for a dip in the stream which ran past the town. Casting his garments upon the 'Shore of Life' Nānak plunged into the Infinite. He suddenly disappeared and was taken as drowned. . . . The waters of the river were combed. Divers were pressed into service. Search parties were organized, but to no avail. In fact hope faded, dwindled and was lost altogether.
>
> At the end of the third day, Nānak reappeared on the scene to the unending joy of the sorrowing citizens of Sultānpur. But he was now a completely changed man with a divine glory on his face and luminous halo around the head. Crowds gathered around him. He was not Nānak now, but Guru Nānak—the Divine Master, the World-Teacher. . . .
>
> When Nānak came out of the water, the words that were on his lips, were: "there is no Hindu, no Mussalman," meaning thereby that there is to be no distinction between man and man. 'Hindu' and 'Muslim' are our names for the 'Mask,' behind the mask is 'Man.' . . .[12]

This popular narrative about Guru Nānak's "enlightenment," told and retold in oral tradition, can be found in the most reliable *janam-sākhīs*.[13] Furthermore, it is even reiterated in more contemporary literary forms, such as the Indian comic series Amar Chitra Katha.[14] The popularity of contemporary forms of the *janam-sākhīs* demonstrates how important hagiographies are in the transmission of Sikh beliefs,[15] even if these beliefs are expressed through symbolism and metaphors.

Although hagiographies can provide information about the nature of a religious figure's character, "critical historians" generally regard them as unreliable legendary accounts. Some contemporary scholars actually view the hagiographies as reflections of how Guru Nānak was actually perceived at the time of their composition; that is, they are regarded as anecdotal accounts reflective of Sikh belief during the seventeenth and eighteenth centuries. Using the textual-critical method, McLeod provides a rigorous analysis of the various *janam-sākhīs*. He considers *Purāntan Janam-sākhī* and *Miharbān Janam-sākhī* as the most reliable hagiographies, but discounts *Bālā Janam-sākhī* and *Gyān-ratanāvalī Janam-sākhī*.[16]

Employing the textual-critical approach in his study of the *janam-sākhīs*, McLeod also provides a detailed schema whereby he classifies the many legendary accounts as "possible," "improbable," "impossible," and "partly probable."[17] For instance, the story about "Guru Nānak's immersion in the river for three days" is an example of a "partly probable" *sākhī*, based on the fact that some of the elements in it may likely have occurred while other supernatural elements surrounding Guru Nānak's spiritual experience are dubious.[18] Indeed, the religious experience and message that "there is no Hindu, there is no Muslim" is probable as it marks the turning point in Guru Nānak's spiritual mission. However, the event of Guru Nānak disappearing in the river for three days is questionable and thus cannot be taken literally.[19]

There are very few historical facts in the scriptural and *janam sākhī* literature on which one can base an accurate biography of Guru Nānak. Tension exists between tradition and scholarship even over the date of Guru Nānak's birth.[20] Modern researchers contend that he was born in the Indian month of Baisākh (April–May).[21] Guru Nānak's birthday as per tradition is, however, celebrated on the day of the largest full moon, which occurs during the month of Kattak (October–November; Kārtik in Sanskrit), an auspicious month in pan-Indian traditions. Having said that, it is agreed on by scholars that Guru Nānak was born in 1469 CE in a town called Rāi Bhoi dī Talvaṇḍī in Shekhupurā *tahsīl* (district) of Lahore—southwest of Lahore city.[22] The town, located in present-day Pakistan, is now referred to as Nānakāṇa Sāhib or Nānakiāṇa Sāhib out of reverence for the Sikh guru.

During the period of Guru Nānak's childhood and early adulthood, the verses of Guru Nānak's life events referred to by Bhāī Gurdās more or less correspond to—or at least do not contradict—either of the two most reliable *janam-sākhīs* (*Purātan Janam-sākhī* and *Miharbān Janam-sākhī*) established by McLeod. It is known that Guru Nānak's father belonged to the merchant caste (*bedī khatrī*) of the larger *kṣatriya* class. Guru Nānak was married at the young age of twelve years (according to *Purātan Janam-sākhī*) or at sixteen years (according to *Miharbān Janam-sākhī*). He had two sons named Lakhmī Dās and Srī Chand, and moved to Sultānpur to work for Governor (*nawāb*) Daulat K̲h̲ān Lodī. It is after Guru Nānak's shift to Sultānpur that there emerges considerable divergence between the two main *janam-sākhīs*, especially in respect of his journeys as an *udāsī*.[23]

*Udāsī* literally means "cool, indifferent, detached or apathetic." The term often refers to someone who withdraws from worldly affairs in the pursuit of higher spiritual goals, such as an ascetic or renunciate. In Sikhism, however, *udāsī* also specifically refers to Guru Nānak's four spiritual journeys or travels. That is, although Guru Nānak is not a renunciate, he has, in a sense, *temporarily* withdrawn from his householder duties in his spiritual pursuit. According to Sikh popular tradition, Guru Nānak traveled in the four directions of the compass as indicated in table 1. Travel in the four directions of the world is a common motif in pan-Indian hagiography and perhaps was a common practice.[24] Guru Nānak is said to have traversed the four directions from Sultānpur, Punjab.

Guru Nānak traveled as an *udāsī* to a great number of places where he sought out religious figures and teachers. He engaged in religious dialogue with many persons belonging to a variety of traditions, including Brahmin priests, Muslim sheikhs, Sufī mystics, Jain and Buddhist monks, Hindu yogis, and the like. Bhāī Gurdās describes Guru Nānak's experience during his religious encounters thus:

> Celebates, ascetics, immortal archorites, the *siddhs*, *nāths* and teacher-taughts were available in abundance . . . many varieties of gods, goddesses, *munis*, *bhairavs*, and other protectors were there . . . seeing *rākṣasas*, demons, *daityas* in their imagination, people were totally in the clutches of duality. All were engrossed with ego and the taughts were getting drowned along with their teachers. Even after minute research, the guru-oriented were nowhere to be found. All the sects, *pīrs*, *paigambars* of the blinds were pushing the blinds into a well. (*Vārāṅ* 1.26)[25]

Guru Nānak's dialogues with various religious figures appear to have crystallized his belief in the recitation of the Divine Name as the means to liberation. According to tradition, it is believed that during his spiritual journeys Guru Nānak attracted many followers, and that several encounters with the Nāth yogis (possibly as related in *Siddh Goṣṭ*) occurred during his travels (*udāsī*).

Guru Nānak did, indeed, travel to a variety of places and interact with people from many different backgrounds. In doing so, he significantly took on the customs of the people with whom he was meeting in order to blend in. Bhāī Gurdās mentions this practice of taking on the

Table 1. Guru Nānak's Travels in the Four Directions*

| *Travel (udasi)* | *Direction* | *Dates* | *Places* | *Function* |
|---|---|---|---|---|
| First | Eastward | ca. 1498–1508<br>1506–1510 | U.P., Bengal and Assam | Visit with Hindu, Jain, and Buddhist centers |
| Second | Southward | ca. 1508–1513<br>1510–1515 | Orissa up to Sri Lanka | Visit with Hindu, Jain, and Buddhist centers |
| Third | Northward | ca. 1513–1518<br>1515–1517 | Kashmir, U.P., up to Mount Kailash | Visit with the *siddhs, lāmas,* and Buddhist centers |
| Fourth | Westward | ca. 1518–1524<br>1517–1520 | Gorakh-haṭaṛī, through Afghanistan, up to Meçca, Medina, and Baghdad | Visit with Islamic and Christian centers |

*Based on McLeod's extensive analysis of the *janam-sākhīs* in *Gurū Nānak and the Sikh Religion* and D. S. Grewal's work on Guru Nanak's travels to the north and east in *Guru Nanak's Travel to Himalayan and East Asian Region, A New Light* (Delhi: National Book Shop, 1995).

customs of the people or "locals." For instance, he narrates, "donning blue attire then Bābā Nānak went to Mecca" (1.32) and "Then Bābā (Nānak) returned to Kartārpur where he put aside his attire of a recluse. Now putting on a householder's dress, he sat splendidly on a cot. . . ." (1.38). Guru Nānak believed that, without compromising one's religious beliefs, one should assimilate by taking on the particular customs and practices of the places one visited. In fact, by changing his dress and taking on local cultural practices, Guru Nānak amplified his spiritual message that one's outer appearance has no bearing on one's interior religious practice or one's spiritual state.

There are numerous accounts of Guru Nānak's *udāsīs* in both Bhāī Gurdās's *Vārāṅ* and the *janam-sākhīs*. While Bhāī Gurdās's *Vārāṅ* does not clearly outline Guru Nānak's four journeys, he does make reference to several lengthy travels and a couple of short trips to pilgrimage places: "Bābā [Nānak] came to the pilgrimage centers and by participating in the ceremonies there he observed them minutely. . . ."

(*Vārāṅ* 1.25). The places which Guru Nānak is said to have visited include Mount Sumeru[26] (1.28), Mecca (1.32), Medina (1.37), Baghdad (1.35), Kartārpur (1.38), Achal Baṭālā (1.39), Multān (1.44), and Kartārpur (1.45).

The descriptions of Guru Nānak's journeys in Bhāī Gurdās's *Vārāṅ* in some ways do not correspond with *Purātan Janam-sākhī* and *Miharbān Janam-sākhī*. For example, according to the *Vārāṅ*, Guru Nānak visited Baghdad during his journey to the west. However, the two main *janam-sākhīs* (*Purātan Janam-sākhī* and *Miharbān Janam-sākhī*) make no reference to this visit. Likewise, according to *Purātan Janam-sākhī*, Guru Nānak visited Laṅka, yet there is no specific reference to such a visit in Bhāī Gurdās's *Vārāṅ* or in the *Miharbān Janam-sākhī*.[27]

On the one hand, the accounts of the eastern and southern travels in the *Purātan Janam-sākhī* and *Miharbān Janam-sākhī* do not strictly correspond with one another.[28] On the other hand, the details on the northern and western journeys are more in agreement, even as there may be some variation.[29] Besides, the *Purātan Janam-sākhī* refers to a short fifth journey to Gorakh-haṭaṛī (even as the *Miharbān Janam-sākhī* describes Guru Nānak as having visited the place twice during his fourth journey to the west). Although there is discrepancy among the sources regarding Guru Nānak's journeys, there is congruence over the fact that Guru Nānak, indeed, ventured out in the four directions, first to the east, then to the south, north and lastly to the west. Moreover, many of the places mentioned are the same, even though the chronology of the visits remains problematic.

Given the historical inconsistencies found in the narrative accounts, important questions emerge, such as: How do these *janam-sākhīs* enhance our understanding of the scriptural hymns? What is the religious significance of these religious journeys (*udāsīs*)? These questions are addressed in the next section, with a specific focus on Guru Nānak's meetings with the Nāth yogis.

Notwithstanding the ambiguity and historical inconsistencies about Guru Nānak's "four journeys," by the time Guru Nānak had established his theological or philosophical system, the first Mug͟hal Emperor—Zahiruddīn Muhammad Bābar (1526–1530 CE)—had commenced his rule in northern India.[30] During Bābar's rule, Guru Nānak was, in fact, temporarily imprisoned.[31] Guru Nānak's "Bābar-bāṇī," contained in the *Gurū Granth Sāhib*, provides an account for Bābar's invasion that had occurred around 1521 CE,[32] which resulted in the establishment of Mug͟hal rule over India (1526 CE):

O Lālo![33]
[Bābar's] wedding party of sin

has come from Kabul,
and demands [our land] as a gift.
O Lālo!
Humanity and righteousness are hidden
and falsehood roams around as the leader.
O Lālo!
The Qāzīs and the Brahmins are no more,
and the devil performs the marriage rites. . . .
O Lālo!
The wedding songs are of blood,
and [the wedded ones] are anointed with blood!
(Tilaṅg, M.1, *GGS*, pp. 722–23)

"Bābar-bāṇī" testifies to Guru Nānak's concern with worldly affairs. Even though most of his hymns focus primarily on existential suffering related to *saṅsār* (*saṃsāra* in Sanskrit) and attachment to the material world, Guru Nānak also clearly viewed suffering as the result of external forces, such as tyranny and oppression.[34] For Guru Nānak, these external forces also need to be acknowledged and addressed. In this way, as argued by Louis E. Fenech, Guru Nānak possessed the potentiality to be a martyr; that is, he saw one had to simultaneously fight social and political injustice, and to renounce one's ego in order to live according to the will of the Guru.[35]

Guru Nānak eventually settled on the banks of river Rāvī in Kartārpur, Punjab, where he spent the last fifteen years of his life with his wife and two sons. He is believed to have spent these remaining years of his life teaching his many followers about the true nature of Reality as he saw it. It is in Kartārpur that Guru Nānak died in 1539 CE.[36] His place of retirement on the Rāvī riverbank is now called Dehrā Bābā Nānak.

One of the significant differences between Guru Nānak and other contemporaneous religious teachers or saints is that, before he died, he appointed a successor—Guru Aṅgad—to continue his religious lineage. It is interesting that, although Guru Nānak appointed a successor, he chose neither of his two sons. Guru Nānak is revered as the first Guru by the Sikhs, and is also revered as a Sant by many Hindus, especially in the northwestern region of India.

## GURU NĀNAK'S ENCOUNTERS WITH THE NĀTH YOGIS

There are important scriptural and hagiographical references to Guru Nānak's encounters with the Nāth yogis or Nāth *siddhs*. However, much ambiguity surrounds the various accounts about Guru Nānak's meetings with the Nāth yogis. Foremost, there is dispute over which actual encounter with the Nāth yogis is the one contained in *Siddh Goṣṭ*. While Guru Nānak does refer to the Nāth yogis in the *Gurū Granth Sāhib,* his encounters with the Nāth yogis are in actuality described in Bhāī Gurdās's *Vārāṅ* and the various hagiographies about Guru Nānak's spiritual journeys (*udāsīs*). These include detailed descriptions about Guru Nānak's meetings with the Nāth yogis, in particular on his third journey to the "north country," where many followers of the Gorakhnāth tradition live. Furthermore, Bhāī Gurdās's *Vārāṅ* describes a short trip in the Punjab, during which Guru Nānak is said to have met a Nāth yogi. In addition, there is a so-called fifth journey, during which Guru Nānak is said to have also met with several Gorakhnāthis, described in *Purātan janam-sākhī* 52.

*Overview of the References to Guru Nānak's Encounters with the Nāth Yogis*

Guru Nānak makes reference to the Nāth yogis in the *Gurū Granth Sāhib* hymn Vār Rāmkalī, *salok* 2–7 of *pauṛī* 12.[37] This scriptural reference neither describes an encounter between Guru Nānak and the Nāth yogis, nor is it written in the form of an actual dialogue (*goṣṭ*). The hymn, however, does cite the Nāth yogis in succession—beginning with Īsar (Īśa or Śiva, the Primal Master), and followed by Gorakh, Gopīchand, Charapaṭ, and Bhartṛharī[38]—in each verse, which has a specific theme regarding the path toward liberation.

The hymn employs some yogic symbolism for the stages of spiritual development (as described in chapter 2). It starts off with a verse that is attributed to Īsar, who speaks of the need for a householder to discipline his sense-desires; the second verse cites Gorakhnāth, who describes the stage of detachment and the "burning of one's ego"; the verse that follows is attributed to Gopīchand, who talks about the *udāsī* experience of "union of the moon (calming) and the sun (arousal)"; the subsequent verse cites Charapaṭ, who speaks of exercising "control over the body and sexual desire"; and the last verse, attributed to Bhartṛharī, discusses the "pillar" connecting one to God:

> One is a *vairāgī* (renunciate),
> if one turns toward the Creator.
> Such a one erects a pillar (tenth gate),
> with the sky (Infinite).

Night and day,
such a one is in [deep] inner meditation.
Bhartṛharī says: The embodiment of Truth,
the quintessence (of Reality) has no form or shape. (6)

It is interesting to note that Gorakhnāth, Gopīnāth, and Charapaṭnāth are frequently included in the various lists of the Nāth immortal teachers. Although there is a general popular belief in the immortal existence of nine Nāths and eighty-four *siddhs* in the Himalayas, the "historical" Gorakhnāth and other Nāth teachers were in fact not contemporaries of Guru Nānak. The inclusion in the *Gurū Granth Sāhib* of the various immortal Nāth yogis or teachers can be interpreted as referring to those religious persons who occupied the seat of the earlier Nāth yogis cited and had also taken on their names—a pan-Indian practice among traditions where guru-disciple lineages exist. Furthermore, each Nāth yogi says the same line: "The embodiment of Truth, the quintessence [of Reality] has no form or shape." It can therefore be inferred that Guru Nānak has inserted the names of the Nāth yogis in his exposition of the path toward liberation in order to show that even the Nāth masters seek the "Truth," which is beyond any form (*nirguṇ*).

Guru Nānak's reference to these religious figures nevertheless indicates his familiarity with the Nāth tradition; possibly, he also had a Nāth yogic audience in mind. The hymn (Vār Rāmkalī *salok* 2–7 of *pauṛī* 12) is, interestingly, cited in a narrative account (*Miharbān Janam-sākhī* 117) within the framework of a dialogue between Guru Nānak and the Nāth yogis. Indeed, the insertion of this hymn from the *Gurū Granth Sāhib* can be viewed as a means of legitimizing the hagiographical account of Guru Nānak's encounter with the Nāth yogis. Such insertion of passages from revered religious or scriptural literature as a means of legitimization is a common practice among Indian religions.[39]

Like this scriptural reference to the Nāth yogis, *Siddh Goṣṭ* also provides very little historical information. *Siddh Goṣṭ* does not indicate whether the discourse occurred during Guru Nānak's third journey, nor does it mention the actual place of the dialogue. The only historical or biographical information *Siddh Goṣṭ* provides is Guru Nānak's reference to two specific Nāth yogis; the religious disciples of Gorakhnāth named Charapaṭ (verse four) and Loharipā (verse seven) are mentioned even though they were not contemporaries of Guru Nānak. The remaining verses (twelve to seventy-three) do not indicate or reveal as to whom Guru Nānak is talking with.

*Siddh Goṣṭ*, however, does describe the purpose of Guru Nānak's journeys. Guru Nānak explains that his motive as an *udāsī* is to search for those who are on the path according to the will of the Guru:

*Siddhs*:
Why have you left your home and become an *udāsī*?
Why have you adopted these religious robes?
What is it that you seek to trade?
How will you carry others across [the ocean of *saṅsār*]? (*SG* 17)

*Nanak*:
I have become an *udāsī* in search of *gurmukhs*.
I have adopted these robes in search of their vision.
I am out to trade Truth.
I am a peddler of Truth.
Nanak says: With the help of *gurmukhs*,
others can be carried across,
[the ocean of *saṅsār*]. (*SG*18)

This verse intimates Guru Nānak's practice of taking on the external customs of those he is visiting in order to blend in ("I have adopted these robes in search of their vision"), without changing his own spiritual orientation. Guru Nanak traveled far for the purpose of religious discourse with various religious figures and teachers during which he could teach his path toward liberation. In fact, the employment of the *goṣṭ* genre itself can be understood as being based on the fact that many philosophers or poet-saints did travel for the purposes of religious discourse.

In contrast to Guru Nānak's hymns that refer to the Nāth yogis (though without providing any historical information about his encounters with them) Bhāī Gurdās's *Vārāṅ* and the hagiographies do provide descriptions of Guru Nānak's meetings with the Nāth yogis. Bhāī Gurdās's commentary on the *Gurū Granth Sāhib* describes Guru Nānak as having definitely met the Nāth yogis or Nāth *siddhs* (*Vāran* I. 28–31). Guru Nānak is portrayed as having climbed up to Mount Sumeru (regarded as the center of the world according to mythological texts).[40] It is at Mount Sumeru that Guru Nānak is said to have encountered a group of Nāth *siddhs*, who consisted of "the mind of the eighty-four *siddhs* and Gorakh et al." (28); that is, the group through Nāth religious practice had attained equivalency with the revered perfected ones. This reference emphasizes the level of accomplishment of those with whom Guru Nānak discoursed. Then a dialogue between the Nāth *siddhs* and Guru Nānak ensues:

> *Siddhs asked (Guru Nānak):* O young boy! Which power brought you here?
>
> *(Guru Nānak):* I have remembered the Lord with loving devotion and meditated upon Him deeply.
>
> *Siddhs said:* O young man, tell us your name.
>
> *Bābā (Nānak) replied:* O respected Nāth! This Nānak has attained this position through remembrance of the name of the Lord. By calling himself lowly, one attains the high position. (*Vārāṅ* I.28)

During this encounter Guru Nānak discoursed with the Nāth *siddhs* on his view of the state of the world:

> *Siddhs asked again:* O Nānak! How the dealings are there on the mother earth?
>
> *Bābā replied:* O respected Nāth, The truth is (dim) like moon and the falsehood like deep darkness. The darkness of the moonless night of the falsehood has spread around and I, in order to search for the (truthful) world, have undertaken this journey. The earth is engrossed with sin and its support, the *dharma* in the form of the ox is crying and wailing (for rescue). In such circumstances, when *siddhs*, the adepts, (by becoming repudiators) have taken refuge in the mountains, how the world could get redeemed. Yogis also bereft of knowledge and simply applying ashes to their bodies are lying down unconcerned. Without the Guru the world is getting drowned. (*Vārāṅ* I.29)
>
> O God! In *kaliyug*, the mentality of the *jīv* has become like the mouth of dog which always seeks the dead to eat. The kings are sinning as if the protective fence were itself devouring the (crop in the) field. Bereft of knowledge, the blind people are uttering falsehood. Now the gurus are dancing variously to the tunes played by the disciples. The taught now sit at home and the teachers go to their abodes. *Qāzīs* enjoy bribes and getting the same they have lost their high regards and position. Man and woman love each other for riches, may they come from anywhere. The sin has become ubiquitous in the whole world. (*Vārāṅ* I.30)

Finally, Guru Nānak engages the *siddhs* in a debate on the "True" system of yoga. He advocates the discipline of the recitation of the Divine Name as opposed to the mental and physical exercises performed by the *siddhs*, just as the *siddhs* believe that Guru Nānak should adopt their theory and practice of yoga.

A popular mythic theme is that one of the Nāth yogis gave Guru Nānak a begging bowl to fetch water. When he went to the stream for the water, there was no water to be found; instead, Guru Nānak saw rubies and jewels in the stream. He was not impressed by the Nāth yogic powers and influence through *māyā*. Furthermore, he was not enticed by the jewels, and thus did not take them (something of which a *manmukh* would have done). Rather, on returning with the bowl, Guru Nanak said to the *siddhs*, "O Nāth, in that stream there is no water." Bhāī Gurdās's commentary adds:

> Through (the power of the word) *śabad* he conquered the *siddhs* and propounded his altogether new way of life. In *kaliyug*, instead of yogic exercises the name of the Lord who is beyond all sufferings (Nānak) is the only source of delight. (*Vārāṅ* I.31)

These stories in the *Vārāṅ* about Guru Nānak's meeting with the Nāth yogis contain two important themes. First, the Divine Name is greater than worldly riches evident in the fact that Guru Nānak was not interested in the jewels. For Guru Nānak, the jewels are the same as the other rocks in the empty stream. Second, the recitation of the Divine Name, as taught by Guru Nānak, is superior to the mental and physical exercises of the Nāth yogis.

Bhāī Gurdās's *Vārāṅ* (I.39–44) also describes a short trip that Guru Nānak took to Achal Baṭālā, Punjab, for the Śivrātrī festival. Amid a group of *siddhs*, Guru Nānak has an intense dialogue with Yogi Bhaṅgar Nāth:

> Said Nānak, 'O Bhaṅgar Nāth, your mother-teacher is unmannerly. She has not cleansed the inner-self of your body-pot and your clumsy thoughts have burnt your flower (of knowledge which was to become fruit). You, while distancing and repudiating household life, go again to those householders for begging. Except their offerings, you don't get anything.'
>
> Listening to this, the yogis snarled loudly and invoked many spirits. 'In *kaliyug*, Bedī Nānak has trampled and driven away the six philosophical schools of Indian philosophy.' . . . (*Vārāṅ* I.40–41)

The yogis are very competitive in the debate on the superior path toward liberation, during which they display their mastery of magical and yogic powers. The passage ends, however, with Guru Nānak demonstrating his ability to subdue and conquer their occult powers.

Table 2. Sources of Guru Nānak's Encounters with the Nāth Yogis

| *Citation* | *Guru Nānak's* Udasi | *Mythic Story* | *Location* | *References to Nāth Yogis* |
|---|---|---|---|---|
| *Gurū Granth Sāhib*, Vār Rāmkalī, salok 2–7 of *pauṛī* 12 | No reference | No story described | No place mentioned | Īsar, Gorakh, Gopīchand, Charapaṭ, Bhartṛharī |
| Bhāī Gurdās *Vārāṅ* I.28–31 | Before travel to Mecca; Third journey | Meeting with *siddhs*; Guru Nānak given an empty bowl to fill with water | Mount Sumeru | General reference to *siddhs*/Nāths |
| Bhāī Gurdās *Vārāṅ* I.39–44 | A short trip after Mecca | Meeting with *siddhs*; Guru Nānak conquers their magical powers | Achal Baṭālā | Yogi Bhaṅgar Nāth |
| *Purātan Janam-sākīi* 18 | First journey | *Siddhs* unsuccessfully attempted to persuade Guru Nānak to join their order | Nānakmāta (also known as as Gorakhmāta in northern U.P. | *Siddhs* |
| *Purātan Janam-sākhī* 50 | Third journey after Kashmir | Nānak sent to fill a bowl with water | Mount Sumeru and Achal Baṭālā | Siva, Gorakhnāth, Bhartṛharī, Gopīchand, Charapṭ |
| *Purātan Janam-sākhī* 52 | Fifth journey | None; meeting with *siddhs*; link made to *SG* | Gorakh-haṭaṛī | *Siddhs* |
| *Miharbān Janam-sākhī goṣṭ* 117 | Third journey after Sultānpur | Meeting with Nāth yogis | Mount Sumeru | Gorakhnāth, Macchendranāth, Īsar, Charapaṭ, Baṅgarnāth, Ghoṛācholī, Bālgundāī, Bhartṛharī, and Gopīchand |
| *Miharbān Janam-sākhī, goṣṭ* 173 | Short trip? | Discourse with the *siddhs* | Achal Baṭālā | "Guru of the yogis" |

Besides the references found in Bhāī Gurdās's *Vārāṅ*, there are several other—albeit inconsistent—hagiographical accounts of Guru Nānak's meeting and discoursing with the Nāth yogis. As indicated in table 2, the *janam-sākhīs* vary in terms of Guru Nānak's departure point, place of discourse, and the events surrounding the meetings with the Nāth yogis and, last, as to which yogis he spoke with. According to *Purātan Janam-sākhī* 50,[41] Guru Nānak set out from Kashmir for Mount Sumeru, and during that trip he discoursed with numerous Nāth yogis. After leaving Kashmir, Guru Nānak ascended to Mount Sumeru, where he is said to have conversed with Śiva, Gorakhnāth, Bhartṛharī, Gopīchand, and Charapaṭ. The Nāth yogis sent him to fill a pot with water. Instead, the pot filled up with jewels. Guru Nānak broke the pot, repaired it, exorcised the spell with a *salok* (*śloka* in Sanskrit) and then filled it with water.

In addition, *Purātan Janam-sākhī* 52[42] describes a short "fifth journey," during which Guru Nānak held a discourse with Nāth yogis. The discourse is said to have taken place at Gorakh-haṭaṛī (a Nāth center in Peshawar, present-day Pakistan),[43] where he is said to have met and discoursed with some Nāth *siddhs*. Similar to the other hagiographies, these Nāth *siddhs* sought to impress him with their displays of occult power, but without success. According to *Purātan Janam-sākhī* 52, it is from Guru Nānak's visit to Gorakh-haṭaṛī that the work entitled *Siddh Goṣṭ* emerged. This reference to *Siddh Goṣṭ* in the account can be interpreted either literally or metaphorically.

According to *Miharbān Janam-sākhī goṣṭ* 117,[44] Guru Nānak set out from Sultānpur for the north. He is said to have climbed Mount Sumeru, where he found all nine *siddhs* seated there—Gorakhnāth, Machhendranāth, Īsarnāth, Charapaṭnāth, Baṅgarnāth, Ghoṛācholī, Bālgundāī, Bhartṛharī, and Gopīchand. When Gorakhnāth asked the identity of the visitor his disciples replied, "This is Nanak Bedī, a *pīr* (muslim mystic) and a *bhagat* (Hindu term for devotee) who is a householder. Nānak Bedī is a great *bhagat*." Gorakhnāth then addressed Guru Nānak, asking him as to where he had come from. The Guru replied that he had come from Āsā-andesā ("hope and fear") and that he dwelt just like a waterfowl floats on water.[45]

### Siddh Goṣṭ *in the Light of the Scriptural and Hagiographical References*

Popular oral tradition states that some dialogues with the yogis belonging to the Nāth tradition (possibly the *Siddh Goṣṭ* itself) occurred during Guru Nānak's third journey (*udāsī*) to the Himalayas. However, there is ambiguity about some of the facts in these narrative accounts. First, the meeting with the Nāth yogis on the third journey is said to have taken place at Mount Sumeru, a place that is mythological. While Mount Sumeru as mentioned in Bhāī Gurdās's *Vārāṅ* and several of the *janam-sākhīs* is mythological, that is not to say that Guru Nānak did not go to Mount Kailash.[46] Second, as aforementioned, neither Gorakhnāth nor his disciples were contemporaries of Guru Nānak. Third, in contrast to the third journey, the fifth journey also talks of a meeting and discourse between Guru Nānak and Nāth yogis, but at either Gorakh-haṭaṛī or Achal Baṭālā, both of which are likely Nāth centers but are not in the Himalayas.

Based on the references in Bhāī Gurdās's *Vārāṅ* and the various hagiographies, there are four important places where Guru Nānak met with the Nāth yogis: (1) Mount Sumeru, (2) Gorakh-haṭaṛī, (3) Achal Baṭālā, and (4) Nānakmāta (Gorakhmāta). According to popular Sikh tradition, *Siddh Goṣṭ* occurred at Mount Kailash on Guru Nānak's third journey to Lake Mansarovar in the Himalayas. In contrast, the traditional Sikh historians hold different views as to which encounter is the one outlined in *Siddh Goṣṭ*.

Bhai Vir Singh, Sher Singh, and Sahib Singh share the same view that *Siddh Goṣṭ* occurred during the Śivrātrī fair at Achal Baṭālā. Their conclusion is based on the fact that Bhāī Gurdās's *Vārāṅ* describes the *siddhs* having gathered around Guru Nānak in formal debate after having had their occult powers subdued by him (*Vārāṅ* I.39–44).[47] By way of contrast, Narain Singh argues that some of the traditional scholars have misinterpreted Bhāī Gurdās's *Vārāṅ*, and have consequently wrongly linked *Siddh Goṣṭ* to Guru Nānak's dialogue with Bhaṅgar Nāth at Achal Baṭālā. Narain Singh contends that *Siddh Goṣṭ* occurred during Guru Nānak's discourses with the Nāth yogis at Gorakh-haṭarī, basing his position on the fact that the *siddhs* in *Siddh Goṣṭ* were similarly not aggressive nor were they preoccupied with acquiring occult powers as they were at Achal Baṭālā.[48] In the like manner, Jodh Singh puts forward the argument that the *siddhs* of *Siddh Goṣṭ* were from Mount Sumeru, relying on their character and disinterest in occult powers as evidenced in *Siddh Goṣṭ*.[49]

Like many of the Sikh traditional historians, one critical historian of Sikhism, W. H. McLeod, also contends that there is a "firmer basis" for the *Siddh Goṣṭ* to have taken place at Achal Baṭālā. McLeod's conclusions are based on the fact that (1) Bhāī Gurdās's *Vārāṅ* (I.39-44) and many hagiographical texts (e.g., *Purātan Janam-sākhī* 50 and *Miharbān Janam-sākhī* 117)[50] record the discourse as having occurred during the Śivrātrī fair at Achal Baṭālā, and (2) Achal Baṭālā is in close proximity to Kartārpur.[51]

Interestingly, notwithstanding the historical inconsistency and ambiguity that surrounds the hagiographies, these accounts often appear to be closer to the sentiments of the common people than the religious philosophy itself. At the mention of *Siddh Goṣṭ*, many Sikhs talk about the hagiographical stories surrounding Guru Nānak's encounters with the Nāth yogis, rather than the actual philosophical teachings that Guru Nānak outlines in the text. Indeed, the hagiographies about Guru Nānak, including his encounters with the Nāth yogis, are an integral part of Sikh oral tradition, reflective of the fact that people belonging to an oral tradition respond more readily and wholeheartedly to stories rather than abstract ideas.[52] For many Sikhs, the stories about Guru Nānak are the ultimate testimony to his spiritual stature and his superiority as a spiritual master. With regard to his meetings with the Nāth yogis, Sikhs give much attention to how Guru Nānak subdued and conquered. their occult powers as described by Bhāī Gurdās:

> . . . the *siddhs* counted all sorts of medicines and started making tantric sounds of the mantras. Yogis changed themselves into the forms of lions and tigers and performed many actions. Some of them became winged and flew like birds. Some started hissing like the cobra and some poured out fire. Bhaṅgar Nāth[53] plucked the stars and may upon deer skin started floating on water. The fire (of desires) of the *siddhs* was inextinguishable. (*Vārāṅ* I.41)
>
> . . . Baba replied 'O respected Nāth! I have nothing worth showing to you . . . I have no support except of the Guru, holy congregation and the Word. That *parātman* who is all full of benedictions (*śivam*) for all is stable and the earth (and material over it) is transitory. . . . The *siddhs* exhausted themselves with the tantra-mantras but the word of Lord did not allow their powers to come up.' (*Vārāṅ* I.42)

Although Sikh followers often understand the "yogis changing into various animal forms" quite literally, it is also plausible that these various animal forms actually refer to different yogic positions, which are named after animals. For instance, a common posture is called the cobra-pose (*bhujaṅg-āsan*), which involves lying on the stomach and raising the torso upward with the arms, during which the *yogi* even hisses like a snake.

As with the stories about Guru Nānak subduing the great powers of the Nāth yogis or *siddhs*, much importance is also placed on the stories about how Guru Nānak fixed the pot and filled it with water. The present authors were surprised at how, on mentioning this present project on *Siddh Goṣṭ*, many Sikhs were quick to narrate the mythic account about Guru Nānak taking a pot to Lake Mansarovar (as described in Bhāī Gurdās's *Vārāṅ* and several of the *janam-sākhīs*) in order to demonstrate his spiritual superiority. Indeed, for many Sikhs this story appears to be the key to demonstrating that the path of the Divine Name is superior to yogic practice and the prerequisite for liberation.

According to a revered Sikh philosopher and preacher, Giani Sant Singh Maskeen, the *Siddh Goṣṭ* dialogue occurred at Mount Kailash during Guru Nānak's travels to Lake Mansarovar in the Himalayas. Sikhs in the oral tradition seemingly focus on the story of the pot being supernaturally being filled with jewels. However, Maskeen claims that it is the actual teachings expounded in *Siddh Goṣṭ* that are of greater importance. He contends that the real significance of *Siddh Goṣṭ* in the development of Sikh thought lies, in fact, in the explanation of the devotional path while "living-in-this-world" that Guru Nānak gives to the renunciates (*siddhs*).[54]

Sikhs often overlook the actual teachings of the *Siddh Goṣṭ* hymn, but rather embrace the events in which Guru Nānak is described as having subdued the great yogic powers of the Nāths and *siddhs*. This has led to incongruence between popular tradition[55] and the Sikh theology based on Guru Nānak's teachings incorporated in the *Gurū Granth Sāhib*. In fact, another philosopher-preacher, Giani Kishan Singh Parwana, contends that such hagiographies can only be verified in the light of the *Gurū Granth Sāhib*. That is, if the hagiography is contrary to the philosophy of the *Gurū Granth Sāhib*, it must then be deemed to be unreliable.[56]

Even though hagiography can be contrary to the teachings of the *Gurū Granth Sāhib*, it is still central to Sikh devotional practice. Unlike the scriptural compositions taken from the *Gurū Granth Sāhib* and Bhāī Gurdās's *Vārāṅ*, which are recited in the form of prayer, the *janam-sākhīs* do not have the status of scripture, and are used in religious sermons (*kathā*) by *giānīs* in the Sikh places of worship (*gurdwārās*). In fact, the accounts about Guru Nānak's meetings with the Nāth yogis—among other central stories—are commonly told on Guru Nānak's birthday (*gurpurb*) in the *gurdwārās*.

Tradition must, indeed, be read in conjunction with the *Gurū Granth Sāhib*. In the case of the stories about Guru Nānak's meetings with the Nāth yogis, there are several points that shed light on the Sikh tradition surrounding *Siddh Goṣṭ*. Notwithstanding the ambiguity and historical inconsistencies (and keep in mind that the *janam-sākhīs* were initially part of an oral tradition, which is bound to contain ambiguity) concerning the place at which the *Siddh Goṣṭ* dialogue occurred, the various stories do reflect the importance of Guru Nānak's journeys during which he interacted with many different religious figures. Guru Nānak was, indeed, familiar with the *siddhs* and Nāth yogis of the Gorakhnāth tradition, with whom he most likely engaged in more than one formal debate. Furthermore, because the local folk tradition places much emphasis on the hagiographical stories surrounding Guru Nānak's spiritual powers that successfully subdued the occult powers of the Nāth yogis, it is important to be familiar with this mythic theme.

The mythic theme found in the *janam-sākhīs* surrounding Guru Nānak and the Nāth yogis underlines that (1) Guru Nānak must have met with Nāth masters at various places on several occasions, and that (2) Guru Nānak was familiar with the practice of hath-yoga and numerous Nāth yogic masters, even as it confirms (3) the hagiographical accounts reinforce Guru Nānak's spiritual superiority not only as a Sant but also in terms of the religious path he teaches. Guru Nānak's spiritual superiority, inadvertently, reinforces the Sikh belief in "living-in-this-world." That is, the narratives about Guru Nānak's meetings with Nāth yogis serve to underline the superiority of the devotional path over the Nāth yogic path of asceticism. They provide the kernel of truth for Sikhs that one does not need to run away from, or renounce, the world in order to attain liberation. Rather, one ought to live in the world and pursue the simple path of the Divine Name. This leads to a redefinition of the term *udāsī*: For Guru Nānak, an *udāsī* refers to someone on the path leading to the Guru and to attaining the experiential Truth within the larger context of "living-in-this-world." Furthermore, even though Guru Nānak may have taken on the *udāsī* attire when interacting with the Gorakhnāthis, his inner condition was untouched by his external garb.

In sum, *Siddh Goṣṭ* was most likely composed after Guru Nānak's journeys—perhaps during his retirement years at Kartārpur, Punjab ca. 1524–1539 CE—at which time he combined the various discourses he had had with the Nāth yogis. Indeed, *Siddh Goṣṭ* most likely consists of the major points he discussed at different times with a variety of Nāth yogis or *siddhs*.

Before proceeding to the analysis of the actual dialogue, it is necessary to first examine the context of *Siddh Goṣṭ*, including the origins and functions of the text, which forms the focus of the next chapter.

# Chapter Four

# The Context of *Siddh Goṣṭ*

*Siddh Goṣṭ* is one of the many hymns contained in the the *Gurū Granth Sāhib*. The *Gurū Granth Sāhib* ("Revered Guru Scripture"), also known as the *Ādi Granth*, is the most revered scripture of the Sikh canon. According to Sikh tradition, the fifth guru, by the name of Guru Arjan Dev (1581–1606 CE), had compiled the first version of the scripture by 1604 CE.[1] in order to establish a permanent and authentic text of the gurus' compositions for what was then called the Nānak Panth.[2] However, the tenth and last human guru, Guru Gobind Siṅgh, is believed to have completed the second and final version of the scripture in 1706 CE. Moreover, according to tradition, along with the proclamation that he was to be the last human guru of the Sikh lineage, Guru Gobind Siṅgh bestowed the status of Guru on the *Gurū Granth Sāhib* in 1708 CE.[3]

Accorded the status of Guru, the *Gurū Granth Sāhib* is regarded as the ultimate authority in the Sikh tradition. The scripture forms the basis for insight and wisdom about the nature of Reality and the human condition. As the central focus of ritual worship, the *Gurū Granth Sāhib* is installed on a raised platform and placed on a regal throne covered by a cloth. Indeed, it occupies the focal point within every Sikh temple (*gurdwārā*) because of its status as the Eternal Guru.

Like the *Gurū Granth Sāhib* of which it is a part, *Siddh Goṣṭ* has the status of ultimate authority for Sikhs. Composed by Guru Nānak, *Siddh Goṣṭ* is written in the form of a discourse so as to teach his philosophical perspective. While *Siddh Goṣṭ* is a religious discourse, it is written according to musical measure (*rāg*; *rāga* in Sanskrit) so as to be used as a hymn for recitation. Therefore, the purpose of *Siddh Goṣṭ* is twofold: (1) it is a philosophical exposition of Guru Nānak's worldview, and (2) it is a devotional hymn meant to be recited as part of daily Sikh religious practice.

This chapter is an analysis of the context in which Guru Nānak wrote *Siddh Goṣṭ* in order to come to a better understanding of its origins, purpose, and ritual function of the text. First, it provides background material on the locus of the *Siddh Goṣṭ* text (*Gurū Granth Sāhib*) and, more specifically, on the origins of *Siddh Goṣṭ*, including authorship, the intended audience of the text, and the dates of its composition. Second, and more important, the chapter explores the purpose and function of *Siddh Goṣṭ*, both as a philosophical exposition and as a hymn to be recited. In doing so, the chapter examines the discourse (*goṣṭ*) literary genre, and discusses the Indian tradition of *rāg* and the musical measure in which the text has been composed.

## SIKH SCRIPTURE AND THE *SIDDH GOṢṬ* TEXT

The Sikh canon consists of the *Gurū Granth Sāhib*, *Dasam Granth*,[4] Bhāī Gurdās's *Vārāṅ*, and Bhāī Nand Lāl's *Dīwān*. For the purpose of this study, the *Gurū Granth Sāhib* and Bhāī Gurdās's *Vārāṅ* are of prime importance. The standardized *Gurū Granth Sāhib* contains 1,430 pages. The hymns are not arranged according to the subject matter; rather, the scripture is organized according to musical measure (*rāg*). The *Gurū Granth Sāhib* can be divided into three distinct sections:

1. The introductory section (pp. 1–13), which consists of the "Mūlmantar" (the mantra viewed as the foundation of Sikh theology is further discussed in chapter 5), "Jap-jī" (the morning hymn), verses used for "Rehrās" (the evening prayer), and "Sohilā" (the night prayer).
2. The *rāg* ("musical measure") (pp. 14–1,353), which reflects its arrangement according to musical measure, whereby each *rāg* begins with a hymn composed by a Sikh guru and ends with hymns composed by one of the many *bhagats* (*bhaktas* in Sanskrit).
3. The ending or final section (pp. 1,353–1,430), which includes hymns composed by the ninth guru, Guru Tegh Bahādur.[5]

Tradition recognizes two versions of the *Gurū Granth Sāhib*. Modern scholarship on Sikh literature has, however, shown that there are three main recensions of the *Gurū Granth Sāhib*, the first two of which are regarded as authentic: (1) the Kartārpur version, which is the original text compiled by Guru Arjan Dev and inscribed by Bhāī Gurdās, (2) the Damdamā version that was compiled during the late seventeenth century by Guru Gobind Siṅgh and the copies made by Bābā Dīp Siṅgh, and (3) the Banno version, which is regarded as inauthentic and deemed to be unreliable.[6]

Composed by Guru Nānak, *Siddh Goṣṭ* is written in a "medieval" form of Punjabi. The *Siddh Goṣṭ* text translated in this present work is taken from the standardized form of the Damdamā version of the *Gurū Granth Sāhib* (pp. 938–946), consisting of seventy-three stanzas. Interestingly, volume two of the *Goindvāl Pothī*—the volume (*pothī*) of hymns collected by Guru Amar Dās[7] and hence considered very reliable—contains *Siddh Goṣṭ*. However, unlike the Kartārpur and Damdamā versions of the *Siddh Goṣṭ* composition, the *Goindvāl Pothī* form of the hymn contains only seventy-two stanzas. While the basic text and meaning has remained the same, "the last stanza [of *Siddh Goṣṭ*] must have been added by Guru Arjan himself."[8]

Along with "Jap-jī,"[9] *Siddh Goṣṭ* is regarded as one of the two most important philosophical texts composed by Guru Nānak.[10] In fact, in terms of their teachings, *Siddh Goṣṭ* and "Jap-jī" complement each other. While the latter has as its focus the actual Sikh practice of repeating the Divine Name (*jap*), the former is concerned with how one can pursue liberation while living in the world. Though the text is a key philosophical work, *Siddh Goṣṭ* is also an expression of experiential Truth uttered by Guru Nānak for the common person, whether he or she is Hindu, Muslim, or a follower of Guru Nānak. Although the *Gurū Granth Sāhib* is now regarded as the scripture of the Sikhs, the original audience of the Sikh gurus would have primarily included the followers of the Nānak Panth, Hindus, and Muslims. It is for this reason that there are many elements of the Hindu and Muslim religions (like myths, symbols, and metaphors) employed in the hymns, along with some allusions to the Buddhist and Jain traditions, all of which reflect the religious landscape of the Indian subcontinent during the time of the Sikh gurus.

Although no doubt exists regarding *Siddh Goṣṭ*'s authorship and audience, there is much ambiguity about the time and place of its composition. *Siddh Goṣṭ* itself does not provide any clue as to the time or place of its composition. According to tradition, the text is believed to have been composed during the later years of Guru Nānak's life (1524–39 CE); that is, during his retirement years in Kartārpur, Punjab.[11] Consequently, the verses may well have been a recollection of the major points made during the discourses Guru Nānak had with the Nāth yogis in the course of his religious travels, set down in verse only after he had retired in Kartārpur, sometime during the last fifteen years of his life.[12]

The ambiguity about the time of the composition of *Siddh Goṣṭ* is directly related to the dispute surrounding the time and place of the actual discourse to the Nāth yogis narrated in the text. As discussed in chapter 3, Bhāī Gurdās's *Vārāṅ* and the hagiographical accounts about Guru Nānak (*janam-sākhīs*) make numerous references to Guru Nānak's various meetings with the Nāth yogis, along with some mention of the dialogues he had with them. Regardless of the ambiguities surrounding the time and place of both the discourse and its composition, *Siddh Goṣṭ* is written in a discourse form, following the pan-Indian literary genre called the *goṣṭ*.

### *The Pan-Indian Genre of the Discourse* (Goṣṭ)

*Siddh Goṣṭ* literally means "A discourse (*goṣṭ*) with the *siddhs*." A *goṣṭ* seeks to explain the respective doctrines of the philosophers, *sants*, or divine religious figures who participate in a discourse. Indian religious or philosophical perspectives are commonly expounded within a dialogic framework as made evident in many philosophical, mythological, or iconographical texts. For example, Hindu mythology in the Epics, Purāṇas or Āgamas is often presented in a *goṣṭ* framework, including the renowned *Bhagavad Gītā*. Set in the larger context of the great Hindu epic *Mahābhārata*, the *Bhagavad Gītā* is the religious discourse between the Pāṇḍava warrior Arjuna and Lord Kṛṣṇa, an incarnation of Viṣṇu.

Philosophical schools also present their viewpoints through a dialogical framework, such as the *Mīmāṃsā Sūtras*. The *Mīmāṃsā Sūtras* expound the orthodox Hindu Mīmāṃsā philosophical school of thought through discourses with other philosophical systems.[13] This literary form is not only a way to expound a particular philosophical or theological viewpoint, but it can also provide a means for debate or comparison in order to highlight differences between two or more schools of thought. In effect, the dialogue framework often serves as a means to establish the superiority of one school of thought over another.

In the corpus of Sikh literature, the *goṣṭ* literary style is used in the *janam-sākhīs* (narrative accounts about Guru Nānak). The *Miharbān Janam-sākhī* is predominantly in the form of dialogues; that is, *goṣṭ* are integrated into the narrative for the exposition of a particular theme.[14] Often, the discourses amount to the recitation or citation of compositions by Guru Nānak in order to put forth his points of view. The inclusion of Guru Nānak's verses can be viewed as a form of legitimization of the narrative material.

*Siddh Goṣṭ*, the text under consideration here, is likewise presented in the form of a religious discourse between Guru Nānak and the Nāth yogis. The Nāth *siddhs* assemble to ask pertinent questions about Guru Nānak's religious pursuits and philosophical orientation.

The introductory verse of *Siddh Goṣṭ* describes the discourse as occurring between the *siddhs* and the sants, one of whom is Guru Nānak:

> A discourse with the *siddhs* . . .
> As the *siddhs* formed an assembly,
> sitting in their yogic postures,
> they saluted the congregation of *sants*.

The dialogue is not one in the literal sense of mutual interaction,[15] since the *siddhs* of the Nāth tradition raise all the questions, while Guru Nānak provides all the answers:

> *Siddhs*:
> Who is hidden? Who is liberated?
> Who is united inwardly and outwardly?
> Who comes and goes [from the cycle of rebirth]?
> Who pervades the three worlds? (*SG* 12)

> *Nānak*:
> [*EkOaṅkār*] is hidden within every heart,
> and the *gurmukh* is liberated.
> Through *śabad*, one is united inwardly and outwardly.
> The *manmukh* comes and goes
> [from the cycle of rebirth].
> Nānak says: The *gurmukh* merges with Truth. (*SG* 13)

Although *Siddh Goṣṭ* begins in the framework of a discourse, as the composition proceeds there are long portions of Guru Nānak explaining his philosophical perspective. In actuality, *Siddh Goṣṭ* is a religious discourse that is meant to convey Guru Nānak's religious and ethical values along with his perception of the world and how one should pursue liberation while "living-in-this-world." Guru Nānak achieves the latter by answering questions put to him by the Nāth yogis in the light of their path of world renunciation as the sole means to liberation. Since the composition is written in the form of Guru Nānak teaching the Nāth yogis, the title *Siddh Goṣṭ* has been translated as "*Discourse to* the Nāth Yogis." Indeed, the *Siddh Goṣṭ* discourse can be viewed as a means to establish Guru Nānak's path as superior to, as well as more practical than, the Nāth yogic way.

As mentioned in chapter 3, *Siddh Goṣṭ* does make specific references to a couple of Nāth yogis with whom Guru Nānak spoke. Only eight verses out of seventy-three, however, actually mention the Nāth

Yogis with whom Guru Nānak discusses religious issues: Verses 4 to 6 consist of the dialogue between Guru Nānak and a Nāth yogi by the name of Charapaṭ, who is believed to have lived around the eleventh to twelfth century CE.[16] Last, verses 7 to 11 are a discourse between Guru Nānak and a yogi of the Gorakhnāth tradition called Loharipā, who is believed to have lived during the tenth century CE.[17] The two yogis—Charapaṭ and Loharipā—thus lived a number of centuries before Guru Nānak. One could hypothesize that the historical inconsistency exists because Guru Nānak may well have met with some contemporary incumbents of the seats of the legendary Nāth masters, who had apparently taken on the names of the latter—a common practice among pan-Indian esoteric traditions.

The remaining verses (12–73) of *Siddh Goṣṭ* do not indicate the name of any particular individual or yogi. Who the persons were and how many they were can be only a matter of speculation. The large portion of *Siddh Goṣṭ* that contains no specific reference to the Nāth yogis or *siddhs* can be regarded as the summation of the various discourses Guru Nānak actually had with a variety of Nāth yogis.

While *Siddh Goṣṭ* has been written in the form of a discourse through which Guru Nānak expounds his philosophical teachings about the path of "True" Yoga, the text was also composed to musical measure in the form of a hymn in order to facilitate its recitation.

## SIKH RELIGIOUS PRACTICE AND THE *SIDDH GOṢṬ* HYMN

The verses of the Sikh scripture, including *Siddh Goṣṭ*, are composed to musical measures that originate in the classical Indian musical tradition in order to both facilitate memorization and enhance spiritual experience. Classical Indian music is based on (1) *rāg* (melodic measure) and (2) *ṭāl* (rhythmic meter), which dates back to ca. 1500 BCE. Musical notes, derived from the ancient Vedic (as well as folk) melodies, are arranged in an ascending to descending scale. The scale is very complex due to its melodic nature; each *rāg* must be performed precisely in order to evoke its own particular mood. There may be variation in the pitch of the tones. The lack of a unified system reflects its dependence on oral traditions throughout the Indian subcontinent.[18]

Each *rāg*, nevertheless, has a function and a mood ascribed to it. As with classical Indian music, in the Sikh tradition the singing of verses to a particular *rāg* has as its primary purpose the evocation of a specific deep emotion (*bhāva*).[19] Guru Nānak wrote his verses to a particular *rāg* in order to awaken deep spiritual emotions that correspond to the actual teachings being sung:

> Guru Nānak wished his hymns to be sung to *rāgas* that express the spirit of the text and performance style to be compatible with the meaning of the hymn. The succeeding gurus followed his example. The *rāgas* named in the Holy Book were selected probably because of their suitability for expressing the ideals represented in the texts for which they were used.[20]

Indeed, in Sikhism divine worship through music is considered to be the paramount way to seek the experience of, or union with, Ultimate Reality. Although devotional singing (*kīrtan*)[21] is an important aspect of Sikh practice, it is to be done in conjunction with reciting the scripture (*pāṭh*), listening to sermons (*kathā*), and remembering (*simraṇ*) the Divine Name. While the *rāg* has a significant role in the Sikh tradition, it is not a mandatory requirement in Sikh devotional practice:

> In the Sikh belief system, a *rāg* is simply an effective carrier of the message, which is the element of primary significance in devotional singing. There is absolutely no provision to deify *rāgs*.[22]

Having said that, each *rāg* has a specific time of the day when it should be performed since the cycle of the day corresponds to the cycle of life and spiritual development.[23] For instance, "Āsā," the popular *rāg* in the Punjab at the time of the Sikh gurus, is a very old devotional *rāg* performed in the early morning just before sunrise in order evoke a mystical mood.[24]

The introductory verse of *Siddh Goṣṭ* provides the *rāg* measure to which the hymn has been written:

> A discourse with the *siddhs*,
> [is composed of] the first *mahalā*
> in the *rāmkalī* meter.
> *EkOaṅkār* is realized
> by the grace of the True Guru.

The *Siddh Goṣṭ* is composed in the Rāmkalī *rāg* (a musical measure used by all the Sikh gurus in over three hundred hymns in the *Gurū Granth Sāhib*). The Rāmkalī *rāg* is meant to be performed after sunrise, especially during the hot season, and functions to rouse highly spiritual thoughts or feelings. Interestingly, many of the hymns composed according to this *rāg* are verses that are for the purpose of teaching the Sikh understanding of "True" yoga,[25] as is the case with *Siddh Goṣṭ*.

In regard to *Siddh Goṣṭ*'s place in devotional practice, it is meant to be recited on a daily basis. *Siddh Goṣṭ* is, significantly, one of the hymns frequently included in the *Pañj Granthī*, an anthology of Sikh daily prayers. The *Pañj Granthī* literally means the "booklet of five"; but there are two common ways that oral tradition interprets the "five."[26] Some Sikh practitioners and traditional scholars regard the word "five" as referring to the fact that the small book (*pothī*) of hymns was compiled by the fifth guru, Guru Arjan Dev; other Sikh scholars[27] contend that the "five" refers to the actual number of hymns that existed in the original version, which then grew larger over time, with the title of the original hymn book retained for its symbolic significance.

While there may be different versions of the anthology of daily Sikh hymns in circulation, it is important to note that the original *Pañj Granthī* only contained selections of hymns taken from the *Gurū Granth Sāhib*.[28] One of the current *Pañj Granthīs*[29] includes ten hymns (*bāṇīs*):

1. *Jap-jī* by Guru Nānak;
2. *Śabad Hajāre* compiled by Guru Arjan Dev—it contains one of his verses, along with six verses composed by Guru Nānak;
3. *Rehrās*, a collection of verses composed by Guru Nānak, Guru Rām Dās, and Guru Arjan Dev;
4. *Kīrtan Sohilā*, a collection of verses written by Guru Nānak, Guru Rām Dās, and Guru Arjan Dev;
5. *Dakhṇī Oaṅkār* by Guru Nānak;
6. *Siddh Goṣṭ* by Guru Nānak;
7. *Ānand* by Guru Amar Dās;
8. *Bāvan Akhrī* by Guru Arjan Dev;
9. *Sukhmanī* by Guru Arjan Dev; and
10. *Āsā dī Vār* by Guru Nānak.

Significantly, *Siddh Goṣṭ* is included in the *Pañj Granthī*. The inclusion of *Siddh Goṣṭ* in the *Pañj Granthī* indicates that the hymn has been traditionally regarded as one of the important texts that should be recited daily.

In view of the aforementioned, it can be concluded that *Siddh Goṣṭ* is indeed a fundamental text found in Sikh canonical literature, which is not only included in the *Gurū Granth Sāhib*, but also contained in the anthology of hymns (*Pañj Granthī*) that is traditionally meant to be recited daily. Although there is ambiguity about the time and place that the *Siddh Goṣṭ* was composed, and about which Nāth yogis that Guru Nānak actually had the religious discourse(s) with, there is certainty about its twofold function: *Siddh Goṣṭ* was composed in the form of a dialogue through which Guru Nānak expounds his religious teachings about his understanding of "True" yoga, and Sikhs are also required to recite daily the hymn in order to evoke a deep spiritual sentiment.

In philosophical terms, Guru Nānak outlines his understanding of "True" yoga in *Siddh Goṣṭ*. In doing so, he modifies several Nāth and hath-yoga terms as he expounds his own path, the yogic discipline of the Divine Name. Chapters 5 and 6 that follow discuss the philosophical framework of *Siddh Goṣṭ*, and the interpretation of it, respectively.

# Part 3

# The Meaning of Guru Nānak's *Siddh Goṣṭ*

# Chapter Five

# Guru Nānak's Worldview: Theory and Practice

The scriptural hymns of Guru Nānak in *Siddh Goṣṭ* and other parts of the *Gurū Granth Sāhib* together provide a philosophical orientation that offers a perspective on the nature of Reality, the concept of the Guru, the relation between Guru and humans, as well as the path toward, and goal of, liberation. Much attention is often given to scriptural teachings for comprehending the nature of a particular religious tradition. However, to understand the practical application of the philosophical beliefs it is necessary to incorporate additional religious sources. According to Donald Lopez Jr., such an approach is useful because it can "provide both more expansive and more focused perspectives on the richness and diversity of religious expressions."[1]

While a philosophical perspective can be delineated from devotional hymns—like *Siddh Goṣṭ*—it is ultimately meant to be "put into practice." Including other religious sources is especially important when the followers of the religious tradition—like the Sikh one—are rooted in oral culture. While Sikhs may remember their scriptural hymns by mere rote, Sikhs, more often than not, depend on the oral transmission of hagiographies (*janam-sākhīs*) and sermons (*kathā*) to learn about their belief system as well as the practices associated with it.

Other pertinent traditional Sikh sources—like religious sermons (*kathā*) and discourses (*vichār*) given by Sikh *giānīs*, hagiographies (*janam-sākhīs*), religious practices, and contemporary scholarship—are indeed helpful in providing a broader or more holistic approach to understanding the practice of the Sikh religion. Therefore, beyond a strictly textual analysis of *Siddh Goṣṭ*, other sources need to be used especially in regard to the practical application of the scriptural beliefs.

Drawing on Guru Nānak's hymns, religious discourses by Sikh *giānīs*,[2] the hagiographical accounts about Guru Nānak, and contemporary Sikh scholarship, this chapter examines the Sikh philosophical orientation formulated by Guru Nānak. The chapter consists of two parts. First, through a thematic analysis, the chapter sets out the philosophical foundation of *Siddh Goṣṭ* (and other major works like "Jap-jī" by Guru Nānak). The analysis outlines the Sikh worldview (*saṅsār*), especially in respect of the path of a Sikh in the pursuit of liberation. Second, the chapter looks at how Guru Nānak's universal scriptural teachings are actually put into religious practice by Sikhs. In doing so, the analysis not only delineates the philosophical perspective from Guru Nānak's *Siddh Goṣṭ* and explicates how these beliefs are put to practice, but it also demonstrates how his religious path pertains to the category of a *renunciate living in the larger context of involvement in society*.

## THE SIKH WORLDVIEW

### *The Nature of Ultimate Reality*

The paramount way of looking at Guru Nanak's understanding of the true nature of Reality is by way of the *mūl-mantar* (literally "root mantra"; *mūla-mantra* in Sanskrit), which is a preamble found at the beginning of the *Gurū Granth Sāhib*. The English translation of the *mūl-mantar* is as follows:

> [*EkOaṅkār*],
> the One primordial essence manifest in all,
> is the Truth,
> is creator,
> is without fear and enmity,
> has a timeless form,
> is beyond the cycle of rebirth, is self-existing,
> and is realized by the grace of the Guru.

Along with the *mūl-mantar* proper,[3] the *purātan* (ancient) tradition contends that the *mūl-mantar* includes the first verse (*salok*), which opens the *Jap-jī*:[4]

> Before all beginning there was Truth,
> when all creation began there was Truth,
> in the present there is Truth,
> Nānak says Truth will be in the future.

While there may be two versions of the constituents of the *mūl-mantar*, many Sikh *giānīs* regard the entire Sikh theology as evolving from, and revolving around, it.[5] That is, all the teachings contained in the *Gurū Granth Sāhib* are but an elaboration of what is taught by the *mūl-mantar*. Hence, as the word *mūl* ("root") indicates, the *mūl-mantar* is considered to be the *foundation or basis of all teachings*.

According to religious hagiography, Guru Nānak recited the *mūl-mantar* after a mystical experience at Sultānpur. *Purātan Janam-sākhī* 10 describes this mystical experience as a direct communion with the Infinite; it is believed to have occurred when Guru Nānak disappeared into a river for three days and transcended the material realm and entered the abode of the Infinite.[6] While immersed in this transcendental state, Guru Nānak is said to have received the *mūl-mantar*.[7]

While critical historians classify the origins of the *mūl-mantar* as "legendary" or tend to discount it altogether as religious hagiography, Sikh *giānīs* approach such narrative accounts as teaching Sikh theology in a concrete thought form. Sikh *giānīs* accept such hagiography as a useful form of metaphorical learning. To them, Guru Nānak's disappearance into the river represents his spiritual union, wherein the ego has dissolved and his path—symbolized by the river—has taken him to the depths of all existence: *EkOaṅkār*,[8] the one primordial essence manifest in all.[9]

The *mūl-mantar* begins with *EkOaṅkār*. In Sikh scripture, the numeral *Ek* ("one") in front of *Oaṅkār* denotes the primordial essence of all existence. The mantra *Oaṅkār* (Punjabi for the Sanskrit mantra *Auṃ*) was recited as early as the Vedic period ca. 1500 BCE.[10] *Oaṅkār* is found in both the Vedic and Buddhist traditions, and is also a sacred mantra in the Jain religion. For example, in the Vedic literature, the *Māṇḍūkya Upaniṣad* describes *Oaṅkār* as:

> *Auṃ*!—This syllable is the whole world.
> Its further explanation is:—
> The past, the present, the future
> everything—is just the word *Auṃ*.
> And whatever else that transcends threefold times—
> that, too, is just the word *Auṃ*. (1.1)

While the numeral *Ek* in front of *Oaṅkār* denotes the oneness of the primordial essence of all existence, *Oaṅkār* has three aspects or qualities: (1) *akār* (creative), (2) *okār* (sustaining), and (3) *mokār* (dissolving). These three qualities attributed to *Oaṅkār* are regarded as one and the same. For this reason, Sikh *giānīs* interpret the iconic representations of *Oaṅkār*—Brahmā (creator), Viṣṇu (sustainer), and Śiva (destroyer)—as an attempt to personify the three qualities of *Oaṅkār*.[11] The following "Dakhṇī Oaṅkār" verse is a fitting example to demonstrate Guru

Nānak's usage of Hindu iconic and religious references to discourse about the abstract Truth of *Oaṅkār*:

> *Oaṅkār* created *Brahmā*.
> *Oaṅkār* created consciousness.
> *Oaṅkār* created the mountains and *yugs* [ages].
> *Oaṅkār* created the *Vedas*.
> *Oaṅkār* liberates with the *śabad*.
> *Oaṅkār* ferries the *gurmukhs* [across *saṅsār*].
> This is the meaning of *Auṃ*.
> The essence of the three worlds. (Rāmkalī, M.1, *GGS*, pp. 929–30)

At first blush, one can easily misinterpret this hymn as endorsing *Brahmā* as a creation of *Oaṅkār*. However, the entire focus of the hymn is to convey the understanding that all existence is a manifestation of *Oaṅkār*. Even though the Sikh texts make references to these Hindu iconic forms, they are not worshiped as gods. In actuality, the iconic forms are employed solely as descriptive terms to understand *EkOaṅkār*.

The Sikh conception of *EkOaṅkār* is better and more accurately conceptualized as a primordial essence emanating from *EkOaṅkār* that resounds throughout the universe. This conception of *EkOaṅkār* allows for the reconciliation between the personal and the absolute in the Sikh tradition.[12] Sikh *giānīs* often use the metaphor of the sun to articulate the nature of *EkOaṅkār*, where there is no essential difference between the sun (creator) and the light rays that it emits (creation).[13]

*EkOaṅkār* is followed in the *mūl-mantar* by a listing of the qualities that reflect its essence. The qualities of *EkOaṅkār* include Truth (*satnām*), creatorship (*kartā purakh*), fearlessness (*nirbhau*), without enmity (*nirvair*), timelessness (*akāl mūrat*), self-existing (*ajūnī saibaṅg*), and is realized by the grace of the Guru (*gur prasād*).[14]

### Saṅsār: *The Sea of Existence*

According to the Sikh tradition, the ultimate source of suffering (*dukh*) is the human condition of being bound to the cycle of transmigration (*saṅsār*).[15] This suffering is metaphorically explained in Sikh texts as a life journey through a chaotic sea storm, in which one has to seek refuge to survive its violent and destructive waves. The world is compared to "an impassable ocean" (*SG* 4). The fierce waves are symbolic of the thoughts that arise from the ego's (*ahaṅkār*) desire for wealth, status, and power.[16] The Sikh tradition is based on the premise that the ego's desires (*tṛṣṇa*) can never be quenched through materialistic endeavors.

The pursuit of the path of the *manmukh* (ego-oriented person) eventually and inevitably causes one to drown in the sea of existence.[17]

The process in which the *manmukh* drowns in the sea of existence is based on the ego's quest to establish itself as a permanent entity that is separate and different from others.[18] In the course of this state, the *manmukh* relies on worldly roles to gain wealth, status, and power:

> Without *nām*,
> people wear many robes
> and stray from the path. . . . (*SG* 72)
> A *manmukh* makes mistakes
> and lives in death's shadow.
> Looking into the home of another,
> he loses.
> A *manmukh* is confused by doubt
> and wanders in the wilderness.
> Straying away from the path,
> he recites mantras at crematoriums.
> Without reflecting on the *śabad*,
> he speaks obscenities.
> Nānak says: Those who are immersed in Truth,
> attain a state of peace. (*SG* 26)

The *manmukh* loses the sense of the authentic self in the illusion (*māya*) that the acquired roles played out in the worldly drama (*līlā*) are at the center of one's existence. As a result, the *manmukh* constructs the notion of the self based solely on these worldly roles that are, in essence, impermanent and ever changing. This false construction of the self causes the *manmukh* to suffer through the cycle of vices as he or she tries to attain permanence through material endeavors.

The cycle of vices involves attachment (*moh*), greed (*lobh*), anger (*karodh*), and lust (*kām*). These four vices, along with the ego, are regarded as the five evils (also spoken of as the five rivals, thieves, or demons) that rob consciousness (*surtī*) from gaining an awareness of the soul (*ātma*):[19]

> They are five and I am one.
> O mind, how can I protect my home?
> They are hitting and robbing me
> over and over [again].
> To whom can I vent my grief?
> (Gauṛī Chetī, M.1, *GGS*, p. 155)

The ego is enmeshed in the cycle of vices, beginning with attachment.[20] Attachment implies attraction, during which the ego is attracted to those people, objects, places, and activities that are perceived as being a source of wealth, status, and power. As the ego's attraction for these external sources strengthens, the attachment transforms into greed—the unquenchable desire to possess.

The acquisition of wealth, status, and power from external sources is almost always beset with obstacles that block the ego from possessing the desired person, object, place, or activity. Such obstacles inevitably lead to anger, creating in the *manmukh* a state of mental and emotional restlessness.[21] This anger takes the place of greed. Anger manifests itself on a continuum ranging from internalized anger to anger expressed verbally and physically. Such anger creates turmoil within the *manmukh* because it infiltrates into both the interpersonal and intrapersonal domains of the *manmukh*'s life.[22]

In this state of anger, the *manmukh* becomes susceptible to lustful indulgence,[23] including the use of mood-altering substances, engaging in gratuitous sex, and other forms of sensory excess. Satisfying the craving associated with lust, however, only provides temporary solace. The *manmukh* remains in the grip of the illusion that the ego is a permanent and separate entity. As a consequence, the *manmukh* remains caught in the clutches of these five evils.

### *The Path of the* Manmukh

The path of the *manmukh* (*manmat mārg*) and the spiritual path of the *gurmukh* (*gurmat mārg*) are the two paths delineated in the Sikh scripture.[24] Everyone pursues the first path—also known as the path of ego reasoning—according to the stages of life. The *manmat mārg* is described by Guru Nānak as having four quarters or phases: (1) infancy, (2) childhood and youth, (3) adulthood, and (4) old age.[25]

In the infancy phase, the mind is not conscious of the eternal soul (*ātma; ātman* in Sanskrit). Rather, the infant's mind is oriented to survival needs, obtained first through the mother's milk.

> O merchant-friend!
> In the first watch of the night,
>     your childlike mind is innocent.
> O merchant friend!
> You drink milk and are caressed,
>     your mother and father love you as their son;
>     your mother and father love their son immensely,

but in *māyā* all are caught in attachment.
You came (into this world)
by the fortune of your past deeds,
and your current deeds
will determine your future.
Without *nām*,
you will not be liberated,
and will drown in your love of duality.
Nānak says: O mortal! In the first watch of the night,
you shall be saved by remembering the All-pervasive One.
(Srī Rāg, M.1., *GGS*, pp. 75–76)

As the infant is nourished with milk, he or she slowly begins to recognize the mother, father, siblings, and other family members as "other." The infant develops the sense that "I am." However, due to the closeness of the mother and father, the infant, remains connected to the parents through a collectivity-orientation.[26]

During the childhood and youth phase, the child learns that he or she belongs to the parents. The parents regard the child as "their" possession. The child thus begins to develop a sense of pride about belonging to a particular family and caste. As the child develops further, there is an exploration of the physical world and the experience of sensual pleasures, including visual beauty, musical sounds, tasty food, fragrances, and sex. During the stage of the youth, there is often indulgence in sensual pleasures. As a consequence, the mental state is that of duality:

O merchant friend!
In the second watch of the night,
you are intoxicated
by the wine of youth and beauty.
O merchant friend!
Night and day,
you indulge in [sensual desire],
and your consciousness is blind to *nām*.
All other tastes are sweet to you
[while] *nām* is not enshrined
within [your heart].
You do not possess wisdom, concentration,
virtue or self-discipline.
In falsehood,
your life is wasted away.

Pilgrimages, fasts, purification,
  and self-discipline are meaningless,
  along with the acts of piety and rituals.
Nānak says: Liberation is attained
  through devotion [of *nām*],
  and all else leads to duality.
(Srī Rāg, M.1., *GGS*, pp. 75–76)

The youth is believed to possess little wisdom and limited ability to concentrate, because the mind is too preoccupied with the desire to experience the sensual pleasures. Even if the youth visits holy places, fasts, or performs acts of piety, these activities are regarded as meaningless, because the mind is not totally absorbed in them. During this phase, it is rare for youth to travel the path of spiritual wisdom (*gurmat-mārg*), because the mind has not been trained to focus inward; rather, the mind is fixed on external experiences.[27]

In the adulthood phase, one is preoccupied with fulfilling household responsibilities (*dharam; dharma* in Sanskrit). Adults perform their duty (*dharam*) as prescribed by their particular familial roles (such as spouse and parent) with the intention of acquiring honor (*izzat*) in society. During the early adulthood phase, the duty of the householder is primarily to accumulate wealth (*arth*) and acquire honor (*izzat*). However, in the late adulthood period, there is a shift in thinking when material riches are no longer experienced as fulfilling:

O merchant-friend!
In the third watch of the night,
  the gooses [white hair] land
  on the pool (head).
Youthfulness wears out,
  and old age is triumphant.
O merchant-friend!
Your days are limited.
At the end,
  you will grieve,
  as Yāma takes you away blind-folded.
You possess everything
  as your own.
But in an instant,
  it will be all lost.
Your intellect will leave you,
  your knowledge will depart,
  and you will repent for your misdeeds.

Nānak says: O mortal!
In the third watch of the night,
  let your consciousness be focused [on *nām*].
(Srī Rāg, M.1., *GGS*, pp. 75–76)

This shift in thinking is also directly related to the facing of one's own mortality; that is, as the body grows old, material wealth is no longer seen as fulfilling. Moreover, people have to reckon with the misdeeds that they have done during their lifetime, which can often lead to feelings of guilt and remorse.

During the old age phase, people are not fit to work, they lack the capacity for sensory pleasure, and they are approaching death. The mental consequences of one's actions (*karam*; karma in Sanskrit) have taken their toll on the body and mind:

O merchant-friend!
In the fourth watch of the night,
  you get old and your body becomes weak.
Your eyes go blind,
  and you cannot see.
O merchant-friend!
Your ears no longer
  hear any words,
  your eyes go blind,
  your tongue loses taste,
  and you live with the help of others.
With no inner virtues,
  how can one find peace?
The *manmukh* comes and goes.
When the crop (physical existence) is ripe,
  it bends, breaks, and perishes.
Then, why be proud over that which comes and goes?
Nānak says: O mortal! In the fourth watch of the night,
  the *gurmukh* recognizes the *śabad*.
(Srī Rāg, M.1, *GGS*, pp. 75–76)

As death approaches, the accumulation of negative actions leads to the mind being wracked by guilt or regret, while goodness and continence cultivated throughout life result in peace of mind. At the time of death, the soul is either liberated (*mukti*), or it remains caught in the cycle of rebirth until it attains liberation in a subsequent life.

This path of the ego (*manmat mārg*) represents Guru Nānak's theological understanding of personal development in the context of the basic life-stages. In contrast, the spiritual path—*gurmat mārg*—is for the attainment of spiritual wisdom and, ultimately, liberation.[28] While the *gurmat mārg* is the ideal religious path for people "living-in-this-world" in order to escape the cycle of rebirth (*saṅsār*), it is actually taken on by only a relatively few. The central teaching of Guru Nānak concerns the path of the *gurmukh* (guru-oriented person) as the sole means to liberation.

## Mukti: *Liberation from the Sea of Existence*

In the Sikh tradition, *jīvan-mukti* or liberation from the worldly sea of existence is the ultimate goal of the *gurmukh* (guru-oriented person), during which there is a break from bondage or the dualistic mode of thinking, so that the individual consciousness is absorbed in the cosmic resonance of *EkOaṅkār*.[29] This state of *jīvan-mukti* is not regarded as the state that the *gurmukh* attains once the *ātma* departs from the physical body (*sarīr; śarīra* in Sanskrit), but rather it is a state that can be attained even while the *ātma* still resides in the human form.[30] This realization or spiritual awakening of the essential unity, *EkOaṅkār*, in all humanity is open to all, irrespective of caste, creed, race, religion, or gender.

Having said that, it should come as no surprise that the Sikh tradition does not define *svarg* or heaven as an independent celestial region that is beyond the material plane of existence.[31] Rather, the Sikh tradition expounds the view that both heaven and hell coexist on earth. Similarly, the goal of the *gurmukh* is to experience the pleasures (*sukh*) and sorrows (*dukh*) of this world as alike while journeying on the path.[32]

In order to explain how the *gurmukh* seeks liberation while living in the worldly sea of existence, Guru Nānak makes reference by way of analogy to the classic Hindu epic *Rāmayaṇ* (*Rāmāyaṇa* in Sanskrit) in *Siddh Goṣṭ*:

> The *gurmukh* is a bridge,
> built by the Creator.
> *Laṅka* [the body] is looted
> by the five demons [five evils].
> Rām Chand [mind] destroys
> Rāvan [the ego].
> The *gurmukh* understands the secret
> that Babhīkan revealed.
> The *gurmukh* can make stones swim
> across the ocean [of *saṅsār*].
> The *gurmukh* saves millions of people. (*SG* 40)

Guru Nānak's reference to the *Rāmayaṇ* is an example of his discourse style where he uses the beliefs and practices of his audience, which was predominantly Hindu, as a means to articulating his own spiritual path. Caught in the web of illusion (*māyā*) or the clutches of the five demons, the *manmukh* has to change by turning to the Guru. The one who is guided or led by the Guru can cross the violent waves of the ocean of *saṅsār*:

> The *gurmukh* crosses over [the ocean of *saṅsār*]
> and carries others across as well.
> Nānak says: The *gurmukh* is liberated through *śabad*. (*SG* 31)

According to Guru Nānak, *śabad* ("word"; *śabda* in Sanskrit) is the means to the Guru:

> The *śabad* is the Guru,
> and the awareness of its sound
> is the disciple. (*SG* 44)

For Guru Nānak, the Guru is not of human form. Rather, the Guru is the Sacred Word (*śabad*). Likewise, the defining mark of the disciple is not religious garbs or symbols, but rather the *gurmukh*'s ability to discipline the mind (*man*) to connect with the Guru *śabad*. Guru Nānak explains the role of *śabad* as that which leads one across the sea of existence:

> The one who meets the Guru is
> carried across [the ocean of *saṅsār*].
> Impurities are erased
> and one becomes virtuous.
> The supreme peace of *mukti*
> is attained
> by contemplating on the Guru's *śabad*. (*SG* 39).

To understand the path of the *gurmukh*, it is necessary to elaborate on the concept of *śabad* as the means and the goal according to Guru Nānak's philosophical perspective.

### Śabad: *The* Gurmukh's *Guru*

*Śabad* ("word") is a central and complex concept found in Guru Nānak's hymns. Guru Nānak does not attempt to precisely define *śabad*. Rather, the focus of his writings is often on the effect that *śabad* has on the *gurmukh*. There are, in fact, several ways in which Guru Nānak uses the term. In general, *śabad* can be viewed as both the means to, and the goal of, liberation.

The first way in which Guru Nānak uses the term *śabad* is as Ultimate Reality itself. In his devotion to the Divine Name of Guru, Guru Nānak refers frequently to Hari (Kṛṣṇa); he is, however, not referring to Kṛṣṇa as the incarnation of the personal Hindu god Viṣṇu with attributes (*sarguṇ; saguṇa* in Sanskrit). Rather, he is referring to the Divine Name of the Guru without attributes (*nirguṇ; nirguṇa* in Sanskrit). Ultimate Reality is ineffable and, therefore, can only be known through Guru's revelation as *śabad*. The Divine Name of Guru is an expression or the embodiment of *EkOaṅkār*.

The second way in which Guru Nānak uses the term *śabad* is as its integral role on the path to liberation. It purifies one's heart in the gradual attainment of spiritual knowledge. For Guru Nānak, *śabad* is the medium through which the *gurmukh* comes to an understanding of *EkOaṅkār*. Indeed, Guru Nānak refers to it as that which carries one across the ocean of *saṅsār* as the "word-ferry":

> Nānak says: The One carries you across
> [the ocean of *saṅsār*].
> True is the great One and True is its *nām*.
> You shall realize this
> by studying the Guru's words. (*SG* 10)

Recitation of the Sacred Word (*śabad*) gradually increases one's awareness of the human condition; it allows one to gradually control the ego, and to inevitably unite with the Ultimate Reality, *EkOaṅkār*. Guru Nānak explains in *Siddh Goṣṭ* that *śabad* is that which unites the soul with *EkOaṅkār*:

> The *gurmukh* is connected to Truth
> through the *śabad*,
> and with love one is united
> [with *EkOaṅkār*].
> One becomes wise,
> perceptive, and,
> through perfect destiny,
> is united. (*SG* 58)

The Sacred Word creates the single-minded desire to meditate on the Divine Name, causing one to become detached from the material world.

It is clear that *śabad*—the eternal Guru—is the true revelation of Guru or Ultimate Reality for Guru Nānak. It seems that Guru Nānak's protest against outward devotion, and his rejection of revelation as a sacred book resulted in his replacing a sacred book with the mystical doctrine of *śabad* as revelation. Revelation must be experienced in the heart; therefore, one attains God through hearing and knowing the Word of the Guru. *Śabad* is also the means to realizing the divine "inner tune" of Reality (on this, more below). In essence, *śabad* can be understood as both the means (*upāya* in Sanskrit) and the goal (*upeya* in Sanskrit). And the means and the goal are, in fact, the same. Guru Nānak describes *śabad* as both the means to, as well as the nectar of, the heart:

> With grace,
>   *śabad* abides deep within the heart,
>   and doubt is removed.
> The body and mind become pure
>   and the pure *śabad* and *nām*
>   are enshrined within the heart.
> The *śabad* is the Guru
>   that will carry one across. (*SG* 59)

Guru Nānak's understanding of the Divine Word has its origins both in the Hindu concept of *śruti*[33] and in the Nāth yogis' notion of the spiritual tune (*anahat-nād*),[34] which is attained through elaborate yogic practices. However, the mystical element that accompanies Guru Nānak's doctrine of *śabad* appears to be an expression of his own spiritual experience of the Guru. Truth is the Sacred Word, and the Word of the Guru leads one to the Truth. *Śabad* is the necessary aid for spiritual pursuit and for attainment of the Truth. This understanding results in complete dependency on the Divine Name. It also results in love for, and devotion to, the Guru (*nirguṇ* God). During Guru Nānak's experience of being fixed on the Divine Name, Ultimate Reality or *EkOaṅkār* is referred to as the un-struck sound:

> Born in the home of the True Guru,
>   my comings and goings
>   [from the cycle of rebirth] have ceased.
> The mind is connected to the unstruck sound (*anahat-nād*).
> *Śabad* has burned away my aspirations and desires. (*SG* 20)

Guru Nānak instructs the *gurmukh* to meditate on and recite the Divine Name, since these spiritual practices contain Divine Presence.

Revelation must be experienced in the heart. Therefore, one attains Ultimate Reality through hearing and knowing the Word of Guru.

Guru Nānak uses the word *śabad* interchangeably with the term *nām* (Divine Name); often he uses both terms, *śabad* and *nām*, together in his devotional writings. Although in some instances *śabad* and *nām* mean the same thing—that is, *śabad* as the Divine Name—some poems express the notion that *śabad* is the means to the goal of *nām*. Guru Nānak explains in *Siddh Goṣṭ*:

> The *gurmukh* attains the pure *nām*.
> The *gurmukh* burns the ego
>   with *śabad*.
> The *gurmukh* sings the praises
>   of the True One.
> Through the True *nām*,
>   the *gurmukh* is honored.
> Nānak says: The *gurmukh* is aware
>   of the mysteries of the world. (*SG* 42)

The preceding verse describes *śabad* as the medium through which the ego is destroyed, allowing the *gurmukh* to experience *nām*. Guru Nānak refers to the Truth attained with the help of the Guru as *śabad*, and Truth uttered by the *gurmukh* as *nām*. *Nām* is the manifestation of *śabad*.[35] The only means to eliminate impurity is by repeating the Divine Name (*nām*) and meditating on the Transcendent Word (*śabad*). The Transcendent Word is contrasted to everyday speech that arises from the deluded self or mind:

> The false ones come into this world
>   and find no refuge,
>   and in duality they come and go.
> This coming and going
>   ends through the *śabad*.
> [*EkOaṅkār*] watches and blesses.
> One suffers from the disease of duality,
>   and the cure of *nām* is forgotten.
> The one who has been inspired to understand
>   is liberated through the *śabad*.
> Nānak says: The Emancipator saves those
>   who have distanced themselves
>   from the ego and duality. (*SG* 25)

*Nām* is not a label or a proper name for Reality, but an ontological category denoting Divine Presence or Ultimate Reality. *Nām* is the expression of the Guru, including the Guru's qualities or attributes (*guṇ*) described in the *mūl-mantar*. *Nām* subsumes within itself the revelation of the essence of the Guru, which ought to be the *gurmukh*'s only object of devotion and contemplation.[36] Furthermore, in the first verse after the introductory verse (*mangla-charan*) of *Siddh Goṣṭ*, Guru Nānak states:

> What use is it to wander?
>    [when] purification is attained through Truth.
> Without the True *śabad*,
>    no one attains *mukti*.
> Pause [to dwell upon this thought.] (*SG* 1)

The fact that this verse is followed by a "pause" indicates that this is the main argument put forward in *Siddh Goṣṭ*. Interestingly, verse 72 of *Siddh Goṣṭ*, which is the last verse in the Goindvāl Pothī version, Guru Nānak concludes:

> . . . Reflect upon this in the mind.
> Nānak says: Without *nām*, there is no *mukti*. (*SG* 72)

While the first verse explains the importance of *śabad* as the means to attaining liberation, the final verse of the Goindvāl version states that without *nām* there is no liberation. The way in which Guru Nānak wrote the *Siddh Goṣṭ* hymn was to amplify how indeed *śabad* is the means (*upāya*) and *nām* is the goal (*upeya*) to liberation.

## SIKH SPIRITUAL PRACTICE

An understanding as to how scriptural beliefs are put into practice can be best achieved through a discussion of the five spheres (*pañj khaṇḍ*) of spiritual development (*gurmat mārg*) outlined by Guru Nānak in his "Jap-jī" hymn. That is, the five spheres provide the theoretical and scriptural foundation for understanding the purpose and meaning of Sikh religious practice. Based on the *pañj khaṇḍ*, the key concepts and practices for the *gurmukh* are (1) selfless service (*sevā*), (2) remembering the Divine Name (*nām-simraṇ*), and (3) meditation techniques (*dhyān sādhan*).

## Pañj Khaṇḍ

Guru Nānak's notion of the five spheres (*pañj khaṇḍ*) of spiritual practice is outlined in "Jap-jī" a popular hymn recited by Sikhs, which begins right after the *mūl-mantar* in the *Gurū Granth Sāhib*.[37] In "Jap-jī" Guru Nānak describes the five spheres (*pañj khaṇḍ*) of spiritual development intended for the *gurmukh*. The *pañj khand* include: (1) the sphere of righteousness (*dharam khaṇḍ*); (2) the sphere of knowledge (*giān khaṇḍ*); (3) the sphere of effort (*saram khaṇḍ*); (4) the sphere of grace (*karam khaṇḍ*); and (5) the sphere of Truth (*sach khaṇḍ*).[38] For most practicing Sikhs, the five spheres are regarded as lying along an ascending path through which the *gurmukh* travels.[39]

The first sphere, the sphere of righteousness (*dharam*), is created through the balance of contentment (*santokh*) and compassion (*dayā*). Just as a bird needs two wings to fly, the *gurmukh* is required to engage in spiritual endeavors that cultivate a balance between contentment and compassion. The two are regarded as equally important, one without the other leads to an unbalanced or incomplete spiritual practice.[40] That is, the inability to be compassionate towards others is regarded as a reflection that one is discontented with oneself.

Contentment cultivates compassion and compassion fosters a sense of service to others. When one is content, one is satisfied with oneself. When one is satisfied, one is naturally compassionate toward others. Similarly, when one engages in selfless service, one becomes filled with love and devotion and this also furthers personal contentment. Indeed, balance is only achievable when both contentment and compassion are equally sought. The emphasis on balance in the relationship between personal contentment and compassion for humanity has the powerful implication that it is neither effective nor even useful to renounce world affairs.

The second sphere, the sphere of knowledge (*giān*), requires the *gurmukh* to participate in religious discourse (*gurbāṇī vichār*) to come to an intellectual understanding of the nature of human suffering and how to ultimately escape it.[41] The *gurmukh* is encouraged to seek the company of others journeying on the path to liberation (*sādh saṅgat*). The company of those on a similar path provides the *gurmukh* with guidance and support. The *gurmukh* can rely on the *sādh saṅgat* for encouragement and energy to help navigate through difficult moments on the spiritual path. Participation in the *sādh saṅgat* can inspire the *gurmukh* toward greater spiritual effort. In fact, to underline the importance of *sādh saṅgat*, Sikh *giānīs* commonly use the metaphor of the river and water droplet.[42] Just as a droplet of water will inevitably and eventually dry up on its own, so, too, will the one who tries to travel alone on a spiritual journey. In contrast, when in the company of the *sādh saṅgat*, the *gurmukh* is believed to become part of a larger group journeying toward the Guru.

Third, the sphere of effort (*saram*) leads the *gurmukh* to put scriptural knowledge into practice. According to Sikh *giānīs*, spiritual practice involves putting the virtues of compassion and contentment into action.[43] The two approaches commonly endorsed in the Sikh tradition are *sevā* (selfless service) and *simraṇ* (meditative remembrance).[44] Provided the *gurmukh* is able to successfully balance a life of *sevā* and *simraṇ*, he or she enters the fourth sphere, the sphere of grace (*karam*).[45] Grace is regarded as a spontaneous flow (*sahaj*) of experience in which there is harmony with the inner resonance of all existence (*sahej dhūnī*), something that occurs through the practice of meditation (*dhyān sādhan*). In this process, the *gurmukh* experiences a state of unconditional bliss (*sahaj ānand*), and inevitably enters the last and fifth sphere, the sphere of Truth (*sach*). The fifth sphere consists of the experience of complete resonance with the Ultimate Reality.

By explicating the *pañj khaṇḍ*, a direct connection emerges between Sikh theology and Sikh spiritual custom, including the practice of *sevā*, *nām-simraṇ*, and *dhyān sādhan*.

## Sevā

The practice of *sevā* (selfless service) is twofold; it (1) cultivates compassion and (2) forms the bridge between the *gurmukh* and society, with the orientation of improving the condition of society or the betterment of humanity. There are three forms of *sevā*: *tan* (physical), *man* (mental), and *dhān* (philanthropy). *Tan* involves the *gurmukh* serving humanity through physical efforts, such as feeding the poor, constructing shelters for the homeless, or cleaning the Sikh place of worship (*gurdwārā*). *Sevā* thus sanctifies and dignifies manual labor in a way that is unique to the Sikh tradition.[46] In traditional Indian society, societal work involving manual labor was regarded with disdain and has traditionally mostly been confined to the lower castes.[47] To counteract this view, Guru Nānak institutionalized *tan sevā* as an integral part of the Sikh tradition when he created the *laṅgar* (community kitchen).[48] The *laṅgar* functions as a place where all are served regardless of caste, religion, race, or creed, and serving others is regarded as a virtuous act.

The second form of *sevā* called *man* involves serving humanity through mental efforts, such as tutoring disadvantaged children, giving managerial support, or teaching *gurmukhī* in the *gurdwārā*. Such talents are not to be used for self-centered pursuits, but rather for the welfare of humanity.[49] Furthermore, the *gurmukh* is also encouraged to cultivate authentic and caring relationships with those whom he or she encounters. In effect, *man sevā* involves sharing or empathizing with the pain of others.

Last, the third form of *sevā* referred to as *dhān* pertains to serving humanity through philanthropic efforts, such as donating money or material goods. *Dasvaṅdh* (tithe) is a common form of personal philanthropy in the Sikh tradition. A crucial aspect of Sikh philanthropic efforts is that they are to be carried out in such a manner so that the acts of giving result in the dissolution of the *gurmukh*'s ego rather than its inflation. The purpose of *dhān sevā* is the breaking of worldly attachments instead of the accumulation of honor.[50] Therefore, true *sevā* must be essentially performed with humility, purity of intention, and sincerity.

## Nām-Simraṇ

While *sevā* is seen as humanitarian practice that cultivates compassion, *simraṇ* (meditative remembrance) is regarded as personal spiritual practice that brings about contentment. The purpose of *simraṇ* is to cultivate a profound connection between the soul and *EkOaṅkār*. The common practice of *simraṇ* in the Sikh tradition is *nām-simraṇ*, meditative remembrance of the Divine Name.[51] *Nām* can be literally translated as name; however, such a loose translation does not capture the philosophical importance of the term, and understates its experiential qualities. In the Sikh tradition, a name is not a mere label to identify a person, object, or phenomenon. *Nām* is the Sacred Word used to express the essence of all existence, that is, *EkOaṅkār*.[52] Thus, one's true nature, form, essence, or name is all *EkOaṅkār*. *Nām* is the primordial essence that binds the entire creation as one integral whole.

The mantra commonly used by Sikhs for *nām-simraṇ* is *Wāhe-gurū*, meaning "the Infinite (*wāhe*) Light (*rū*) [that dispels] all darkness (*gu*)," darkness being the mind's ignorance of its true essence.[53] *Nām-simraṇ* involves a systematic process that requires the *gurmukh* to discipline the mind and body. The mind is metaphorically described by Sikh *giānīs* as a fallow field waiting to be cultivated.[54] The farmer (consciousness) can either routinely plow the field to maintain its vegetation potential, or he or she can allow weeds to destroy its utility. The seed of *nām* can only flourish if the *gurmukh* routinely practices mental cleansing. This involves control over the sensory stimuli that enter the mind through the nine openings or gates of the body:

genitals, anus, mouth, nostrils, eyes, and ears. For *nām-simraṇ* to begin there has to be complete control over sensory stimuli and the subsequent thoughts of desire that arise or erupt out of sensory perception. Control over the senses can be achieved through meditation.

### Dhyān Sādhan

A common meditation technique (*dhyān sādhan*) used among Sikh practitioners is breath control. One is instructed to sit in a comfortable position on the ground, such as cross-legged with a straight spine, and to mentally follow the breath flowing in through the nose, filling the lungs, and exhaling through the nose. As in *prāṇayam yoga*, many Sikh practitioners hold that breathing and mental states are interconnected. By calming, and focusing on, the breath, it is believed that the mind can enter a state of stillness and tranquillity. This state of mind is a requisite for *nām-simraṇ;* just as the farmer plants a seed in a fallow field, the seed of *nām* can only be absorbed in a quiet and still mind.

Once the mind has attained a state of tranquillity, the chanting aspect of *nām-simraṇ* begins. The *gurmukh* recites the *Wāhegurū* mantra in a clear and concise fashion. Chanting requires the *gurmukh* to affix his or her attention (*dhyān*) on the audible sound current or *ahat nād*.[55] This sound is perceptible to the auditory faculty of the mind, where the sound waves are believed to invoke a conscious state that enables the *gurmukh* to tune-in to a higher frequency. In this state, the consciousness slowly transcends the mind and connects with the *anahat-nād* or unstruck sound.[56] *Anahat-nād* is the cosmic resonance that is experienced through the *dasam duār* (tenth gate), which functions as a spiritual conduit between the *gurmukh* and *EkOṅkār*.[57] As the *gurmukh* becomes absorbed in the *anahat-nād*, the mind is in a habitual state of meditation (*ajapa jap*), even though the mechanical chanting has stopped.[58] Guru Nānak explains this transcendental process in the *Siddh Goṣṭ*:

> By blocking the nine gates,
> one arrives at the tenth gate.
> It is here that the unstruck sound (*anahat-nād*)
> resounds in the state of emptiness (*sunn*). (*SG* 53)

This stage in meditation is regarded as a critical one according to Sikh *giānīs*. It is believed that once the *gurmukh* attains this state, he or she is susceptible to slowly withdrawing from worldly responsibilities and humanitarian efforts, and becoming disconnected from the world.[59] To sit alone in the absorbed state or experience of emptiness (*sunn;*

*śūnya* in Sanskrit) is not encouraged in the Sikh tradition. Rather, emptiness has a paradoxical meaning; the mind has to be emptied to become fully aware of the primordial essence that unifies all existence:

> One attains peace when uniting in a state of *sahaj*.
> The *gurmukh* remains awake and does not fall asleep.
> The *śabad* is enshrined deep within *sunn*.
> One is liberated by chanting *śabad* and liberates others as well.
> Those who practice the Guru's teachings are immersed in Truth.
> Nānak says: Those who lose their ego are united [with
> *EkOaṅkār*] rather than separated. (*SG* 54).

Truth is the ultimate realization and experience that the *ātma* is at the core of one's being. As this realization arises, the *ātma* is liberated (*mukti)* from the cycle of births and deaths, as it merges with the Supreme Universal Soul (*paramātma*). There is no longer the sense that "I" is separate from the "other," but rather there is the experience of unity with the all-pervasive Universal Soul, *EkOaṅkār*.

These aforementioned spiritual practices are to be followed by the *gurmukh* while living in society. The *gurmukh* is required to be dispassionate about, and detached from, material endeavors while at the same time living in the world.[60] In *Siddh Goṣṭ*, Guru Nānak metaphorically describes the *gurmukh*:

> As the lotus flower remains untouched by water,
> and as a duck floats above the water;
> when the mind is connected to the *śabad*,
> one crosses over the world ocean.
> Nānak chants the *nām*.
> A person who lives detached and enshrines the One,
> in the mind,
> remains desireless amidst desires.
> [The disciple] who sees and inspires others to see the Ineffable,
> Nānak is such a [disciple's] servant. (*SG* 5)

For Guru Nānak, the distinctive mark of a *gurmukh* is that he or she works for *sarbat da bhalā* or the welfare and liberation of all humanity.[61] The virtues of compassion and contentment, which are the prerequisites for *sevā* and *simraṇ*, need to be continuously balanced in the *gurmukh*'s life.

Like Hinduism, Buddhism, and Jainism, Sikhism adheres to the worldview of birth, death, and rebirth (*saṅsār*) and the goal of liberation (*mukti*) from it. However, according to the Sikh tradition, *saṅsār* is like an impassable ocean, where one is easily caught in the clutches of the five evils. Human beings, led by their ego (*manmukh*), are driven by their quest for permanence and power, resulting in a cyclical state of suffering. One can, however, alleviate suffering by following the way of the *gurmukh*, which leads one across this ocean of illusion (*māyā*). One ought to be oriented to *EkOaṅkār* in order to attain liberation. The process of resonating with *EkOaṅkār* within one's own heart is a process of ridding or moving away from the ego through the spiritual practices of involving oneself in selfless service to humanity (*sevā*), remembering the Divine Name (*nām-simraṇ*), and meditation (*dhyān sādhan*).

Guru Nānak's path of the *gurmukh* falls into the category of the *renunciate in the larger context of involvement in society*. The path toward self-realization is to be pursued while "living-in-this-world" and is achievable by all, based on the understanding that all persons have the potential to be a *gurmukh*. The Sikh worldview (based on the key concepts of *EkOaṅkār*, *śabad*, and *gurmukh*) and Sikh religious practice (including *seva*, *nām-simraṇ*, and *dhyān sādhan*) provides the theoretical foundation necessary for a critical look at the *Siddh Goṣṭ* debate about renunciation as a valid means to liberation.

# Chapter Six

# Renunciation and Social Involvement in *Siddh Goṣṭ*

*Siddh Goṣṭ* is a key Sikh philosophical text that describes Guru Nānak's understanding of "True" yoga in the context of the issue of whether or not renouncing mundane existence is necessary for the attainment of liberation (*mukti*). The effort to arrive at a more accurate reading and interpretation of the *Siddh Goṣṭ* discourse can benefit considerably from knowledge of the four aspects used to understand a primary text. The first aspect involves background material about the people with whom the author is having the discourse, in this case, the Nāth yogis who are regarded as the pioneers of hath-yoga. As *renunciates living outside society*, the Nāths engage in the twofold pursuit of (1) acquiring occult powers (*siddhis*), especially for the purpose of conquering evil spirits/omens, and (2) immortality (*jīvan-mukti*) through mental and physical exercises that awaken the *kundalinī śakti* to unite with the supreme Śiva-consciousness.

The second aspect is concerned with the life-situation of the author. In respect of *Siddh Goṣṭ*, Guru Nānak's life story and accounts of his meetings with the Nāth yogis are mainly described in the hagiographical *janam-sākhī* literature. Although there are historical inconsistencies in the *janam-sākhīs* and there is ambiguity surrounding the exact location where the *Siddh Goṣṭ* dialogue took place, the accounts nevertheless do reflect Guru Nānak's spiritual orientation to the world, his familiarity with the Nāth yogic tradition, and his rejection of the ascetic lifestyle.

The third aspect involves the larger aim or function of the text. The *Siddh Goṣṭ* text seems to have a twofold function: (1) it is a philosophical work that expounds the Sikh worldview, and (2) it is a hymn that is intended to be recited as part of daily Sikh practice in order to develop spiritual insight into the nature of "True" yoga. While the text is included in both the *Gurū Granth Sāhib* and some versions of the *Pañj Granthī*, the actual audience for which the text was composed was Hindu, and Muslim as well as the followers of the Sikh Panth.

Last, the fourth aspect entails knowledge about the philosophical framework within which the text is situated. In respect of *Siddh Goṣṭ*, it involves the nature of Reality (*EkOaṅkār*) and the practical application of Sikh scriptural belief. While the *gurmukh* path to union with *EkOaṅkār* entails remembering (*nām-simraṇ*) and meditating (*dhyān sādhan*) on the Divine Name, this path simultaneously requires partaking in selfless service (*sevā*) while remaining in society. Indeed, one ought to pursue Sikh religious practice in the context of "living-in-this-world."

Having discussed the four criteria in the previous chapters, this chapter explores the central issue in *Siddh Goṣṭ*—whether or not renunciation should be a prerequisite for attaining liberation from the cycle of rebirth (*saṅsār*). Drawing on *Siddh Goṣṭ* and other relevant hymns by Guru Nānak, this chapter looks at Guru Nānak's critique of world renunciation and his understanding of "True" yoga. While Guru Nānak teaches the path of yoga, he distinctively prescribes following it, in line with the Sikh worldview, while living in society. Moreover, even though he teaches that one ought to remain living in society, Guru Nānak at the same time critiques the traditional householder path.

The chapter begins by specifically analyzing Guru Nānak's critique of world renunciation. Second, it analyzes Guru Nānak's exposition of "True" yoga in the light of the references he makes to the Nāth practice of world renunciation and hath-yoga. Third, the chapter investigates what constitutes "living-in-this-world" by exploring Guru Nānak's perspective on the path of the householder. Last, and more important, the chapter puts forth the argument that Guru Nānak prescribes the religious lifestyle of the *renunciate living in the larger context of involvement in society*, which forms the last of the four categories of religious lifestyles described in chapter 1. Indeed, while the analysis shows that Guru Nānak (and Sikhism at large) rejects the lifestyle of the *renunciate living outside society*, it also demonstrates that he rejects as well the two householder religious lifestyles—the *householder living in society* and the *householder living in the larger context of eventual withdrawal from society.*

In order to fully grasp the essence of Guru Nānak's argument for the path of the *renunciate living in the larger context of social involvement*, it is necessary to first discuss Guru Nānak's critique of world renunciation.

## CRITIQUE OF WORLD RENUNCIATION

The *janam-sākhīs* about Guru Nānak's encounters with the Nāth yogis asserts Guru Nānak's spiritual superiority not only as a Sant but also in terms of the religious path he teaches. These *janam-sākhīs* need, however, to be verified against Sikh scriptural teachings like the *Siddh Goṣṭ* text. There is no evidence in *Siddh Goṣṭ* that there was any competition between Guru Nānak and the Nāth yogis as some of the hagiographies seek to present. Rather, even though the Nāth yogis addressed Guru Nānak as "child" twice in the *Siddh Goṣṭ* text (verses 2 and 43), they ask him questions as if seeking his realized Truth. Consequently, the *Siddh Goṣṭ* discourse can be taken to have been intended to convey Guru Nānak's philosophical orientation of the world along with guidance by him as to how one should pursue liberation while living in society. Guru Nānak achieves the latter by answering questions put to him by the Nāth yogis in the light of their path of world renunciation as the sole means to liberation.

The *Siddh Goṣṭ* discourse can be viewed not only as a means to establish Guru Nānak's path as superior to, as well as more practical than, the Nāth yogic way, but also as his attempt to counteract the general mind-set of the laypeople. At the time of Guru Nānak, there was the common belief among the laypeople that world renunuciation was the sole means to liberation. As a consequence, the common people had the tendency to emulate or give high esteem to *renunciates living outside society* like the Nāth yogis.

There is no ambiguity in *Siddh Goṣṭ* about whether or not Guru Nānak valued or agreed with world renunciation as a necessary requirement to achieve liberation. As made evident first and foremost in *Siddh Goṣṭ* and his other devotional compositions, Guru Nānak explicitly rejects renunciation as a requisite for liberation. Guru Nānak's rejection of worldly renunciation, or of the ascetic practices associated with it, is made evident in his own use of the term *udāsī*. While *udāsī* usually refers to a renunciate who has withdrawn or is detached from society (as in the case of the Nāth yogis), in *Siddh Goṣṭ* it is used to mean the *gurmukh*'s quest for the Truth. When the *siddhs* ask Guru Nānak about the nature of his status as an *udāsī*, Guru Nānak replies thus:

> I [Nānak] have become an *udāsī* in search of *gurmukhs*.
> I have adopted these robes in search of their vision.
> I am out to trade Truth.
> I am a peddler of Truth.
> Nānak says: With the help of *gurmukhs*,
> others can be carried across
> [the ocean of *saṅsār*] (*SG* 18)

*Udāsī*, according to Guru Nānak, is not about taking a vow of asceticism. Rather, *udāsī* is actually the spiritual journey for realizing the

Truth. And, in undertaking it, there is the search for others with whom one can travel on this venture.

In the case of Guru Nānak, he was a renunciate in that as a *gurmukh* he had ventured out on his spiritual travels, leaving his family behind. The redefinition of *udāsī* lies in the fact that after his long journeys in the four directions of the world, Guru Nānak returned to his family, where he combined spiritual piety with worldly living:

> In the compositions of Guru Nānak there are verses which can be interpreted as supporting renunciation (*udās*), and Guru Nānak himself had travelled widely, leaving his family behind. His decision to return to the life of a house-holder, therefore, was important. It demonstrated his basic ideal that true renunciation consisted in living pure amidst the impurities of attachment. The followers of Guru Nānak at Kartārpur and elsewhere pursued honest occupations for livelihood. They demonstrated thus how to combine piety with worldly activity. A disciplined worldliness was the hallmark of this new community.[1]

Indeed, even though Guru Nānak ventured out in the four directions for the purpose of religious discourse, he did not technically renounce the world to attain liberation since "leaving his family behind" was only temporary.

In his devotional hymns, Guru Nānak also explicitly denounces the religious lifestyle of the *renunciate living outside society* as a futile means for self-realization or liberation, because, for him, it is merely a form of attachment:

> Yoga is not the patched coat,
>   or smearing the body with ashes.
> Yoga is not the earrings, shaven head,
>   or the blowing of the horn.
> To remain pure
>   amid the impurities [of the world]
> is the way yoga is attained.
> Yoga is not attained
>   by conversing [about it].
> The one,
>   who looks upon all as one,
> shall be known as a yogi.
> Yoga is not [achieved]
>   by visiting memorials at cremation sites

Yoga is not [about] sitting in a trance.
Yoga is not wandering in the world.
Yoga is not bathing at pilgrimage sites.
To remain pure,
  amid the impurities [of the world],
is the way yoga is attained.
(Sūhī Rāg, M.1, *GGS*, p. 730)

In Guru Nānak's view, the path and goals related to world renunciation are futile because, instead of enhancing the spiritual quest, they divert one to a sectarian way rather than aid in realizing the Divine Name.

Guru Nānak makes reference to his path of the *gurmukh* as yoga; however, he discounts hath-yoga and the ascetic practices associated with it. In fact, his hymns explicitly critique the Nāth practice of hath-yoga for its futility:

Restraint through hath [-yoga] wears off the body:
Fasting and austerities do not soften the mind.
There is nothing that equals *nām*.
Serve the Guru!
O mind! Associate with
  those connected with the All-pervasive One! . . .
(Rāmkalī, M.1, *GGS*, p. 905.)

According to Guru Nānak, strenuous yogic exercises are counterproductive because they "harden," instead of enlighten, the mind. In effect, the discipline of rigorous mental and physical yogic exercises fail in guiding one toward liberation from the cycle of rebirth (*sańsār*):

When you drink the essence (*nām*),
  the messenger of death cannot touch you,
  and the serpent [of *māyā*] cannot sting you.
The world is in conflict,
  and is softened by [false] music.
Abiding in the three modes [of *māyā*]
  one comes and goes.
Without *nām*,
  there is only suffering.
The yogi inhales his breath upwards [to awaken the *kundalinī*]
[The yogi] performs inner cleansing and six purification rituals.
Without *nām*, the breath the yogi inhales is meaningless. . . .
(Rāmkalī, M.1, *GGS*, p. 905.)

While, for the Nāths, hath-yoga is the primary practice for subduing the senses and self-realization, for Guru Nānak it is ineffective in cleansing the mind from the influence of *māyā*. Moreover, Guru Nānak disagrees with the Nāth practice of acquiring occult powers because it misleads one in the search for Truth. Guru Nānak argues that the acquisition of occult powers through yogic practices leads to futile results:

> If I dressed myself with fire,
> lived in a house of snow,
> and ate iron for food;
> [so what!]
> [If I] drank suffering like water,
> and drove the earth before me,
> weighed the earth on a scale with a copper coin;
> [so what!]
> [If I were] to become so great that
> I could not be contained,
> and lead all,
> to have mental power to control others;
> so what!
> Great is the Master,
> great are the blessings,
> upon whom they are bestowed.
> Nānak says: Those blessed with grace
> attain the glory of the True *nām*.
> (Salok, M.1, *GGS*, 147)

According to Guru Nānak, the occult powers acquired by hath-yoga—like enlarging the body, influencing others or controlling others—are meaningless for the ultimate goal of liberation. In fact, occult powers are but a distraction from the ultimate experience of Ultimate Reality. It is only the *gurmukh*, liberated through *śabad*, who can discriminate the Truth from falsehood, including the difference between occult powers acquired by the Nāth renunciates living outside society and the universal wisdom attained by the *gurmukhs*:

> The *gurmukh* attains the eight occult powers and universal wisdom.
> The *gurmukh* crosses the ocean [of *saṅsār*]
> and attains true understanding.
> The *gurmukh* can discriminate
> between Truth and falsehood.
> The *gurmukh* recognizes worldliness and renunciation.

The *gurmukh* crosses over [the ocean of *saṅsār*]
and carries others across as well.
Nānak says: The *gurmukh* is liberated through *śabad*. (*SG* 31)

Guru Nānak in *Siddh Goṣṭ* rejects the Nāth path of *the renunciate living outside society* even as he uses Nāth "ascetic" or "yogic" terminology to illustrate his devotional path while "living-in-this-world." Although he rejects world renunciation and ascetic practices, and he does not follow the hath-yoga practices of the Nāth tradition, Guru Nānak modifies the term yoga even as he incorporates in his worldview the Nāth notion of the "inner tune" (*anahat-nād*), the breaking away from duality (*sahaj*), and the larger context of emptiness (*sunn*) that has to be realized, the topic of the following section.

## THE CONCEPT OF "TRUE" YOGA

*Siddh Goṣṭ* provides a description of what Guru Nānak understands by yoga. While he teaches the path of the *gurmukh*, Guru Nānak also refers to it as "True" yoga. Interestingly, he also describes his own conception of "True" yoga by making references to the Nāth practice of hath-yoga. Guru Nānak's *Siddh Goṣṭ* expounds the path of "True" yoga as one of self-renunciation based on the premise that it is the ego that ought to be renounced while "living-in-this-world." For Guru Nānak, the *gurmukh* path of yoga consists of renouncing the ego through single-minded contemplation on *śabad* and remembrance of *nām*. The following verse (*vār*) by Bhāī Gurdās most effectively summarizes Guru Nānak's viewpoint on yoga:

> Illusion cannot be erased without yoga. It is similar to the fact where we know that without cleansing of the mirror, the face cannot be seen in it. Yoga is cleansing praxis through which the *surati* [consciousness] gets absorbed into the unstruck melody. Eighteen *siddhis* and nine treasures fall at the feet of a *gurmukh* yogi. In *kaliyug*, Patañjali talked about the fulfillment of desires that remained unfulfilled in the three ages. The complete achievement of yogic *bhakti* is that you get every thing hand to hand. The *jīv* should cultivate the nature of remembrance of God, charity and ablution (internal and external). (Bhāī Gurdās, *Vārāṅ*, 1.14)[2]

For Guru Nānak, "True" yoga involves meditative remembrance of the Divine Name (*nām-simraṇ*) while at the same time taking to selfless service (*sevā*) in the pursuit of liberation.

Guru Nānak disagrees with Nāth belief and practices, yet he incorporates Nāth terminology in his exposition of "True" yoga. How is it that Guru Nānak can use the concepts associated with renunciation in general, and makes references to Nāth yogic belief and practices in particular, when he disagrees with them? In actual fact, Guru Nānak *modifies* the concepts and terms associated with the Nāth practice of hath-yoga so that they can fit in with his own philosophical orientation.[3]

First, Guru Nānak makes general references to the Nāth dress code and practice of yoga, especially the earrings, the primary mark of the Nāth yogi:

> O yogi! Let your vision be
> the patched coat, earrings, and [begging] bag.
> [Concentrate on] the One dwelling
> within the twelve branches of yoga,
> and let the path of the One teach
> the wisdom of the six philosophical schools.
> If the mind understands this, then one will not suffer.
> Nānak says: The *gurmukh* understands that
> this is the way yoga is attained. (*SG* 9)

In discussing the external symbols of the Nāth yogis, Guru Nānak teaches that one needs to go beyond the external symbols or forms of religion. That is, the mind of the *gurmukh* has to be disciplined and has to be in tune with the *śabad* of Guru.

*Siddh Goṣṭ* contains several references specific to Nāth practices, especially those associated with hath-yoga. *Siddh Goṣṭ* makes a couple of references to the yogic imagery of balancing the moon and sun in order to reverse the aging process (i.e., mortality). In *Siddh Goṣṭ*, the *siddhs* ask Guru Nānak:

> How does the moon
> cool life like snow?
> How does the sun blaze?
> How can death be turned away? . . . (*SG* 48)

Guru Nānak answers:

> When one chants *śabad*,
> the moon
> [that is the mind] is infinitely illuminated.

When the sun [of wisdom] dwells
in the home of the moon
[that is the mind]
darkness is dispelled.
Pleasure and suffering are alike,
when one has the support of *nām*.
[*EkOaṅkār*] itself carries us
across [the ocean of *saṅsār*].
With the Guru's wisdom,
the mind merges in Truth.
Nānak says: Such a one is not consumed by death. (*SG* 49)

Guru Nānak however teaches that *śabad* is the means to liberation since it illuminates the mind (moon) and dispels darkness (sun), whereas for the hath-yogi it is the physical and mental exercises that bring forth a balance of the calming (moon) and arousal (sun) energy channels, reversing the physiological processes of aging and death.

*Siddh Goṣṭ* also refers to the three central hath-yogic exercises of (1) breathing (*prāṇaya*) [verses 44 and 67], (2) posturing (*āsan*) [verses 3 and 50], and (3) hand gesturing (*mudrā*) [verse 61]:

*Siddhs:*
The air is said to be the life of the mind,
but what does the air feed on?
What is the hand posture (*mudrā*) of wisdom?
What is the practice of the enlightened one (*siddh*)? (*SG* 61)

Guru Nānak replies to the *siddhs:*

Without the *śabad*
the essence is not attained,
nor does the thirst of the ego depart. (*SG* 61)

For Guru Nānak, the *anahat-nād* resonating in the *śabad* is the source of all existence, including the yogic concept of *prāṇa* or life force energy, while meditation on the *śabad* is regarded as the paramount practice.

Guru Nānak also refers to the hath-yogic energy channels—the three central pathways (*nāḍīs*) of the subtle body (*suṣumanā-nāḍī* [*sukhmanā* in Punjabi], *iḍā-nāḍī*, and *piṅgalā-nāḍī*) in his discussion on the nature of Reality:

One understands the *sukhmanā*, *iḍā*, and *piṅgalā*,
when the ineffable is realized.

> Nānak says: The True One is above
> the three energy channels.
> Through the True Guru's *śabad*,
> one is united [with *EkOaṅkār*] (*SG* 60)

While the hath-yogi aims to raise the *kundalinī*-Śakti through each of the seven central *cakras* to ultimately unite with Śiva-consciousness, Guru Nānak reinterprets the underlying notion to advance his own understanding of yoga. That is, meditation on the *śabad* awakens the consciousness to destroy the ego, and to ultimately experience *EkOaṅkār*. In Guru Nānak's approach, the ego is viewed as the deficiency that prevents one from experiencing *EkOaṅkār*, whereas hath-yoga views a dormant *kundalinī*-Śakti and imbalanced *iḍā* and *piṅgalā* as the deficieny (as described in *Gorakṣa Śataka* 47–50 and *Haṭha-yoga Pradīpikā* chapters 2 and 4).

Guru Nānak writes about the ten gates of the human body, where the "nine doors" refer to physical or sensory experiences (two eyes, two ears, two nostrils, the mouth, the anus, and the genitals), and the "tenth door" refers to the transcendental or spiritual channel that unites the *gurmukh* and *EkOaṅkār*. In the following verse, Guru Nānak explains that one needs to block the nine gates in order to reach the "tenth door":

> By blocking the nine gates,
> one arrives at the tenth gate.
> It is here
> that the unstruck sound (*anahat-nād*)
> resounds in the state of *sunn*.
> . . . The hidden *bāṇī* is revealed.
> Nānak says: The True One is realized. (*Siddh Goshth* 53)

This verse makes reference to the "tenth door" as the place where one has the yogic experience of the unstruck sound (*anahat-nād*), which is attainable through meditation on the *śabad*. The difference between Guru Nānak and the Nāth yogi in their understanding of the "tenth door" is that, the latter see it as an actual subtle energy channel located within the body,[4] while the former views it as an intangible spiritual experience.

As discussed in the verse earlier quoted (Salok, M.1, *GGS*, p. 147), Guru Nānak dismisses the strenuous practices associated with hath-yoga. Yet, we see Guru Nānak referring to hath-yoga terminology in *Siddh Goṣṭ* and other relevant hymns. However, for Guru Nānak, his perspective involves the belief that one will understand all, including yogic processes, once one transcends duality, which—in his view—is attainable only through the meditation of the *śabad*. The one recurrent theme throughout *Siddh Goṣṭ* is that the *śabad* is the only means to the goal of union with *EkOaṅkār*:

> The True One supports the breath
> that extends the distance
> of three and seven fingers.
> The *gurmukh* speaks about the essence,
> and realizes the ineffable and infinite.
> By erasing the three *guns*,
> the *śabad* is enshrined in the mind
> and the ego is removed.
> When the One is seen
> inside and out,
> the love of *nām* is present.
> One understands the *sukhmanā, iḍā,* and *piṅgalā,*
> when the ineffable is realized.
> Nānak says: The True One is above
> the three energy channels.
> Through the True Guru's *śabad,*
> one is united [with *EkOaṅkār*]. (*SG* 60)

This hymn accurately describes Guru Nānak's perspective on the "True" yoga. The central argument that Guru Nānak puts forward is that meditation on the *śabad* is the practice that ultimately enables the *gurmukh* to become absorbed in *nām-simraṇ* and experience the Divine Essence of *nām*.

Guru Nānak's understanding of the *śabad* has its origins both in the Hindu concept of the Vedic mantra *Auṃ* as well as in the Nāth yogis' understanding of the spiritual tune *(anahat-nād)*. For instance, the ancient Vedic mantra *Auṃ* is the eternal sound considered as the highest realization sought through meditation. Similar to the *Auṃ* mantra, *EkOaṅkār*, "One Primordial Essence manifest in all" is also regarded as the eternal sound that is to be experienced as the unstruck sound. Indeed, *Auṃ* (*Chāndogya Upaniṣad* 1.1; *Māṇḍūkya Upaniṣad* 1.1) and *EkOaṅkār* are identified with Ultimate Reality, and spiritual attainment is the experiential realization of the equation of the ātma with Ultimate Reality or the merging of the eternal soul with Ultimate Reality (*Chandogyā Upaniṣad* 6). There is, however, a significant difference between the Upaniṣad and Sikh understanding of the eternal sound; while the eternal sound of *Auṃ* is limited to Vedic learning and practice, accessible to only the privileged males belonging to the three upper classes (*dvija*), the eternal sound in Sikhism is a cosmic resonance, meant to be experienced by all. According to Guru Nānak, no one can take ownership over the eternal sound (*EkOaṅkār*) nor is it attainable by a certain group of people (*dvija*). The prerequisite to experiencing the eternal sound is devotion and the personal relationship one has with Ultimate Reality.

The pan-Indian concept of *śabad*, similarly, has great importance in the yogic traditions with their practice of mantra, in which *śabad* is the means to experience the inner divine tune of Reality. The concept of *śabad* is inextricably connected with the concept of the unstruck sound (*anahat-śabad* or *anahat-nād*), or pure or eternal sound. According to W. H. McLeod, the Tantric use of *śabad* as the musical sound that needs to be experienced has influenced the Sant tradition, with which Guru Nānak is associated.[5] Although the Sant and Sikh traditions do not follow the hath-yoga practices of the Nāth tradition, they have incorporated in their worldview the notion of the "inner tune" that has to be realized. However, for Guru Nānak, the only means to realizing the inner tune is *nām*:

> Immersed in *nām*,
> the ego is distant.
> Immersed in *nām*,
> one merges in Truth.
> Immersed in *nām*,
> one can contemplate the way of yoga.
> Immersed in *nām*,
> one finds the door of liberation.
> Immersed in *nām*,
> one understands the three worlds.
> Nānak says: Immersed in *nām*,
> one attains eternal peace. (*SG* 32)

Therefore, the concept of the unstruck sound is derived from the Nāth yogis, who practice hath-yoga as the means to experience the unstruck melody, which resonates in the tenth door from where the nectar of *nām* trickles down.

The Nāth concept of experiencing the spiritual tune—which is attained through elaborate yogic practices and results in the break from dualistic thinking (*sahaj*)—concurs with the *gurmukh* experience of union with *EkOaṅkār*. It is important to emphasize, however, that, unlike the Nāth yogis, for Guru Nānak it is only *EkOaṅkār* that produces the Sacred Sound. Sikhism believes in a nondual dynamic of Reality, which is realized through devotional remembrance, rather than Tantric yoga's dualistic realism and its orientation of world renunciation, focus on the physical body and technical methods of *prāṇayam*, *āsan*, and *mudrā*. While Guru Nānak's understanding of *śabad* has its roots in both the Upaniṣadic and Nāth traditions (both of which view world renunciation as a prerequisite for attaining liberation), the mystical element in Guru Nānak's doctrine of *śabad* appears, however, to be an expression of his own spiritual experience of Ultimate Reality.

Modern scholarship has demonstrated how Sikhism has—through the Sant tradition—been influenced by the devotionalism of Hindu (Vaiṣṇava) Bhakti, the hath-yoga of the Nāth tradition, and the mysticism of Sufism.[6] While the argument on the influence of the Sant tradition on the Sikh tradition has, for the most part, been accepted, the notion of possible Nāth influence *via* the Sant tradition has been a point of contention among some scholars. For instance, several traditional Sikh scholars contend that Guru Nānak was not, in actuality, influenced by the Nāth tradition, basing their argument on the fact that Sikhism is founded on the path of the householder that values social involvement, such as selfless service (*sevā*).[7]

Guru Nānak, however, does incorporate the popular yogic concepts concerning self-realization—including the notion of mystical union (*sahaj*) or transcending the dualistic mode of thinking within his Sikh philosophical system—even as he may modify them. As discussed in chapter 5, Guru Nānak's philosophical system includes concepts, such as the spontaneous realization of one's innate nature (*sahaj-dhūnī*); blissful state (*sahaj-ānand*); and the unstruck sound (*anahat-nād*). *Siddh Goṣṭ* makes several references to mystical union that emerges out of emptiness (*sunn*):[8]

> When the heart and body did not exist,
> the mind resided detached
> in *sunn*.
> When there was no support
> of the naval lotus,
> the life breath resided within itself,
> immersed in love. . . . (*SG* 67)

For Guru Nānak, mystical union not only consists in breaking all duality, but also unites one with *EkOaṅkār*.

While appropriating the Nāth terminology of hath-yoga, Guru Nānak modifies it for the sake of teaching his own spiritual message. In presenting the spiritual path of *self-renunciation while living in the world*, Guru Nānak actually transforms the traditional system of yoga. Guru Nānak does use terms associated with the Nāth tradition, but he changes them to fit the larger context of his Sikh perspective on the world and liberation. However, the very incorporation of the concepts from the Nāth tradition suggests a certain degree of influence regardless of the modification of the terms by Guru Nānak in the larger context of Sikhism.

While it has discounted hath-yoga as a means to self-realization, the Sikh tradition has, in fact, not been against yoga in relation to the physical benefits that it provides. For instance, *gaṭkā*—the Sikh martial arts started by the sixth guru, Guru Hargobind—involves physical, mental, and breathing practices derived from Ancient Indian exercises that were appropriated by the formalized school of yoga. However, the physical discipline of *gaṭkā* is by no means regarded as a spiritual practice.[9] Indeed, spiritual development is considered achievable only through the devotional recitation of the Divine Name.

While the Sikhs and the Nāth yogis (or renunciates in general) share the same larger religious worldview of *saṅsār* along with the goal of escape from the cycle of rebirth, Guru Nānak's exposition of the path of self-renunciation while living in the world adheres to the belief that one ought to live in the world or at least not run away from it. However, since Guru Nānak at the same time critiques the traditional path of the householder, it is necessary first to explore his actual position on it in order to come to a precise understanding as to what Guru Nānak means by living in the world.

## CRITIQUE OF THE TRADITIONAL HOUSEHOLDER PATH

As a consequence of Guru Nānak's explicit rejection of world renunciation as a valid means to liberation, his discounting of world renunciation has at times been misinterpreted as supporting the traditional householder religious lifestyle. While Sikhism is often described as a "householder religion," Guru Nānak's teachings in *Siddh Goṣṭ*, in actuality, reject the traditional path of the householder, that is, the householder path as traditionally understood in Indian thought and prescribed by Brahmanism and Classical Hinduism.

The householder path, at first blush, can be considered to be the way of the Sikh. And, if one uses the two common polarities of "living-in-this-world" and "renouncing-this-world," it would seem inevitable that Sikhs would be regarded as falling in the householder category. In fact, the writings of traditional Sikh scholars, as well as the beliefs or attitudes held by many Sikh practitioners, often emphasize that Sikh teachings promote the householder path to liberation. One such scholar, for instance, states: "The religion of Guru Nānak is the religion of householders."[10]

There is, no doubt, often a tendency to use theological concepts to legitimize cultural norms about achieving materialistic goals of wealth and progeny for security and status. However, "living-in-this-world" and the traditional householder paths—a *householder living in society* and a *householder living in the larger context of eventual withdrawal from society*—are not synonymous. Guru Nānak, no doubt, holds a firm position against the path of renunciation as a valid means to liberation, and he indeed teaches self-renunciation in the context of living in the world. But, importantly, he also simultaneously denounces—rather than supports—the orientation and goals sought after by a householder. In fact, Guru Nānak equates the householder path with the renunciate one in the sense that he considers them both as forms of attachment to *māyā*:

> The people of the world (householders) are entangled
> in the three modes [of the material world] (*māyā*);
> so too are the yogis.
> By reflecting on *śabad*,
> sorrows are dispelled.
> One becomes radiant and true
> through *śabad*.
> Thus, a yogi is the one
> who reflects on the way [of the *gurmukh*].
> (Rāmkalī, M.1, *GGS*, p. 903)

For Guru Nānak, then, the paths of both the traditional householder and the traditional renunciate are dissimilar from that of the *gurmukh* path, which is based on self-renunciation through the practice of the recitation and meditation on the Divine Name.

It is of central importance to underline here that Guru Nānak explicitly rejects the two ideal householder religious lifestyles—a *householder living in society* and a *householder living in the larger context of eventual withdrawal from society*. First, Guru Nānak critiques the socioreligious norms associated with the traditional role of the householder, especially in regard to its ego-oriented goals of acquiring the "fruits" of (1) wealth (*arth*), (2) sensual-pleasures (*kām*), and (3) religious merit (*dharam*). Fundamentally, according to Guru Nānak, humans pursuing the goals of the householder are blinded by illusion (*māyā*) and driven by ego:

The desire for *māyā* attaches one
  to one's son, relatives, household and wife.
The world is deceived and robbed
  by attachment, greed, and ego.
Attachment has robbed me,
  and the ego has destroyed the world.
O my beloved One!
I have no one but You.
Without You, nothing pleases me.
I am in peace with Your love.
I sing the praises of *nām*
  with love,
  and I am content with *śabad*.
Whatever is seen will eventually pass away.
So, do not be attached to this false vision! . . .
(Srī Rāg, M.1, *GGS*, p. 61)

For Guru Nānak, the experience of honor (*izzat*), such as begetting a son or accumulating wealth, is attachment to *māyā*. And, for him, it is this desire of acquiring worldly goals that brings suffering or enmeshes the individual in the cycle of five evils.[11] Guru Nānak not only explicitly critiques the specific socioreligious goals associated with the householder path—like begetting a son or acquiring *izzat*—but, in doing so, he also mocks the patriarchy of the traditional household.[12]

Guru Nānak likewise disagrees with the concept of religious pursuit according to the four life-stages outlined in the classical Hindu law books. This is most evident in Guru Nānak's discussion of the "Four Watches of the Night," which describes personal development in the context of the different life-stages. In all four stages in life, the respective goals desired are but a form of attachment, whether it be the child who is attached to the mother, the adult who is clinging to a sense of permanency or superiority through the materialistic goals of wealth and power, or the elders who are preoccupied with their accumulated good deeds for the fruit of a better rebirth. In effect, the desire for the goals sought during the four stages of life all result in suffering.

Guru Nānak's "Four Watches of the Night" does not only reflect his rejection of the various forms of attachment that the *manmukh* experiences during the four stages of life, but it is also an implicit critique of the religious lifestyle of the *householder living in the larger context of eventual withdrawal from society*. For Guru Nānak, renunciation is of the ego; that is, it does not depend on one's stage in life or ascribed *dvija* status. This stance is most evident in Guru Nānak's own return to his family and farming livelihood after his spiritual journeys. His own act of returning to the household near the end of his life further indicates that Guru Nānak did not value or live in accordance with the classical Hindu schema of the four stages of life (during which one renounces worldly affairs during the last stage in life). For Guru Nānak, the path of the *manmukh*, which can be understood to be that of the four phases or stages of life, is wholly different from the path of the *gurmukh*.

It is erroneous or—at the very least—misleading therefore to refer to Sikhism as a "householder religion," given that Guru Nānak rejects the two householder religious lifestyles. Nevertheless, Guru Nānak in *Siddh Goṣṭ* teaches self-renunciation in the context of remaining involved in society. Since he discounts the traditional path of the householder, as to what, then, Guru Nānak actually means by remaining involved in society is yet to be explored.

## SELF-RENUNCIATION AND SOCIAL INVOLVEMENT

If Guru Nānak rejects the paths of world renunciation and the householder, what does Guru Nānak exactly mean by living in the world? According to the Sikh worldview as expounded by Guru Nānak, one must live in the world while seeking liberation but to do so in accord with the genuine theological understanding of self-renunciation. Indeed, for Guru Nānak, the *gurmukh* or "True" yogi is one who has renounced the ego and lives in accordance with the will of the Guru while living in society:

> *Nānak*:
> The stores and highways do not let one sleep
> [not allowing the mind to rest].
> One should not be swayed
> by another's home.
> Without *nām*, the mind cannot be still,
> Nānak says: Nor is one's hunger satisfied.
> The Guru has revealed to me the stores, cities, and homes,
> in which I deal with the true trade.
> Sleep little and eat little.
> Nānak says: This is the essence of wisdom. (*SG* 8)

In Guru Nānak's thinking, one must not be guided by one's own ego (*manmukh*) under the influence of *māyā*. Rather, one ought to live amidst the *māyā* of the world—such as the competition among others over material possessions—but one must not live under its influence. Indeed, the ideal is to renounce the ego and live according to the will of the Guru even while living in the world. That is, one is *to be in the world, but not to be of the world*.

The goal and the means of the *gurmukh* are attainable even while living in the world, since liberation is solely dependent on recitation of the Divine Name. It is only through recitation that one's heart and mind are purified:

*Nānak*:
Born in the home of the True Guru,
  my comings and goings
  [from the cycle of rebirth] have ceased.
The mind is connected to the unstruck sound.
*Śabad* has burned away my aspirations and desires. . . . (*SG* 20)

For Guru Nānak, renunciation consists of renouncing the ego so that one can resonate with the unstruck sound (*anahat-nād*). In the same manner, one breaks away from duality or the dualistic mode of thinking. As a consequence of the breaking away from duality, pleasure and pain are seen as the same.

Guru Nānak views the fulfillment of one's duties while detached from the fruits of one's actions as further developing one's mental concentration, which is necessary for meditative remembrance of the Divine Name. In fact, he teaches that the process of mental discipline is improved more by living in the midst of *māyā* as opposed to running away from it.

One popular story belonging to the oral tradition talks of Guru Nānak teaching the *siddhs* about how one can live in the world amid *māyā* and still be connected to Reality. In response to the *siddhs* questioning him as to why he was giving a religious discourse at a fair, Guru Nānak asks a *siddh* to carry a full cup of water around the fair without spilling it. What occurs then is that the *siddh* was unable to pay attention to the material things at the fair because he was too focused on not spilling the water. In effect, Guru Nānak demonstrates that, with mental discipline, one automatically cultivates concentration, and that can all be done amid the *māyā* of the world.

In Guru Nānak's teachings, living amid *māyā* and the material world is viewed as a necessary challenge for spiritual development (like the cultivation of discipline and concentration). The common pan-Indian metaphor for living amid *māyā* is that of the lotus, which floats in the sticky mud but remains undefiled by it:

As a lotus flower remains untouched by water,
  and as a duck floats above the water;
when the mind is connected to *śabad*,
  one crosses over the ocean of this transitory world. . . . (*SG* 5)

Like the lotus, one ought to live in the world without being touched by the illusory nature of the material realm.

Continuous with the way Guru Nānak led his life in the world as a *renunciate living in the larger context of involvement in society*, Article III of the contemporary *Sikh Rahit Maryādā* ("Sikh Code of Conduct and Conventions") requires Sikhs to live according to three fundamental principles:

1. meditation on Divine Name (*nām-japo*),
2. hard work and honest living (*kirat karo*), and
3. sharing one's earnings with the needy (*vanḍ ke chhako*).

In this injunction, along with *nām-japo*, one ought to work hard and honestly as well as share one's earnings, since it is important to remain connected with society in order to help humanity. While there may be some dispute about the instituting of the *Sikh Rahit Maryādā*—since it occurred during the early twentieth century when the Sikh governing body had as its aim to emphasize a "K̲h̲ālsā" Sikh identity[13]—for the purposes of this study, it is nonetheless important to note that the *janam-sākhīs* describe Guru Nānak as having valued and lived by precisely these principles.[14]

The central point of *Siddh Goṣṭ* is that one ought to fulfill one's familial or social duties in the pursuit of liberation, but social involvement does not mean to strive only for householder goals. Of course, through self-renunciation and meditative remembrance of the Divine Name, one can become detached from worldly pursuits, such as attaining wealth, begetting a son, and enjoying sensual pleasures. As with the teachings of the *Bhagavad Gītā*, the basic aim would be to renounce the fruits of one's actions (*niṣ-kāma-karma*-yoga). The fundamental difference here, however, is that, for Guru Nānak, this path of action and self-renunciation ought to be pursued while "living-in-this-world," and not in the context of the *varṇa-āśrama-dharma* schema, nor according to the concept of *dvija*. While Classical and Bhakti Hindu philosophers or theologians contended that everyone is equal at the spiritual level, they accepted, unlike Guru Nānak, the caste system at the social level. On the other hand, Guru Nānak teaches the path of self-renunciation in the context of *social involvement in order to improve the state of humanity* (as, for example, the *laṅgar* institution, through which was a radical break from the brahminical notions of religious and social purity). Social involvement, then, goes beyond the accomplishment of householder goals; rather, it ought to find expression in the practice of selfless service (*sevā*) in the community.

Every human is a social being. As a social being, one has social responsibilities, including the moral responsibility to contribute to society. Rather than removing oneself from society, one has to remain connected with humanity (as manifest in one's community or society). Therefore, according to Guru Nānak, a *gurmukh*—a *renunciate living in the larger context of involvement in society*—ought to achieve a balance between self-renunciation through meditation on the Divine Name and remaining involved with society through selfless service. While self-renunciation through *nām-simraṇ* (remembrance of the Divine Name) brings one closer to the ultimate goal of contentment, it is best sought in conjunction with the performance of *sevā* (selfless service in the household and in society in general) since it cultivates compassion. Indeed, the *gurmukh* requires maintaining a balance between achieving contentment and compassion:

> The mythical bull [of Hindu mythology] is actually *dharam*
> which is born out of compassion
> and holds the earth in order through contentment.
> (*Jap-jī*, *GGS*, p. 3)

Besides, for Guru Nānak, when people are simultaneously content and compassionate, the world stands on an even keel. With Guru Nānak (as with the later interpretations of the *Bhagavad Gītā* written during the nineteenth and twentieh centuries),[15] the spiritual teaching of self-renunciation is not to be interpreted to mean conformity with or complacency about the existing social order when such an order is unjust or oppressive. Rather, in the state of having renounced one's ego in order to live according to the will of the Guru, one must simultaneously fight against social and political injustice. That is, involvement in society is for the betterment of society or humanity. Guru Nānak held the view that suffering was related to both internal forces (such as ego, attachment, and the cycle of rebirth), and external forces (such as tyranny and oppression). According to Guru Nānak, both the internal and external forces need to be tackled.

Paradoxically, a *gurmukh* is that ideal person who pursues the religious path that consists of one being socially involved in the pursuit of the Truth of Ultimate Reality. Indeed, a *gurmukh* is a "socially involved renunciate." According to Guru Nānak, this paradox is reconcilable because (1) it is by overcoming the challenges of living amid *māyā* that one is able to fully achieve self-renunciation through *nām-simraṇ*, and (2) as one contributes to society, one can simultaneously remain connected with *EkOaṅkār*, because the resonance of *EkOaṅkār* vibrates through all humanity:

> The essence of *nām* is in all.
> Without *nām*,
> one is afflicted by pain and death.
> When one's essence [soul] merges with the Essence [*EkOaṅkār*],
> the mind is fulfilled.
> Duality disappears,
> and the mind returns home.
> Nānak says: The unmoved state is attained in *sahaj*. (*SG* 50)

## SUMMING UP

### *The Paradox of the Socially Involved Renunciate*

Guru Nānak's "Discourse to the Nāth Yogis" deals with the popular question about whether or not renouncing mundane existence is necessary for the attainment of liberation (*mukti*). While it takes a strong position against the path of renunciation as a valid means to liberation, it also denounces the orientation and goals sought by the traditional householder path.

Sikhism has often been described as a "householder religion," yet Guru Nānak's teachings in *Siddh Goṣṭ*, in actuality, reject the traditional path of the householder. In his rejection of the first three types of religious lifestyles—including *renunciate living outside society, householder living in society* and the *householder living in the larger context of eventual withdrawal from society*—Guru Nānak uses Nāth "ascetic" or "yogic" terminology to illustrate his path of self-renunciation while "living-in-this-world." That is, Guru Nānak advocates the path of the *renunciate in the larger context of involvement in society*; a *gurmukh* pursues liberation through self-renunciation even as he or she remains in the world. For Guru Nānak, the ideal is to become a *socially involved renunciate*.

The paradox of the socially involved renunciate encompasses the two polarities—the path of the renunciate, and the path of the householder—for attaining liberation that are found in Indian religions. It is most profoundly expressed through Hindu mythology, as in the iconic figure Śiva. Śiva is portrayed sometimes as an ascetic and at other times as a householder accompanied by his consort Pārvatī. As mentioned in chapter 1, Wendy Doniger contends that the ascetic and erotic depictions of Śiva are not diametrically in opposition to each other. Rather, the images reflect Śiva as the mediating principle between the renunciate and the householder lifestyle models.[16] The opposing depictions of Śiva, no doubt, reflect the tension that exists between the ascetic and domestic ideals in the pursuit of the ultimate religious goal of liberation from *sańsār*.

While Hindu mythology provides concrete and vivid imagery of the tension or mediation between the desires of the human soul for liberation and for being connected with the world or humanity, Guru Nānak provides a reconciliation of the two polarities in his philosophical worldview as expounded in *Siddh Goṣṭ*. Guru Nānak not only reconciles the polarities of the ascetic and householder ideals, but he provides a practical means to achieve it, in a seemingly paradoxical way, renunciation while existing in the social world through becoming a socially involved renunciate. For Guru Nānak, one ought to renounce the ego while "living-in-this-world." In doing so, one needs to attain a balance between the quest for contentment achieved by self-renunciation through meditation on the Divine Name (*nām-simraṇ*) and the cultivation of compassion through the practice of selfless service (*sevā*). That is, according to Guru Nānak, the *gurmukh* or "True" yogi is *to be in the world, but not be of the world*!

# Part 4

# *Siddh Goṣṭ*
# *Discourse to the Nāth Yogis,*
# An English Translation

## I. THE MEETING

A discourse with the *siddhs,*[1]
[is composed of] the first *mahalā*[2]
in the *rāmkalī* meter.[3]
*EkOaṅkār*[4] is realized
by the grace of the True Guru.[5]

As the *siddhs* formed an assembly,
sitting in their yogic postures,
they saluted the congregation of *sants.*[6]

*Nānak:*
Salutations to the True One,
who is infinite,
and beyond reach.
I remove my head as an offering
and surrender my body and mind.
Nānak says: Truth is attained by meeting the *sants,*
and glory is experienced in *sahaj.*[7] [1]

What use is it to wander?
[when] purification is attained through Truth.
Without the true *śabad,*[8]
no one attains *mukti.*[9] [1]
Pause [to dwell upon this thought].

*Siddhs:*
Who are you? What is your name?
What is your path? What is your goal?

*Nānak:*
I speak of nothing but Truth,
when I said I surrendered myself to the *sants.*

*Siddhs:*
Where do you sit?
O child![10] Where do you live?
Where did you come from? Where are you going?
O Nānak, the detached one! What is your path? [2]

*Nānak:*
I abide in the Eternal [One],[11]
who resounds in the hearts of all,
and walks according to the True Guru's will.
I came and will depart according to the *hukam*,[12]
and, I, Nānak, will forever live according to the *hukam*.
The posture[13] of the Supporter is stable;
this is the teaching I received from the Guru.
The *gurmukh*[14] is wise
and understands the Self is merged in Truth. [3]

## II. THE PATH

*Siddhs:*
The world is like an impassable ocean.
How can one cross it?
Charapaṭ[15] says: O Nānak! Give us your thoughtful reply.

*Nānak:*
What answer can I give to someone
who claims to know all?
How can I discourse on the Truth
when you believe you have [already] crossed
the world ocean [of *saṅsār*[16]]? [4]

As a lotus flower remains untouched by water,
and as a duck floats above the water;
when the mind is connected to *śabad*,
one crosses over the ocean of this transitory world.
Nānak chants the *nām*.[17]
A person who lives detached and enshrines the One,
in the mind,
remains desireless amidst desires.
[A disciple is one] who sees and inspires others to see the ineffable,
Nānak is such a [disciple's] servant. [5]

*Siddhs:*
[O] holy one,
listen to our prayer!
We ask your true opinion.
Don't be angry with us.

Please tell us how we
 can find the door to the Guru?

*Nānak:*
Nānak says: With the support of *nām*,
the wavering mind can become focused
 in its true home [i.e., aware of the true nature of the
 soul and *EkOaṅkār*].
The Creator unites us with itself
 and inspires us to love the Truth. [6]

*Siddhs:*
Away from the stores and highways,
 we abide in the woods among the plants and trees.
Our food is fruit and roots;
 [To live thus] is the wisdom spoken of by the wise ones.
We bathe at sacred pools and attain fruits of peace,
 so that our minds are free from filth.
Gorakh's disciple Loharipā[18] says:
This is the way of yoga. [7]

*Nānak:*
The stores and highways do not let one sleep
 [not allowing the mind to rest].
One should not be swayed
 by another's home.
Without *nam*, the mind cannot be still.
 Nānak says: Nor is one's hunger satisfied.
The Guru has revealed to me the stores, cities, and homes,
 in which I deal the true trade.
Sleep little and eat little.
Nānak says: This is the essence of wisdom. [8]

O yogi! Let your vision be
the patched coat, earrings, and [begging] bag.[19]
[Concentrate on] the One dwelling
 within the twelve branches of yoga,[20]
and let the path of the One teach
 the wisdom of the six philosophical schools.[21]
If the mind understands this, then one will not suffer.
Nānak says: The *gurmukh* understands that
 this is the way yoga is attained. [9]

Let *śabad* deep within you be your earrings,
and become distant from the ego and attachment.
Discard lust, anger, and egoism,
and learn from the Guru's *śabad*.
Let the patched coat and [begging] bag be the Pervasive One.
Nānak says: The One carries you across
[the ocean of *saṅsār*].
True is the great One and True is its *nām*.
You shall realize this
by studying the Guru's words. [10]

Let the [begging] bag be the turning away of the mind,
and the cap be the lessons of the five elements.[22]
Let the body be the meditation mat,
and the mind the loincloth.
Let Truth, contentment, and self-discipline be your companions.
Nānak says: The *gurmukh* cherishes the *nām*. [11]

### III. A *GURMUKH*

*Siddhs:*
Who is hidden? Who is liberated?
Who is united inwardly and outwardly?
Who comes and goes [from the cycle of rebirth]?
Who pervades the three worlds?[23] [12]

*Nānak:*
[*EkOaṅkār*] is hidden within every heart,
and the *gurmukh* is liberated.
Through *śabad*, one is united inwardly and outwardly.
The *manmukh*[24] comes and goes
[from the cycle of rebirth].
Nānak says: The *gurmukh* merges with Truth. [13]

*Siddhs:*
How is one bound and eaten by the snake of illusion[25]?
How does one lose? How does one win?
How does one become pure? How is one in darkness?
The one who knows the essence of these questions,
is our Guru. [14]

*Nānak:*
The mind is bound by evil
  and eaten by the snake of *māyā*.
The *manmukh* loses and the *gurmukh* wins.
Meeting with the True Guru [*śabad*] dispels darkness.
Nānak says: The destruction of the ego
  allows one to merge [with *EkOaṅkār*]. [15]

If one is connected with the inner *sunn*,[26]
  the goose (soul) does not fly and the wall (body) does not break.[27]
One's true home is the cave of *sahaj*.
Nānak says: The True [One] loves those who are true. [16]

*Siddhs:*
Why have you left your home and become an *udāsī*?[28]
Why have you adopted these religious robes?
What is it that you seek to trade?
How will you carry others across [the ocean of *saṅsār*]? [17]

*Nānak:*
I have become an *udāsī* in search of *gurmukhs*.
I have adopted these robes in search of their vision.
I am out to trade Truth.
I am a peddler of Truth.
Nānak says: With the help of the *gurmukhs*,
others can be carried across
  [the ocean of *saṅsār*]. [18]

## IV. THE SOURCE

*Siddhs:*
How did you change the course of your life?
To what is your mind connected?
How did you still your aspirations and desires?
How did you discover the light deep within you?
Without teeth, how can one eat iron?
O Nānak! Give us your true opinion. [19]

*Nānak:*
Born in the home of the True Guru,[29]
  my comings and goings
  [from the cycle of rebirth] have ceased.

The mind is connected to the unstruck sound.[30]
*Śabad* has burned away my aspirations and desires.
As a *gurmukh*,
  I have found the light deep within.
By destroying the three *guns*,[31]
  one eats iron.
Nānak says: The liberated one liberates others. [20]

*Siddhs:*
What can you tell us about the beginning?
Where does *sunn* reside?
What are the earrings of wisdom?
Who dwells in the hearts of all?
How can one avoid the stroke of death,
  and enter the home of fearlessness?
How can one learn the posture of *sahaj* and contentment,
  and overcome one's bad habits?

*Nānak:*
As the Guru's *śabad* destroys the ego,
  one dwells in the home of the Self within.
The one who recognizes the *śabad* of the Creator,
  Nānak is such a one's servant. [21]

*Siddhs:*
Where did we come from?
Where are we going?
Where will we merge?
Whoever knows the answer to these questions
  is detached
  and a guru.
How can one discover the essence of the ineffable?
How does the *gurmukh* experience devotional love?
It is consciousness and it is the Creator.
O Nānak! Tell us your wisdom.

*Nānak:*
Through *hukam* we come,
  go,
  and merge.
Through the perfect Guru,
  Truth is learned

and through the *śabad*,
  one's state and measure are understood. [22]

As for the beginning,
  a sense of wonder can be expressed.
*Sunn* abides deep within itself.
Let freedom from desire be the earrings
  of the Guru's wisdom.
The True Universal [One] dwells in the hearts of all.
Through the Guru's word,
  one merges in *sahaj*
and intuitively attains the essence of the Absolute.
Nānak says: The learner who discovers the path
  does not serve any other.
*Hukam* is wonderful,
  and the one who discovers *hukam*
  understands the truth about the life of all creatures.
The one who destroys the ego is desireless,
  enshrines the Truth within,
  and is a yogi. [23]

From the absolute state,
  [*EkOaṅkār*] assumed
  both a *nirguṇ* and *sarguṇ* form.[32]
By knowing the True Guru,
  one attains the highest state
  and merges in the True *śabad*.
By distancing oneself
  from the ego and duality,
  the True One is realized.
One is a yogi
  if the *śabad* is realized
  and the inner lotus blossoms.
If one destroys the ego,
  everything is understood,
and by realizing [the soul] within,
  one has compassion for all.
Nānak says: One is praised if one sees
  oneself in all beings. [24]

We emerged from the Truth
  and will merge with the Truth,

The true one identifies with the One.
The false ones come into this world
  and find no refuge,
  and in duality they come and go.
This coming and going
  ends through the *śabad*.
[*EkOaṅkār*] watches and blesses.
One suffers from the disease of duality,
  and the cure of *nām* is forgotten.
The one who has been inspired to understand
  is liberated through the *śabad*.
Nānak says: The Emancipator saves those
  who have distanced themselves
  from the ego and duality. [25]

## V. TRUTH

A *manmukh* makes mistakes
  and lives in death's shadow.
Looking into the home of another,
  he loses.
A *manmukh* is confused by doubt,
  and wanders in the wilderness.
Straying away from the path,
  he recites mantras at crematoriums.
Without reflecting on the *śabad*,
  he speaks obscenities.
Nānak says: Those who are immersed in Truth,
  attain a state of peace. [26]

A *gurmukh* lives in fear
  of the Truth.
Through *bāṇī* (*śabad* or Sacred Word),
  the *gurmukh* refines the unrefined.
A *gurmukh* sings the praises
  of the pure One.
A *gurmukh* attains the sacred high state.
A *gurmukh* meditates on
  the pervasive One
  which resides within every cell of the body.
Nānak says: The *gurmukh* merges with Truth. [27]

Depth allows the *gurmukh*
to discuss the Vedas.[33]
Depth enables the *gurmukh*
to be carried across
[the ocean of *saṅsār*].
Depth is attained when the *gurmukh*
has knowledge of *śabad*.
Depth allows the *gurmukh* to discover
the inner secret.[34]
The *gurmukh* attains the unseen and infinite.
Nānak says: The *gurmukh* enters the door of *mukti*. [28]

The *gurmukh* speaks about the unspoken wisdom.
The *gurmukh* practices righteousness in the household.
The *gurmukh* meditates deeply with love.
The *gurmukh* [realizes] the *śabad*
and practices a righteous lifestyle.
The mystery of *śabad* is understood,
and the *gurmukh* inspires others
to understand.
Nānak says: By burning the ego,
one merges [with *EkOaṅkār*]. [29]

The earth was created by Truth
for the *gurmukhs*.
This is the play of creation and destruction.
One is immersed in love
by enshrining the *śabad*.
Immersed in Truth,
one goes home with honor.
Without *śabad*,
one does not attain honor.
Nānak says: Without *nām*,
how can one attain Truth? [30]

The *gurmukh* attains the eight occult powers[35] and universal wisdom.
The *gurmukh* crosses the ocean [of *saṅsār*]
and attains true understanding.
The *gurmukh* can discriminate
between Truth and falsehood.
The *gurmukh* recognizes worldliness and renunciation.

The *gurmukh* crosses over [the ocean of *saṅsār*]
and carries others across as well.
Nānak says: The *gurmukh* is liberated through *śabad*. [31]

## VI. IMMERSION

Immersed in *nām*,
the ego is distant.
Immersed in *nām*,
one merges in Truth.
Immersed in *nām*,
one can contemplate the way of yoga.
Immersed in *nām*,
one finds the door of liberation.
Immersed in *nām*,
one understands the three worlds.
Nānak says: Immersed in *nām*,
one attains eternal peace. [32]

Immersed in *nām*,
one can converse with the *siddhs*.
Immersed in *nām*,
one can practice meditation forever.
Immersed in *nām*,
one lives a truthful lifestyle.
Immersed in *nām*,
one can contemplate
the *guns* and wisdom.
Without *nām*,
all that one utters is meaningless.
Nānak says: Those immersed in *nām*
are celebrated as being victorious. [33]

Through the perfect Guru,
one attains *nām*.
The path of yoga leads one to merge in Truth.
The yogis are divided into twelve schools of yoga,
and the *saṅiyāsī* into six and four.[36]
The one who destroys the ego through *śabad*,
finds the door of liberation.
Without *śabad*, all become attached to duality.
Reflect upon this thought.

Nānak says: Blessed and fortunate are those
who have enshrined Truth in their hearts. [34]

The *gurmukh* attains the jewel [of *nām*]
through focused attention.
The *gurmukh* intuitively understands
the value of this jewel.
The *gurmukh* practices Truth
in action.
The mind of the *gurmukh* is absorbed
in Truth.
The *gurmukh* sees the unseen.
Nānak says: The *gurmukh* does not suffer. [35]

The *gurmukh* is blessed
with *nām*, compassion, and purity.
The *gurmukh* undergoes a natural process
of meditation.
The *gurmukh* attains honor
in the court [of *EkOaṅkār*].
The *gurmukh* merges with the Supreme Being,
the destroyer of fear.
The *gurmukh* performs good deeds
and inspires others to do the same.
Nānak says: The *gurmukh* is united [with *EkOaṅkār*]. [36]

The *gurmukh* understands
the Smṛtis, Śāstras,[37] and Vedas.
The *gurmukh* knows the secrets
within the hearts of all.
The mind of the *gurmukh* is rid
of hate and envy.
The *gurmukh* keeps no count
[of deeds].
The *gurmukh*,
with *nām*,
is immersed in love.
Nānak says: The *gurmukh* realizes the Master. [37]

Without the Guru,
one wanders about the coming and going [in *saṅsār*].

Without the Guru,
  one's aspirations bear no fruit.
Without the Guru,
  the mind spills over
  [like water flowing in all directions].
Without the Guru,
  one is never satisfied
  and feeds on poison.
Without the Guru,
  one is stung
  by the poisonous snake [of *māyā*]
  and dies.
Nānak says: Without the Guru, all is lost. [38]

The one who meets the Guru is
  carried across [the ocean of *saṅsār*].
Impurities are erased
  and one becomes virtuous.
The supreme peace of *mukti*
  is attained
  by contemplating on the Guru's *śabad*.
The *gurmukh* is never defeated.
The body is a store
  and the mind is a merchant.
Nānak says: With poise,
  the mind deals in Truth. [39]

The *gurmukh* is a bridge,
  built by the Creator.
Lanka [the body] is looted
  by the demons [five evils].[38]
Rām Chand [mind] destroys
  Rāvaṇ [the ego].
The *gurmukh* understands the secret
  that Babhikhen revealed [*śabad*].[39]
The *gurmukh* can make stones swim
  across the ocean [of *saṅsār*].
The *gurmukh* saves millions of people. [40]

The *gurmukh* is not subject
  to entering and leaving [this world].
The *gurmukh* is honored
  in the court [of *EkOaṅkār*].

The *gurmukh* can distinguish
between Truth and falsehood.
The *gurmukh* concentrates naturally.
The *gurmukh* is immersed in praises.
Nānak says: The *gurmukh* is not bound [by *saṅsār*]. [41]

The *gurmukh* attains the pure *nām*.
The *gurmukh* burns the ego
with *śabad*.
The *gurmukh* sings the praises
of the Truth.
Through the True *nām*,
the *gurmukh* is honored.
Nānak says: The *gurmukh* is aware
of the mysteries of the world. [42]

## VII. CREATION

*Siddhs:*
What is the root of all existence?
What are the teachings of the present era?
Who is your guru? Whose disciple are you?
What is that sermon,
by which you remain detached?
O child Nanak! Listen to what we have to say!
Give us the answer to our questions.
How can *śabad* carry us across
the ocean [of *saṅsār*]? [43]

*Nānak:*
From the life-breath (*prāṇ*) was the beginning;
This is the era of the Guru's teachings.
The *śabad* is the Guru,
and the awareness of its sound
is the disciple.
By speaking the unspoken,
I remain detached.
Nānak says: Era after era,
the Caregiver has been my Guru.
I contemplate only the words of the one *śabad*.
Thus the *gurmukh* extinguishes the fire of ego. [44]

*Siddhs:*
How can one break iron with wax teeth?

What can be eaten to take away pride?
How can one live in a palace of snow
  while wearing robes of fire?
Where is that cave
  in which one remains stable?
Who pervades here and there?
What is that meditation
  by which the mind can abide
  within the Self? [45]

*Nānak:*
By destroying the ego and individualism,
  and by erasing duality,
  there is only One.
The world is difficult for the *manmukh*
  because such a one is unwise.
When one meditates on *śabad,*
  iron can be chewed.
The inner and the outer are seen as One.
Nānak says: The fire is extinguished
  through the True Guru's grace. [46]

When one fears Truth,
  pride is taken away.
The One is realized
  by contemplating on *śabad*.
When *śabad* dwells
  deep within the heart of Truth;
  the mind and body are comfortable
  and one is colored in love.
The fire of sexual desire, anger, and corruption
  are extinguished.
Nānak says: The beloved One bestows grace upon us. [47]

*Siddhs:*
How does the moon
  cool life like snow?
How does the sun blaze?
How can death be turned away?
What is the wisdom
  by which the *gurmukh*'s honor
  is preserved?

Who is the warrior
who battles death?
O Nānak! Reply with your thoughts. [48]

*Nānak:*
When one chants *śabad*,
the moon
[that is the mind] is infinitely illuminated.[40]
When the sun [of wisdom] dwells
in the home of the moon
[that is the mind]
darkness is dispelled.
Pleasure and suffering are alike,
when one has the support of *nām*.
[*EkOaṅkār*] itself carries us
across [the ocean of *saṅsār*].
With the Guru's wisdom,
the mind merges in Truth.
Nānak says: Such a one is not consumed by death. [49]

The essence of *nām* is in all.
Without *nām*,
one is afflicted with pain and death.
When one's essence [soul] merges with the Essence [*EkOṅkār*],
the mind is fulfilled.
Duality disappears,
and the mind returns home.
Nānak says: The unmoved state is attained in *sahaj*. [50]

Inner *sunn* and outer *sunn* fill the three worlds as well.
The one who attains the fourth state[41]
is neither sinful nor virtuous.
The one who sees the mystery
residing in the hearts of all
knows the Primal Pure Being.
The humble one is immersed
in the purity of *nām*.
Nānak says: Such a one is the Creator. [51]

## VIII. EKOAṄKĀR

*Nānak:*
Everyone speaks about
the state of *sunn*.
How can one attain this state
of *sunn*?
Who are those,
who are connected to this state
of *sunn*?
They are like the One
from whom they have originated.
They are not born,
they do not die,
and they do not come and go.
Nānak says: The *gurmukh* can instruct the mind. [52]

By blocking the nine gates,
one arrives at the tenth gate.[42]
It is here
that the unstruck sound (*anahat-nād*)
resounds in the state of *sunn*.
Merged in Truth,
one sees [*EkOaṅkār*] in everything.
The Truth pervades the hearts of all.
The hidden *bāṇī* is revealed.
Nānak says: The Truth is realized. [53]

One attains peace
when uniting in a state of *sahaj*.
The *gurmukh* remains awake
and does not fall asleep.
The *śabad* is enshrined
deep within *sunn*.
One attains *mukti*
by chanting *śabad*,
and liberates others as well.
Those who practice the Guru's teachings
are immersed in Truth.

Nānak says: Those who lose their ego
  are united [with *EkOaṅkār*]
  rather than separated. [54]

What refuge can one find,
  when one's words are unwise?
One does not understand
  the essence [of the soul]
  and lives in grief.
Bound down at death's door,
  no one can help.
Without the *śabad*,
  no one can be honored or trusted.
How is one to understand,
  and cross over [the ocean of *saṅsār*]?
Nānak says: The *manmukh* does not understand this. [55]

Unwise thoughts are erased
  by contemplating the Guru's *śabad*.
When one meets the True Guru,
  the door of liberation is attained.
The *manmukh* does not know the essence,
  and thus is burnt away.
Unwise thoughts separate one
  [from the soul],
  and suffering arises.
Accepting the *hukam*,
  one is blessed
  with virtues and wisdom.
Nānak says: Such a one is honored
  in the court [of *EkOaṅkār*]. [56]

If one gathers the wealth of Truth;
one crosses over
  [the ocean of *saṅsār*]
and carries others as well.
The one who understands *sahaj*
is honored.
No one can estimate such a one's worth.
Wherever one looks,
[*EkOaṅkār*] is manifest.

Nānak says: With true love,
  one crosses over. [57]

## IX. THE SACRED WORD

*Siddhs:*
Where does the *śabad* reside
  that will carry us across?
What supports the breath
  that extends the distance
  of three and seven fingers?[43]
How can one be stable,
  while speaking and playing,
  to realize the ineffable?
Listen holy Nānak!
  How do you instruct the mind?

*Nānak:*
The *gurmukh* is connected to Truth
  through the *śabad*,
and with love one is united
  [with *EkOaṅkār*].
One becomes wise, perceptive, and,
  through perfect destiny,
  is united [with *EkOaṅkār*]. [58]

The *śabad* is deep
  within the hearts
  of all beings,
  and wherever one looks,
  [*EkOaṅkār*] is seen.
As air is [pervasive]
  so is [*EkOaṅkār*]
  pervasive in *sunn*.
[*EkOaṅkār*] is without attributes (*nirguṇ*)
  and with attributes (*sarguṇ*) as well.
With grace,
  *śabad* abides deep within the heart,
  and doubt is removed.
The body and mind become pure
  and the pure *bāṇī* and *nām*
  are enshrined within the heart.

*Śabad* is the Guru
  that will carry one across.
Realize that there is One
  here and hereafter.
[*EkOaṅkār*] has no color,
  no form,
  and is not an illusion (*māyā*).
Nānak says: The *śabad* shall reveal this. [59]

The True One supports the breath
  that extends the distance
  of three and seven fingers.
The *gurmukh* speaks about the essence,
  and realizes the ineffable and infinite.
By erasing the three *guṇs*,
  the *śabad* is enshrined in the mind
  and the ego is removed.
When the One is seen
  inside and out,
  the love of *nām* is present.
One understands the *sukhmanā, iḍā,* and *piṅgalā,*[44]
  when the ineffable is realized.
Nānak says: The True One is above
  the three energy channels.
Through the True Guru's *śabad*,
  one is united [with *EkOaṅkār*]. [60]

## X. GRACE

*Siddhs:*
The air is said to be the life of the mind,
  but what does the air feed on?
What is the hand posture (*mudrā*) of wisdom?
What is the practice of the enlightened one (*siddh*)?

*Nānak:*
Without the *śabad*,
  the essence is not attained,
  nor does the thirst of the ego depart.
Immersed in *śabad*,
  one discovers *amṛt*,
  and remains immersed in Truth.

*Siddhs:*
What knowledge can hold the mind steady?
What type of food is satisfying?

*Nānak:*
Nānak says: When one feels pain
and pleasure as alike,
through the True Guru's grace,
one does not taste death. [61]

If one is not immersed in love,
does not taste the essence,
and is without the Guru's *śabad*,
one is consumed by the fire [of desire].
Such a one does not preserve the sperm
and does not chant the *śabad*.
The breath is not controlled and Truth
is not contemplated.
But the one who speaks
the unspoken wisdom
remains balanced.
Nānak says: Such a one attains the Supreme Soul. [62]

By the Guru's grace,
one is immersed in love,
drinks the nectar (*amṛt*)
and merges in Truth.
By contemplating the Guru,
the fire [of desire]
is extinguished.
By drinking the *amṛt*
the soul dwells in peace.
By contemplating the Truth,
the *gurmukh* crosses over
[the ocean of *saṅsār*].
Nānak says: After deep contemplation,
this is understood. [63]

## XI. AWARENESS

*Siddhs:*
Where does the mind that wanders like an elephant reside?
Where does the breath live?

Where does *śabad* reside?
  How can the wandering mind be stilled?

*Nānak:*
With grace,
  one meets the Guru,
  and the mind dwells
  in the home within.
When one eliminates the ego,
  one becomes pure
  and the mind is stilled.

*Siddhs:*
How can the root of all existence be recognized,
  in which the soul can be realized?
How can the sun [of wisdom] enter
  the home of the moon [that is the mind]?

*Nānak:*
When the *gurmukh* eliminates the ego,
Nanak says: The sun [of wisdom] naturally
  enters the home of the moon [that is the mind]. [64]

When the mind becomes steady and stable,
  it abides in the heart,
and the *gurmukh* realizes
  the root of all existence.
When the breath is seated
  in the home of the navel,
the *gurmukh* discovers the essence
  [of the soul].
*Śabad* resides in the home
  within the heart,
  and through *śabad*
  the light of the three worlds is seen.
Hunger for the Truth
  eliminates suffering,
  and satisfaction is attained
  through the True One.
The *gurmukh* is aware
  of the unstruck sound of *bāṇī*,
  and rare are those who understand this.
Nānak says: The one who speaks the Truth is immersed
  in the never-fading color of Truth. [65]

*Siddhs:*
When the heart and body did not exist,
where did the mind reside?
When there was no support
of the navel-lotus,[45]
where did the life-breath[46] reside?
When there was no form or shape,
to whom was *śabad* connected to?
When there was no tomb [of the body]
made from egg and sperm,[47]
how could one understand
the measure and value [of *EkOaṅkār*]?
When there was no color, dress, or form,
how could the Truth be realized?

*Nānak:*
Nānak says: Those who are immersed in *nām*
are detached from the past and the present,
and see only the True One. [66]

When the heart and body did not exist,
the mind resided detached
in *sunn*.
When there was no support
of the navel-lotus,
the life-breath resided within itself,
immersed in love.
When there was no form, shape, or caste,
*śabad* resided in the Supreme Being.
When the earth and sky did not exist,
the light of the Formless One
pervaded the three worlds.
Color, dress, and form were contained
in the One,
as was *śabad* contained
in the Wondrous One.
Nānak says: Without Truth,
no one can be pure,
this is the unspoken speech. [67]

## XII. LIBERATION

*Siddhs:*
O man!

How did the world come into existence?
How does suffering end?

*Nānak:*
The world came into existence
  through the ego,
and when *nām* is forgotten,
  suffering arises.
The *gurmukh* contemplates
  the essence of wisdom,
and burns away the ego
  with *śabad*.
Body, mind, and speech become pure,
  and one is immersed in the Truth.
Through the *nām*,
one remains detached
and enshrines Truth
  within the heart.
Nānak says: Without *nām*,
  yoga is not attained.
Reflect upon this and see. [68]

The *gurmukh*,
  who reflects upon the true *śabad*,
is rare.
The true *bāṇī* is revealed to the *gurmukh*.
The mind of the *gurmukh* is immersed
  in love,
but rare are those
  who understand this.
The *gurmukh* dwells deep
  inside the home.
The *gurmukh* is a yogi
  who has realized yoga.
Nānak says: Only the *gurmukh* knows the One. [69]

Without serving the True Guru,
  yoga is not attained.
Without meeting the True Guru,
  no one attains *mukti*.
Without meeting the True Guru,
  *nām* is not attained.
Without meeting the True Guru,
  one suffers in pain.

Without meeting the True Guru,
one is enveloped
  in the darkness of ego.
Nānak says: Without the True Guru,
one loses the opportunity
  of human life (i.e., liberation). [70]

When the *gurmukh* conquers the mind,
  the ego is destroyed.
The *gurmukh* enshrines Truth
  within the heart.
The *gurmukh* conquers the world,
  and destroys the messenger of death.
The *gurmukh* does not lose
  in the court of [*EkOaṅkār*].
The *gurmukh* is united
  [with *EkOaṅkār*],
  and only he or she knows this.
Nānak says: The *gurmukh* understands *śabad*. [71]

Listen renunciates!
This is the essence of my words (teaching).
Without *nām*,
  there can be no yoga.
Those immersed in *nām*
are in a state of bliss
  night and day,
And with *nām*,
  they find peace.
Everything is revealed and understood
  through *nām*.
Without *nām*,
  people wear many robes
  and stray from the path.
*Nām* is attained
  from the True Guru,
  and the way of yoga is attained.
Reflect upon this in the mind.
Nānak says: Without *nām*,
  there is no *mukti*. [72]

You [*EkOaṅkār*] know your status and measurement.
What can anyone say about it?
You are hidden,
  you are revealed,
  and You enjoy all pleasures.
Many seekers, *siddhs*, gurus, and disciples
  search for You
  according to Your will.
They beg for *nām*
  and You bless them [with it];
I sacrifice myself for Your vision.
The Eternal Sovereign One
has staged this play,
  and the *gurmukh* understands it.
Nānak says: You existed
  throughout the ages,
  and never was there another. [73][48]

# Notes

## NOTE ON TRANSLATION

1. *Sree Gurū Granth Sāhib*, translated and annotated by Gopal Singh (Delhi: World Book Center, 1993 [1964]), p. 903.

## CHAPTER 1

1. The Hindu definition of the term "guru" is simply spiritual master or teacher. The Sikh meaning of "Guru," on the other hand, denotes Ultimate Reality or the embodiment of that reality, such as the Sacred Word. In Sikhism, Guru also refers to the ten human gurus, who uttered the Sacred Word, and the scripture (*Gurū Granth Sāhib*), which contains the Sacred Word. See chapter 5 for a discussion on the nature of Ultimate Reality in Sikhism.

2. *Siddha* (literally "realized, accomplished, or perfected one") is a broad term for an ascetic who has, through specific practices, realized (1) superhuman powers (*siddhis*) and (2) immortality (*jīvan-mukti*). The Nāth yogis are one class of ascetics who practice hath-yoga. Although *siddha* is a broad term and Nāth yogi refers to someone belonging to a specific group of ascetics, Guru Nānak uses both terms interchangeably. In the case of *Siddh Goṣṭ*, "*siddh*" (in Punjabi) refers to the teachers or practitioners of the Nāth tradition. For an elaboration on the Nāth yogis or *siddhas*, see chapter 2.

3. Wendy (Doniger) O'Flaherty, *Śiva: The Erotic Ascetic* (London: Oxford University Press, 1973), pp. 35–38.

4. It is commonly accepted that Hinduism has no founder, no creed, nor a governing organizational structure, hence making it a difficult religion to define. The term "Hinduism" can nonetheless be understood as consisting of a complex network of pan-Indian and local religious streams—the many traditions or layers of thought and practice found among the majority of people in India. Kamala Elizabeth Nayar, *Hayagrīva in South India: Complexity and Selectivity of a Pan-Indian Hindu Deity* (Leiden: Brill, 2004), pp. 3–4. See also Günther D. Sontheimer and Hermann Kulke, eds., *Hinduism Reconsidered* (New Delhi: Manohar Publishers, 1989).

5. For instance, O'Flaherty, *Śiva*; Patrick Olivelle, "Ascetic Withdrawal of Social Engagement," in Donald S. Lopez Jr., ed., *Religions of India in Practice* (Princeton: Princeton University Press, 1995), pp. 533–46.

6. For example, Surinder Singh Kohli, *Yoga of the Sikhs* (Amritsar: Singh Brothers, 1991), p. 10. See also, Daljeet Singh, *The Sikh Ideology* (Amritsar: Singh Brothers, 1990), pp. 74–77.

7. Hindu traditions are often related back to the Vedas (ca. 1500–900 BCE), the ancient scripture referred to as *śruti* ("that which is heard"), reflecting its character as unauthored (*apauruṣeya*) and thus eternal. Indeed, for Hindus, the Vedas are regarded as *śruti* and, therefore, authoritative.

8. *The Hymns of the Ṛg Veda, translated with a popular commentary*, J. L. Shastri, ed. (Delhi: Motilal Banarsidass, 1973), p. 329.

9. For a discussion on the relation of the Vedas to the Hindu tradition, see: Louis Renou, *Le Déstin du Veda dans l'Inde* (Paris: Adrien Maisouneuve, 1960); Brian K. Smith, *Reflections on Resemblance, Ritual and Religion* (New York: Oxford University Press, 1989); and Wilhelm Halbfass, *Tradition and Reflection: Exploration in Indian Thought* (Albany: State University of New York Press, 1991).

10. Patrick Oliville, *The Early Upaniṣads: Annotated Text and Translation* (New York: Oxford University Press, 1998), pp. 16–27.

11. *Upaniṣat-Saṃgrahaḥ*, J. L. Shastri, trans. (Delhi: Motilal Banarsidass, 1984). All *Upaniṣad* translations are taken from *The Thirteen Principal Upanishads*, Robert Ernest Hume, trans. (2nd ed., reprint; Delhi: Oxford University Press, 1989).

12. During the Buddha's own spiritual quest, he became disenchanted with various yogic practices, including self-denial (which he found to be exhausting and thus ineffective), and yogic trances (which he experienced to be transient in nature and thus futile). In effect, the Buddha promulgated the Middle Way of renunciation, based on the Four Noble Truths and the Eightfold Path. After attaining enlightenment he dedicated his life to teach those striving for liberation from *saṃsāra*.

13. The Buddha's Four Noble Truths acknowledge that (1) life is suffering (*dukkha* in Sanskrit, *dukka* in Pali), (2) the source of suffering is desire for permanence, when in fact everything is impermanent (*anicca* in Pali), (3) suffering can be extinguished (*nirvāṇa* in Sanskrit, *nibbāna* in Pali), and (3) the cessation of suffering is attainable through the Eightfold Path.

14. The Eightfold Path consists of: (1) Right View, (2) Right Intention, (3) Right Speech, (4) Right Action, (5) Right Livelihood, (6) Right Effort, (7) Right Mindfulness, and (8) Right Concentration.

15. *Dhammapada*, John Ross Carter and Mahinda Palihawadana, trans. (Oxford: Oxford University Press, 2000).

16. *The Middle Length Sayings (Majjhima-Nikāya)*, vol. 1 *The First 50 Discourses*, I. B. Horner, trans. (London: Luzac and Company), pp. 328–29.

17. In the Jain tradition, twenty-four perfected beings (*jinas*) are venerated. The most recent *jina* is Mahāvīra (540–468 BCE), the founder of Jainism, whose life story is considered exemplary by Jain followers pursuing liberation. At the age of thirty, Mahāvīra gave up his family connections and took on ascetic practices. He went wandering in the wilderness in order to subdue his passions and desires through giving up all of his possessions, fasting (he ate one meal a day at the most), begging for food, and practicing meditation. After twelve years of extreme asceticism, Mahāvīra is believed to have at-

tained liberation from *saṃsāra*, which Jains call *nirvāṇa*. Then, during the remaining thirty years of his life, he taught the gradual path of renunciation. John E. Cort, *Jains in the World: Religious Values and Ideology in India* (New York: Oxford University Press, 2001). Padmanabha Jaini, *The Jaina Path of Purification* (Berkeley: University of California, 1979).

18. *Jaina Sutras*, part 1, Hermena Jacobi, trans. (Oxford: Clarendon Press, 1884).

19. See James Laidlaw, *Riches and Renunciation: Religion, Economy and Society Among the Jains* (Oxford: Clarendon Press, 1995).

20. *Smṛti* ("that which is remembered") literature (such as the Epics and socioreligious law books) integrates Vedic ritualism and Upaniṣadic philosophy forming the body of classical Hindu literature.

21. The *Bhagavad Gītā* is a section of the *Mahābhārata* (ca. 500–100 BCE), one of the two great Hindu epics. *Rāmāyaṇa* (ca. CE) is the other epic. These epics are of primary importance as they are in fact at the heart of Hindu belief and devotional ritual practice. The *Bhagavad Gītā* has twofold importance for Hindus: (1) the notion of Kṛṣṇa revealing himself as an incarnation of God (*avatāra*) (*Bhagavad Gītā* 4.6.), and (2) Kṛṣṇa's teachings to the warrior Arjuna, who does not want to fight in the battle (*Bhagavad Gītā* 2).

22. *The Bhagavad Gita*, W. J. Johnson, trans. (Oxford: Oxford University Press, 1994).

23. The Bhakti interpretations of the *Bhagavad Gītā* by Indian philosophers like the ŚrīVaiṣṇava *ācārya* Rāmānuja (*Gītā-bhāṣyam*). The modern interpretations of the *Bhagavad Gītā* by Indian thinkers like Mohandas K. Gandhi (*The Bhagavadgītā According to Gandhi*) or Bal Gangadhar Tilak (*Śrīmad Bhagavadgītā rahasya*) could conceivably be placed in category four.

24. The four stages of life (*āśrama*) are: (1) *brāhmaṇa* "studenthood" stage, (2) *gṛhastha* "householder" stage, (3), *vānaprastha* "forest-dweller" stage, and (4) *saṃnyāsa* "renunciation" stage.

25. The four *varṇas* are: (1) *brahmin* "priesthood" class, (2) *kṣatriya* "warrior" class, (3) *vaiśya* "agriculturalist" class, and (4) *śūdra* "serving" class.

26. *Manusmṛti*, M. N. Dutt, trans. (Varanasi: Chowkhamba Press, 1979).

27. Edward Conze, *Buddhist Thought in India: Three Phases of Buddhist Philosophy* (reprint [1962]; Ann Arbor: University of Michigan Press, 1967), pp. 195ff. For introductory literature on Buddhism, see Peter Harvey, *An Introduction to Buddhism: Teaching, History and Practice* (Cambridge: Cambridge University Press, 1990) and Donald S. Lopez Jr., ed., *Buddhism in Practice* (Princeton: Princeton University Press, 1995).

28. *Buddhist Mahāyāna Texts Part II*, Max Müller, ed. and trans. (reprint [1849]; Delhi: Motilal Banarsidass, 1968), pp. 89–102, 101.

29. Buddha not only refers to the historical Gautama Buddha but also to a universal Buddha and celestial ones, as well.

30. *Buddhist Mahāyāna Texts Part II*, pp. 1–72, 62–63.

31. Hindu Bhakti began in South India where it flourished beginning in the sixth century CE (e.g., the Tamil Nāyaṉmars, the Tamil Āḻvārs and Śrī Vaiṣṇavism). The devotional movement spread to the North and flourished

there during the fifteenth to sixteenth century CE. Friedhelm Hardy, *Viraha-Bhakti: The Early History of Kṛṣṇa Devotion in South India* (Delhi: Oxford University Press, 1983); Nancy Ann Nayar, *Poetry as Theology: The Śrīvaiṣṇava Stotra in the Age of Rāmānuja* (Wiesbaden: Otto Harrassowitz, 1992).

32. The Sant movement emerged out of both a Hindu and Islamic environment: that is, it was affected by the religious landscape of Vaiṣṇava Bhakti (which originated in South India), the Nātha yogic tradition of Northern India, and Sufism, the mystical tradition in Islam. Karine Schomer, "The Doha as a Vehicle of Sant Teachings," in Karine Schomer and W. H. McLeod, eds., *The Sants: Studies in the Devotional Tradition of India* (Delhi: Motilal Banarsidass, 1987), pp. 61–90; W. H. McLeod, "The Meaning of Sant in Sikh Usage," in Karine Schomer and W. H. McLeod, eds., *The Sants: Studies in the Devotional Tradition of India* (Delhi: Motilal Banarsidass, 1987), pp. 251–263.

33. *The Bījak of Kabir*, Linda Hess and Sukhdev Singh, transls. (Delhi: Motilal Banarsidass, 1983).

34. McLeod's statement of influence on the Sikh tradition through the Sant tradition is a point of contention among some scholars. The debate surrounding this statement is explored in chapter 6. W. H. McLeod, *Gurū Nānak and the Sikh Religion* (Delhi: Oxford University Press, 1976), pp. 151–53.

35. *Ādi Srī Gurū Granth Sāhib* (Sri Damdami Bir) (Amritsar: Sri Gurmat Press, standard pagination).

36. For a thorough analysis on the polarized nature of Sikh Studies, see J. S. Grewal, *Contesting Interpretations of the Sikh Tradition* (Delhi: Manohar Publishers, 1998); W. H. McLeod, "Cries of Outrage: History Versus Tradition in the Work on the Sikh Community," in *Exploring Sikhism: Aspects of Sikh Identity, Culture and Thought* (Delhi: Oxford University Press, 2000), p. 269.

37. For examples of the viewpoint of "traditional historians," see Trilochan Singh, *Ernest Trumpp and W. H. McLeod as Scholars of Sikh History, Religion and Culture* (Chandigarh: International Centre of Sikh Studies, 1994); Gurdarshan Singh Dhillon, *Researchers in Sikh Religion and History* (Chandigarh: Sumeet, 1989); Daljeet Singh, *The Sikh Ideology* (Amritsar: Singh Brothers, 1990).

38. For examples of the viewpoint of "critical historians," see W. H. McLeod, *Guru Nānak and the Sikh Religion*; Harjot Singh Oberoi, *The Construction of Religious Boundaries: Culture, Identity, and Diversity in the Sikh Tradition* (Chicago: University of Chicago Press, 1994); Pashaura Singh, *The Guru Granth Sahib: Canon, Meaning and Authority* (Delhi: Oxford University Press, 2000).

39. Pashaura Singh, *The Guru Granth Sahib: Canon, Meaning and Authority*, p. 221.

40. Ernest Trumpp, *The Ādi Granth* (reprint [1989]; New Delhi: Munisharam Manoharlal, 1989); Arthur Max Macauliffe, *The Sikh Religion: Its Gurus Sacred Writings and* Authors, 6 vols in 3 (reprint; Delhi: DK Publishers, 1998).

41. J. D. Cunningham, *A History of the Sikhs* (reprint; Delhi: S. Chand, 1955).

42. Teja Singh, *Sikh Dharam* (reprint [1952]; Amritsar, Khlasa Brothers, 1977); Professor Sahib Singh, *Srī Gurū Granth Sāhib Darpaṇ* 10 vols. (Jalandhar, 1962–64).

43. The main contentious issues surrounding Sikh studies are: (1) the use of the textual-critical method to Sikh literature (both scripture and religious literature, including the *Gurū Granth Sāhib, Dasam Granth* and *janamsākhīs*); (2) the correlation made between Jat cultural and Śakti religious patterns with the emergence of militancy in the Sikh tradition and the creation of the K̲h̲ālsā; (3) the codification of the *Sikh Rahit Maryādā*; and (4) the discrepancy between social equality in theory and the use of caste in practice. For an elaborate analysis of the debate surrounding these contentious issues, see J. S. Grewal, *Contesting Interpretations of the Sikh Tradition*.

44. For a discussion on the historical Jesus and the Christ of faith, see Rudolf Karl Bultmann, *Jesus Christ and Mythology* (New York: Scribner, 1958); and Jaroslav Pelikan, *Jesus through the Centuries: His Place in the History of Culture* (New Haven: Yale University Press, 1985).

45. J. S. Grewal, *Contesting Interpretations of the Sikh Tradition*, pp. 132–67.

46. For a discussion on the methodology in religious studies, see Wilfred Cantwell Smith, *Towards a World Theology: Faith and the Comparative History of Religion* (London: MacMillan, 1981).

## CHAPTER TWO

1. David Gordon White, *The Alchemical Body: Siddh Traditions in Medieval India* (Chicago: University of Chicago Press, 1996), pp. 1–4, 9.

2. Recent scholarship has shown that the Nātha Siddhas and Rasa Siddhas, in fact, belonged to the same group of ascetics. The difference between the Nātha Siddhas and Rasa Siddhas has been their socioreligious function: while the former were the pioneers of hath-yoga, the latter were the alchemists. White, *The Alchemical Body*, pp. 2–9.

3. White, *The Alchemical Body*, pp. 335–52.

4. White, *The Alchemical Body*, p. 6; George Weston Briggs, *Gorakhnāth and the Kānphaṭa Yogīs* (reprint [1938]; Delhi: Motilal Banarsidass, 2001), pp. 4–5.

5. White, *The Alchemical Body*, pp. 8–9, 78.

6. The Tantra practices are for the purification of the body and mind, self-consecration, and the visualization of the deity. While Hindu and Buddhist Tantra are similar in their set of practices for the purpose of self-purification and self-consecration, the two Tantric traditions differ in terms of their goals. On the one hand, for Hindu Tantra, the goal is the merging of one's soul (*ātman*) with the underlying source of reality (*brahman*) or union with one's particular deity. On the other hand, in Buddhist Tantra the aim is to achieve buddhahood. Elizabeth Ann Benard, *Chinnamastā: The Aweful Buddhist and Hindu Tantric Goddess* (Delhi: Motilal Banarsidass, 1994), pp. 23–46, 77–78.

7. For example, the internationally acclaimed *qawwali* singer, Nusrat Fateh Ali Khan, whose mother tongue was Punjabi, sung a Punjabi folk song called *jogī de nāl* ("with the yogi"), which even makes references to the yogi's earrings (*muṇḍrā*). A famous contemporary Punjabi folk singer, Harbhajan Mann, sings a tune called *jogī lageyā merā kalejā khadeke* ("The yogi who stole my heart").

8. For a discussion on Kashmir Śaivism, see Lilian Silburn, *Kundalinī: The Energy of the Depths, A Comprehensive Study Based on the Scriptures of Non-Dualistic Kashmir Śaivism* (Albany: State University of New York Press, 1988); Paul Eduardo Muller-Ortega, *The Triadic Heart of Śiva: Kaula Tantricism of Abhinavagupta in the non-Dual Shaivism of Kashmir* (Albany: State University of New York Press, 1989); and Mark S. G. Dyczkowski, *The Doctrine of Vibration: An Analysis of the Doctrines and Practices of Kashmir Śaivism* (Albany: State University of New York Press, 1987).

9. Briggs, *Gorakhnāth and the Kānphaṭa Yogīs*, pp. 1–2.

10. The word *tantra* is derived from the Sanskrit verbal root *tan* "to shine, extend, spread, spin out, manifest" (Monier-Williams, *Sanskrit-English Dictionary*, pp. 435–436), and literally means "thread or loom." Tantra refers to a lineage of gurus through whom the disciple is given the esoteric teachings of a particular sect or to the extensive body of theory and practice that is viewed as heterodox and quite unsystematic.

Tantrism took shape around the first century CE and was well established by the sixth to seventh centuries CE, although it really flourished during the period from the eighth century to the fourteenth century and later. Although there are Tantric elements in the Vedas (ca. 1500–500 BCE), the actual Tantric tradition is a later development. At times, it is difficult to clearly distinguish between what has its origins in Tantra and what does not. The Tantra tradition is often viewed according to its sectarian orientation (Śaiva, Vaiṣṇava, Śākta, Buddhist, Jain). For a good discussion of the relationship between Vedic and Tantric worship, see Alexis Sanderson, "Śaivism and the Tantric Tradition," in Steward Sutherland, et al., eds., *The World's Religion* (Boston, Mass.: G. K. Hall, 1988), pp. 660–704.

11. White, *The Alchemical Body*, pp. 1–2; Tuen Goudriaan, *Hindu Tantrism* (Leiden: E. J. Brill, 1979), pp. 13–46. Douglas Renfrew Brooks, *The Secret of the Three Cities: An Introduction to Hindu Śākta Tantrism* (Chicago: University of Chicago Press, 1990), p. 3; White, *The Alchemical Body*, pp. 1–2.

12. Buddhist Tantra also known as Vajrayāna Buddhism derived many of its practices from Mahāyāna Buddhism, including *mudrā*, mantra, *maṇḍala*, *dharāṇi*, yoga, and *samādhi*. There are three main elements *śūnya*, *vijñāna*, and *mahāsuka*. Teachings are passed down to 84 *siddhas* and their disciples. Benoytosh Bhattacharya, *An Introduction to Buddhist Esotericism* (reprint [1980]; Delhi: Motilal Banarsidass, 1989), p. 166.

13. White, *The Alchemical Body*, p. 2.

14. White, *The Alchemical Body*, p. 78. For a thorough discussion on the various lists of the "nine" Nath teachers and other listings of the *siddhas*, see White, *The Alchemical Body*, pp. 78–92.

15. White, *The Alchemical Body*, pp. 91–92.

16. Briggs, *Gorakhnāth and the Kānphaṭa Yogīs*, pp. 136–37; Hazari Prasad Dwivedi, *Nātha Sampradāya* (Varanasi, 1966), p. 16.

17. According to field research by Briggs at Ṭilla (where a large Nāth centre exists), there are twelve recognized subsects connected with Gorakhnātha (even though several different ones are not actually traceable to Gorakhnātha).

While there were formerly eighteen sects under Śiva, a conflict among them resulted in the destruction of twelve Śiva subsects and six Gorakhnātha subsects. As a result, there remain only six Gorakhnātha subsects. Briggs, *Gorakhnāth and the Kānphaṭa Yogīs*, p. 63.

18. For a thorough discussion on the various lists of the founders of the "twelve" subdivisions, see White, *The Alchemical Body*, pp. 92–122.

19. White, *The Alchemical Body*, pp. 92–93.

20. Briggs, *Gorakhnāth and the Kānphaṭa Yogīs*, pp. 179–83.

21. White, *The Alchemical Body*, p. 78.

22. Briggs, *Gorakhnāth and the Kānphaṭa Yogīs*, p. 181.

23. Briggs, *Gorakhnāth and the Kānphaṭa Yogīs*, pp. 2–5.

24. White, *The Alchemical Body*, p. 335.

25. Briggs, *Gorakhnāth and the Kānphaṭa Yogīs*, pp. 179–207.

26. Briggs, *Gorakhnāth and the Kānphaṭa Yogīs*, pp. 26–27.

27. Briggs, *Gorakhnāth and the Kānphaṭa Yogīs*, pp. 10, 27.

28. Briggs, *Gorakhnāth and the Kānphaṭa Yogīs*, pp. 32–33.

29. Devotees of the malevolent forms of Śiva like Bhāirava often cover themselves with ashes, leaving their hair uncut and mat-locked, wear a necklace of skulls, and so on. See Diana Eck, *Banaras: City of Light* (Princeton: Princeton University Press, 1982).

30. *Liṅga-yoni* is the aniconic form of Śiva representing the union of Śiva and Śakti.

31. Briggs, *Gorakhnāth and the Kānphaṭa Yogīs*, p. 103.

32. There is a Nāth shrine at Hiṅg Lāj, which is in present-day Pakistan (the Hindu shrine farthest west) eighty miles from the mouth of the Indus River and twelve miles from sea. Briggs, *Gorakhnāth and the Kānphaṭa Yogīs*, pp. 103–6.

33. Briggs, *Gorakhnāth and the Kānphaṭa Yogīs*, pp. 15–16.

34. Briggs, *Gorakhnāth and the Kānphaṭa Yogīs*, p. 144.

35. Briggs, *Gorakhnāth and the Kānphaṭa Yogīs*, pp. 131–41.

36. Ayodhyā is the important Hindu pilgrimage place, especially for Vaiṣṇavas. It is the location King Daśratha and Prince Rāma ruled in the classical Hindu epic *Rāmāyaṇa*.

37. Vārāṇasī is a major Hindu pilgrimage place for Śaivas and Śāktas. It lies on the Ganges River, and is the place where a famous annual Kumba Mela occurs.

38. An important Hindu pilgrimage place (in present-day Uttar Pradesh) that is situated on the Ganges River in the foothills of the sacred Himalaya Mountains.

39. Ṭilla or Gorakh Ṭilla is a Nāth center in the Punjab, twenty-five miles northwest of Jhelum (now in present-day Pakistan). As one of the oldest religious sites in Northern India and one of the first Nāth centers, it is considered to be the chief seat of the Gorakhnāthis. There is a special annual festival (*mela*) held in March. Briggs, *Gorakhnāth and the Kānphaṭa Yogīs*, p. 34, 101–3.

40. Briggs, *Gorakhnāth and the Kānphaṭa Yogīs*, p. 10.

41. Briggs, *Gorakhnāth and the Kānphaṭa Yogīs*, p. 78.

42. Karen L. Merry, "The Hindu Festival Calendar," in Guy R. Welbon and Glenn E. Yocum, eds., *Religious Festivals in South India and Sri Lanka* (New Delhi: Manohar Publishers, 1982), pp. 1–25.

43. Briggs, *Gorakhnāth and the Kānphaṭa Yogīs*, pp. 142–144.

44. We have chosen a more exact transliteration of the Hindu mantra, although readers may have or may in the future see the Sanskrit syllable written as *Oṃ*, a familiar and accepted form used in the West.

45. Briggs, *Gorakhnāth and the Kānphaṭa Yogīs*, p. 143.

46. Briggs, *Gorakhnāth and the Kānphaṭa Yogīs*, p. 125; White, *The Alchemical Body*, pp. 3–11.

47. Briggs, *Gorakhnāth and the Kānphaṭa Yogīs*, pp. 125–28.

48. Briggs, *Gorakhnāth and the Kānphaṭa Yogīs*, pp. 131–41.

49. The *Gorakṣa Śataka* (The Hundred [Verses] of Gorakhnātha) is a Sanskrit hymn that consists of 101 verses. The hymn focuses on the mental and physical practices of hath-yoga, which reverse the physiological processes of aging and death. The celebrated author of *Gorakṣa Śataka* is *Gorakhnātha* (vs. 3, 4, 101). All quotations from the *Gorakṣa Śataka* are taken from: Briggs, *Gorakhnāth and the Kānphaṭa Yogīs*, pp. 284–304.

50. White, *The Alchemical Body*, p. 39ff.

51. The Nāth tradition has been influenced by Tantra. Early Tantrism (ca. sixth century CE) practiced approaching godhead in a sexual manner resulting in the bliss of sexual orgasm as realizing one's god-consciousness. The Tantric practices involved the use of magical formulae and erotic rituals as means to get in touch with the cosmic powers, and supernatural experiences were deemed as heterodox. During the tenth to eleventh century CE there was a move to clean up the sexual practices associated with Tantra, evident in Abhinavgupta's reconfiguration of Tika Kaulism. The sexual practice became an esoteric path, transmitted in secret form from teacher to student. As a consequence, the most renowned division in Tantra occurred: the left-handed school (*vamācara*) and the right-handed school (dakṣinācara). While the Vamācara school is associated with inauspicious and impure practices (such as alcohol consumption, eating meat, and rituals involving sexual intercourse), the latter is more conservative and more accepted in other Hindu circles. Douglas Renfrew Brooks, *The Secret of the Three Cities: An Introduction to Hindu Śākta Tantrism* (Chicago: University of Chicago Press, 1990), p. 3.

52. Mantra means "sacred sound, sacrificial formula, or prayer," derived from the Sanskrit verb root *man* "to think, believe, imagine, conjecture." One of the most popular and least complex forms of worship—the chanting of mantras—is related to this notion of speech (*śabda*). The most famous Hindu mantra is *Auṃ*.

53. For an elaboration of the concept of vibration, see Dyczkowski, *The Doctrine of Vibration*.

54. Similarities exist between Vedic and Tantric meditative and ritual practices; the most important of these is the equation of *śabda* (speech/word/sound) with divine cosmic energy.

55. G. Fuererstein, *The Philosophy of Classical Yoga* (Manchester: University of Manchester Press, 1982); Mircea Eliade, *Yoga: Immortality and Freedom*, Bollingen Series 41 (Princeton: Princeton University Press, 1969).

56. B. K. S. Iyenger, *The Tree of Yoga* (Boston: Shambhala Publications, 1989), p. 106.

57. Briggs, *Gorakhnāth and the Kānphaṭa Yogīs*, p. 259.

58. *Śatapatha Brāhmaṇa* 10.5.8.1. See also, *Taitirīya Brāhmaṇa* 11.2.3.

59. For example, *Kaṭha Upaniṣad* 2.12, 3.4, 6.11; *Taittirīya Upaniṣad* 2.4; *Śvetāśvatara Upaniṣad* 2.11, 6.13.

60. *Yogatattva Upaniṣad* is the forty-third Upaniṣad in the list of 108. *Upaniṣad-saṃgrahaḥ* (Delhi: Motilal Banarsidass, 1984), pp. 297–303. Subsequently, smaller "Tantric" compositions took on the Upaniṣadic genre form in order to legitimize later religious developments as belonging to Vedic or Vedāntic religion. Kamala Elizabeth Nayar, *Hayagrīva in South India: Complexity and Selectivity of a pan-Indian Hindu Deity* (Leiden: Brill, 2004), pp. 193–94.

61. Mantra-yoga employs the repetition of sacred syllables (mantras) and texts.

62. *Laya-yoga* revolves around subduing the senses in order to create a trance (*laya*) state, ultimately resulting in a "quiet mind."

63. Mircea Eliade, *Yoga*; G. Feuerstein, *The Philosophy of Classical Yoga* (Manchester: University of Manchester Press, 1982).

64. The six orthodox Hindu philosophical schools are: Pūrva Mīmāṃsā, Vedānta (Advaita, Viśiṣṭādvaita, Dvaita), Nyāya, Vaiśeṣika, Sāṃkhya, and Yoga. The Hindu philosophical systems (except for Pūrva Mīmāṃsā) are based on the condensed version of the *Upaniṣads* in the form of aphorisms called the *Vedānta Sūtras*.

65. Klaus Klostermaier, *A Survey of Hinduism* (Albany: State University of New York Press, 1989), pp. 358–67.

66. *Bhāgavata Purāṇa* 3.26.1–72 and 3.27.1–30. *Bhāgavata Purāṇa* is a later Hindu text that has an Advaita Vedāntic perspective, which is evident even in its exposition of Sāṃkhya philosophy.

67. The three *guṇas* are *sattva* (being, true, pure, illumination), *rajas* (passion, excitement, activity), and *tamas* (dark, inertia).

68. *Patañjali's Yoga Sūtras with the commentary of Vyāsa and the Gloss of Vācaspati Miśra*, Rama Prasada, transl. (reprint [1912]; New York: AMS, 1974).

69. *Yoga-sūtra* 3.36–37.

70. The most important texts of hath-yoga include *Haṭha-yoga Pradīpikā* (Light on the Yoga of Force), *Gheraṇḍa Saṃhitā* (Text of Gheraṇḍa) and the *Śiva-saṃhitā* (Text of Śiva). *Haṭha-yoga Pradīpikā* is the oldest text that was compiled ca. fourteenth or fifteenth century CE by Śvatmarāma. And, it remains to be the most renowned and important text on hath-yoga. *Haṭha-yoga Pradīpikā* consists of four chapters: Chapter one concerns itself with postures (*āsanas*) as a practice for cleansing the impurities of the 72,000 *nāḍīs*. The second chapter discusses the regulation of the breath (*prāṇayama*) as a way to control the *nāḍīs*. Chapter three is about the practice of hand gestures (*mudrās*)

and its practice to awaken the *kundalinī*. Last, chapter four is about the transcendental experience (*samādhi*), wherein the breath becomes thin and the mind thus becomes absorbed (which corresponds to illumination in *rāja-yoga* as described by Patañjali).

71. For example, *Haṭha-yoga Pradīpikā* 3 describes the reversal of old age and death with the practice of hand gestures (*mudrās*). See also *Gorakṣa Śataka* 82.

72. *Gorakṣa Śataka* 75–76.

73. *Gorakṣa Śataka* 97–100.

74. *Haṭha-yoga Pradīpikā* 1.

75. *Haṭha-yoga Pradīpikā*, Pancham Singh, transl. (reprint [1915]; New York: AMS, 1974).

76. *Haṭha-yoga Pradīpika* 1.41, 2.7–23, 4.18. See also *Gorakṣa Śataka* 47–50.

77. L. Silburn, *Kundalinī: Energy of the Depths* (Albany: State University of New York Press, 1988).

78. *Haṭha-yoga Pradīpikā*, especially chapters 2 and 4.

79. White, *The Alchemical Body*, pp. 39–45.

## CHAPTER THREE

1. J. S. Grewal, *Sikhs of the Punjab* (Cambridge: Cambridge University Press, 1991), pp. 28–30.

2. Classical Hindu philosophers like Śaṅkara of the Advaita Vedānta school and Rāmānuja of the Viśiṣṭādvaita Vedānta school.

3. For instance, "Investiture of the sacred thread" (*Miharbān Janam-sākhī* 7; *Gyān-ratanāvali Janam-sākhī* 44) and "Instruction by the Hindu Pandit" (*Purātan Janam-sākhī* 2; *Miharbān Janam-sākhī* 5; *Bālā Janam-sākhī* 3; *Gyān-ratanāvali Janam-sākhī* 33–34).

4. Paul Valliere, "Tradition," in Mircea Eliade, ed., *The Encyclopedia of Religion*, vol. 14 (New York: MacMillan, 1987), p. 4.

5. "Bābar-bāṇī" refers to the random hymns that depict Mugẖal Bābar's invasion of India. See, *Gurū Granth Sāhib*, Āsā 1.5–5, p. 360; Tilaṅg 1.5–3, pp. 722–23; Āsā 1. 1–11, p. 417.

6. Besides the *Gurū Granth Sāhib*, Bhāī Gurdās's (1551–1636 CE) commentary on the *Gurū Granth Sāhib* also forms part of the Sikh canon. Bhāī Gurdās, the initial scribe of the *Gurū Granth Sāhib*, wrote the most revered commentary on the *Gurū Granth Sāhib* called the *Vārāṅ* during the guruship of Arjan Dev, who designated the *Vārāṅ* as the "key" to the understanding of the Sikh scripture. Accordingly, Bhāī Gurdās's commentary on the *Gurū Granth Sāhib* is regarded as the "key." In fact, as per tradition, it is held that one should actually read the *Vārāṅ* before reading the *Gurū Granth Sāhib*. The *Vārāṅ*'s primary focus is on the spiritual teachings of the Sikh gurus, although there are references to several historical events. Giani Sant Singh Maskeen, personal communication January 22, 2003. See also Khushwant Singh, *A History of the Sikhs*, vol. 1 (Princeton, NJ: Princeton University Press, 1963), p. 310 and Max Arthur Macauliffe, *The Sikh Religion: Its Gurus Sacred Writings and Authors*, vols. 3–4 (reprint [1909]; Delhi: DK Publishers, 1998), p. 64.

7. McLeod, *Gurū Nānak and the Sikh Religion*, p. 34.

8. Kamala Elizabeth Nayar, *The Sikh Diaspora in Vancouver: Three Generations amid Tradition, Modernity and Multiculturalism* (Toronto: University of Toronto Press, 2004), pp. 129–30.

9. John Stratton Hawley and Mark Juergensmeyer, *Songs of the Saints of India* (New York: Oxford University Press, 1988), pp. 68–70; Nayar, *The Sikh Diaspora in Vancouver*, pp. 129–30; W. H. McLeod, *Gurū Nānak and the Sikh Religion* (Delhi: Oxford University Press, 1976), pp. 8–13.

10. McLeod, *Gurū Nānak and the Sikh Religion*, p. 12.

11. Nayar, *The Sikh Diaspora in Vancouver*, pp. 130, 142.

12. Ranbir Singh, *Glimpses of the Divine Masters* (New Delhi: International Traders Corporation, 1965), pp. 82–83. See also W. H. McLeod, *The B40 Janam Sākhī* (Amritsar: Guru Nanak Dev University, 1980).

13. *Purāntan Janam-sākhī* 10 and *Miharbān Janam-sākhī* 28–29.

14. "Guru Nanak," *Amar Chitra Katha*, no. 47 (Delhi: India Book House), pp. 17–19.

15. For an example of a symbolic interpretation of a hagiography, see chapter 5.

16. McLeod outlines the criteria he uses for discerning fact from legend as (1) miracle or fantastic stories, (2) testimony of external sources such as of Mug͟hal Bābar or Daulat K͟hān Lodī, (3) Guru Nānak's own writing in the *Gurū Granth Sāhib*, (4) agreement or disagreement among the various *janam-sākhīs*, (5) relative reliability of the different *janam-sākhīs*, (6) genealogical consistency, and (7) based on geographic sensibility. McLeod, *Gurū Nānak and the Sikh Religion*, pp. 68–70.

17. McLeod, *Gurū Nānak and the Sikh Religion*, pp. 77–94.

18. McLeod, *Gurū Nānak and the Sikh Religion*, p. 92.

19. The metaphorical interpretation of Guru Nānak's disappearance for three days is given in chapter 5.

20. Harbans Singh, *The History of the Sikhs*, p. 12.

21. Max Arthur Macauliffe, *The Sikh Religion: Its Gurus Sacred Writings and Authors*, vol. 1 (reprint Delhi: DK Publishers, 1998), p. 1; McLeod, *Gurū Nānak and the Sikh Religion*, p. 146.

22. Hawley and Juergensmeyer, *Songs of the Saints of India*, p. 67.

23. McLeod, *Gurū Nānak and the Sikh Religion*, p. 143.

24. The epic *Rāmāyaṇa* refers to a tour called *dig-vijaya* "conquer of the four (directions)." Likewise, Indian poet-saints are often described as having toured in the four directions, such as Śaṅkara and Rāmānuja.

25. All quotations from Bhāī Gurdās's *Vārāṅ* are taken from: *Vārāṅ Bhāī Gurdās: Text, Transliteration and Translation*, 2 vols., Jodh Singh, trans. (New Delhi: Vision and Venture, 1998).

*Muni* is a sage. *Bhairav* refers to the Hindu god Śiva. *Rākṣasa* and *daitya* are two types of demons in Hindu mythology. *Pīr* is a Persian word for a Sufi master or teacher. *Paigambar* is a prophet or messenger of God.

26. See footnote 40, for the discussion surrounding Mount Sumeru as a mythological place.

27. This is based on McLeod's extensive analysis of the *janam-sākhīs* in *Gurū Nānak and the Sikh Religion.*

28. According to the *Purātan Janam-sākhī*, the eastern and southern journeys were to: Pāṇīpat, Delhi, Vārāṇasī, Nānakmāta, Kāmrūp (Assam), Talvaṇḍī, Pākpaṭṭan, Goindvāl, Saidpur, Lahore, Kartārpur, and Laṅka. On the other hand, according to *Miharbān Janam-sākhī*, Guru Nānak visited Delhi, Hardwār, Allahābād, Vārāṇasī, Hājīpur, Paṭṇā, Ayodhyā, Jagannātha Purī, Rāmeśwaram, beyond Setu-bandha entered a foreign land (possibly Laṅka), Ujjain, Vindhyā Mountains, Narabad river, Ujjain, Bīkāner, Sauraāhtra, Mathurā, Kurukshetra, and Sultānpur.

29. According to the *Purātan Janam-sākhī*, the northern and western journeys were to: Kashmir, Mount Sumeru, Achal Baṭālā, Mecca. Whereas, according to *Miharbān Janam-sākhī*, Guru Nānak visited Mount Sumeru, Gorakh-haṭaṛī, Multān, Mecca, Hiṅg Lāj, Gorakh-haṭaṛī, Saidpur, Ṭillā Bālgundāī, Talvaṇḍī, Pāk Paṭṭan, Dīpālpur, Khokhovāl, Pokho, and Kartārpur.

30. Grewal, *The Sikhs of Punjab*, p. 39. Harbans Singh, *The History of the Sikhs*, pp. 19–20.

31. Louis E. Fenech, *Martyrdom in the Sikh Tradition: Playing the 'Game of Love'* (Delhi: Oxford University Press, 2000), p. 81.

32. According to the "Bābar-bāṇī," the invasion (or at least one of them) occurred: in "seventy-eight" (1578 Vikram), which is 1521 CE. (*GGS*, p. 723.)

33. Bhāī Lālo was a carpenter by profession, who lived in Saidpur (which is now Eminābād in present-day Pakistan). The *Bālā Janam-sākhī* describes Bhāī Lālo as a devoted Sikh whom Guru Nānak stayed with for three nights. Harbans Singh (ed.), *Encyclopedia of Sikhism*, vol. 2, p. 561.

34. *GGS*, p. 417. See also Jaswinder S. Sandhu, "Existential Themes in Eastern Spirituality: A Thematic Analysis of the Sikh Spiritual Tradition," in D. Sandhu (ed.) *Alternative Approaches to Counseling and Psychotherapy* (New York: Nova Science, in press).

35. Fenech, *Martyrdom in the Sikh Tradition*, pp. 66–69.

36. Grewal, *The Sikhs of the Punjab*, pp. 39–41.

37. *GGS*, pp. 952–53.

38. Bhartṛharī is a disciple of Gorakhnāth, who found the Bhairāj subsect. Briggs, *Gorakhnātha and the Kānphaṭa Yogīs*, p. 65.

39. Kamala Elizabeth Nayar, *Hayagrīva in South India: Complexity and Selectivity of a Pan-Indian Hindu Deity* (Leiden: Brill, 2004), pp. 191–98.

40. Mount Sumeru (Sumeru Parbat) is referred to in the Hindu Purāṇic mythological texts (*Matsya Purāṇa* 113; *Padma Purāṇa* 128) as being at the center of the world. It is situated in the Himalayan mountain range in northeastern India. According to D. S. Grewal, Mount Sumeru is the name of a peak on Mount Kailash in western Tibet. The highest body of fresh water in the world is found on Mount Kailash called Lake Mansarovar. While Hindus revere Mount Kailash as the throne of Lord Śiva, Buddhists see it as representing the father mountain that leads one to enlightenment (and Lake Mansarovar as the mother pearl). For Sikhs, Lake Mansarovar at Mount Kailash is the place where Guru Nānak met with some of the Nāth yogis. D. S. Grewal, *Guru*

*Nanak's Travel to Himalayan and East Asian region, A New Light* (Delhi: National Book Shop, 1995), p. 44. Giani Sant Singh Maskeen, interview by authors, Surrey, BC, 22 January 2003.

41. McLeod, *Gurū Nānak and the Sikh Religion*, p. 49.

42. McLeod, *Gurū Nānak and the Sikh Religion*, p. 49.

43. Jodh Singh, *The Religious Philosophy of Gurū Nānak*, p. 18.

44. McLeod, *Gurū Nānak and the Sikh Religion*, pp. 59–60.

45. Guru Nānak responds to Gorakhnāth's question regarding the *kaliyug* with three verses that describe its degeneracy: Vār Āsā, *salok* 1 of *pauṛī* 11, *GGS*, p. 468; Vār Mājh, *salok* 1 of *pauṛī* 16, *GGS*, p. 145; Vār Rāmkalī, *salok* 1 of *pauṛī* 11, *GGS*, p. 951. The discourse also includes the Rāmkalī, *salok* 2–7 of *pauṛī* 12, discussed at pp. 12–13.

46. McLeod, *Gurū Nānak and the Sikh Religion*, p. 121.

47. Jodh Singh, *The Religious Philosophy of Gurū Nānak*, pp. 19–22.

48. Jodh Singh, *The Religious Philosophy of Gurū Nānak*, pp. 21–22.

49. Jodh Singh, *The Religious Philosophy of Gurū Nānak*, pp. 24–25.

50. See McLeod, *Gurū Nānak and the Sikh Religion*, pp. 75, 141.

51. McLeod, *Gurū Nānak and the Sikh Religion*, p. 141.

52. Nayar, *The Sikh Diaspora in Vancouver*, pp. 128–130.

53. Bhaṅgar Nāth is one of the yogis of the Gorakhnāth tradition who, according to the *Vārāṅ*, is believed to have met with Guru Nānak during the Śivarātrī fair at Achal Baṭālā, now in Gurdāspur district of the Punjab.

54. Giani Sant Singh Maskeen, interview, 22 January 2003.

55. For a detailed analysis of the various streams of belief in the development of the Sikh tradition, see Harjot S. Oberoi, *The Construction of Religious Boundaries: Culture, Identity, and Diversity in the Sikh Tradition* (Chicago: University of Chicago Press, 1994).

56. Giani Kishan Singh Parwana, *gurdwārā* lecture, Sri Guru Singh Sabha, Toronto, 1991.

## CHAPTER FOUR

1. *Sree Gurū Granth Sāhib*, Gopal Singh, transl. reprint [1964]; Delhi: World Book Center, 1993), p. xviii. W. H. McLeod, *Gurū Nānak and the Sikh Religion* (Delhi: Oxford University Press, 1988), p. 7.

2. Guru Arjan Dev collected the hymns of the first five Sikh gurus (Guru Nānak, Guru Aṅgad, Guru Amar Dās, Guru Rām Dās, and Guru Arjan Dev), all of which are cited as *mahalā* "majestic palace" with their respective order in the guru lineage. Also included in the *Gurū Granth Sāhib* are selected hymns from both Hindu *bhagats* (such as, Ravidās and Nāmdev) and Muslim mystics (such as, Kabīr and Bābā Farīd).

3. The belief that Guru Gobind Siṅgh bestowed the status of Guru upon the *Gurū Granth Sāhib* has been historically challenged by scholars like W. H. McLeod, *Gurū Nānak and the Sikh Religion*, p. 2. For an elaboration on McLeod's perspective, see *The Evolution of the Sikh Community* (New Delhi: Oxford University Press, 1975).

4. Along with the *Gurū Granth Sāhib*, equally authoritative, although less read, is the *Dasam Granth* ("the Tenth Sacred Book"). The *Dasam Granth* is a collection of writings attributed to Guru Gobind Siṅgh. Some scholars, however, do not accept his authorship for the entire volume. There are four theories about the authorship of the *Dasam Granth*: (1) the entire book was written by Guru Gobind Siṅgh; (2) the first three parts are written by Guru Gobind Siṅgh; (3) Guru Gobind Siṅgh only wrote the "Zafar-nāmā," even though the other portions reflect his ideas, and (4) Guru Gobind Siṅgh wrote the "Zafar-nāmā," but the remaining portions should not be considered a reflection of his beliefs. W. H. McLeod, *The Sikhs: History, Religion and Society* (New York: Columbia University Press, 1989), pp. 90–91; and Harjot S. Oberoi, *The Construction of Religious Boundaries: Culture, Identity, and Diversity in the Sikh Tradition* (Chicago: University of Chicago Press, 1994), pp. 92–103, 137.

5. Pashaura Singh, *The Guru Granth Sahib: Canon, Meaning and Authority* (Delhi: Oxford University Press, 2000), pp. 46–53; W. H. McLeod, *Textual Sources for the Study of Sikhism* (Chicago: University of Chicago Press, 1984), p. 4; *Sree Gurū Granth Sāhib*, Gopal Singh, transl. (Delhi: World Book Center, 1993), p. xix.

6. For a more detailed and critical discussion on the different recensions of the *Gurū Granth Sāhib*, see Pashaura Singh, *The Guru Granth Sahib*, pp. 28–82, 201–235. See also, Gurinder Singh Mann, *The Making of Sikh Scripture* (New York: Oxford University Press, 2001), pp. 82–101, 121–125.

7. In reaction to the many hymns circulating, Guru Amar Dās (1479–1574) took the initiative to prevent the forged or "unripe utterances" (*kachī bāṇī*) from infiltrating into the Nānak Panth as parts of the text. Hence, Guru Amar Dās collected his hymns, along with those of the previous two gurus and some selected compositions by several *bhagats*, and compiled a volume (*pothī*) of hymns known as the *Goindvāl Pothī*. When Guru Arjan Dev assumed Guruship in 1581, he received a large body of sacred hymns, some of which had initially been collected by the third guru, Guru Amar Das, including the *Goindvāl Pothī*. It is said that the *Goindvāl Pothī* had been incorporated in the *Ādi Granth* (Kartārpur) by Guru Arjan Dev. There are at least two extant *Goindvāl Pothīs*. Pashaura Singh, *The Guru Granth Sahib*, pp. 18–19. Mann, *The Making of Sikh Scripture*, pp. 40–50. For a thorough examination of the *Goindvāl Pothī*, see Gurinder Singh Mann, *The Goindvāl Pothīs: The Earliest Extant Source of the Sikh Canon* (Cambridge: Harvard University Press, 1996).

8. Pashaura Singh, *The Guru Granth Sahib*, p. 102.

9. Guru Nānak's "Jap-jī" is discussed in chapter 5.

10. Jodh Singh, *The Religious Philosophy of Gurū Nānak: A Comparative Study with Special Reference to Siddha Goṣṭi* (Delhi: National Book, 1989), p. 16.

11. Jodh Singh, *The Religious Philosophy of Gurū Nānak*, p. 24. Harbans Singh, ed., *Encyclopedia of Sikhism*, vol. 4 (Patiala: Punjabi University, 1998), p. 124.

12. J. S. Grewal, *Sikhs of the Punjab* (Cambridge: Cambridge University Press, 1991), p. 39.

13. *The Mīmāṃsā Sūtras of Jaimini*, Mohan Lal Sandal, trans. (reprint [1923–25]; New York: AMS Press, 1974).

14. Harbans Singh, ed., *Encyclopedia of Sikhism*, vol. 2, pp. 338–39.

15. Jodh Singh, *The Religious Philosophy of Gurū Nānak*, p. 17.

16. Charapaṭ is regarded as one of the disciples of Gorakhnāth and is revered as one of the immortal Nāth teachers. David Gordon White, *The Alchemical Body: Siddh Traditions in Medieval India* (Chicago: University of Chicago, 1996), pp. 78–92.

17. Loharipā is the Punjabi name for Luipā, the Tibetan name for Matsyendranāth, one of the nine immortal teachers of the Gorakhnāth lineage. White, *The Alchemical Body*, pp. 78–92.

18. Alain Danielou, *The Rāgas of Northern Indian Music* (London: Barrie and Rockliff, 1968). Harbans Singh (ed.), *Encyclopedia of Sikhism*, vol. 2, pp. 156–79.

19. At the end of the standardized version of the *Gurū Granth Sāhib*, there is an "appendix-like" list of the classifications of the eighty-four *rāgs* called the *Rāgmālā* (p. 1430). According to the editorial perspective of the *Gurū Granth Sāhib*, only one-fourth of the *Rāgmālā* list is accepted in the scripture. This exclusion of the other sixty-three *rāgs* in the *Gurū Granth Sāhib* may reflect the orientation of the Sikh gurus. Pashaura Singh, *The Guru Granth Sahib*, p. 148.

Some infer or speculate that the *Rāgmālā* was not primarily written for the *Gurū Granth Sāhib*, based on the fact that the classification of the Indian *rāg* does not directly correspond with the types of *rāgs* used in the scripture. (The followers of Bhāī Randīr Siṅgh, the Akhaṇḍ Kīrtanī Jathā sect, and several academic scholars contend that the *Rāgmālā* is not an authentic hymn of the *Gurū Granth Sāhib* because it does not consist of Sikh teachings.) However, others contend that it is part of the scripture based on the importance that the *rāg* has in the *Gurū Granth Sāhib*. Moreover, the authorship of the *Rāgmālā* is disputed, with some arguing that it was composed by a Muslim by the name of Ālam, who was a contemporary of Guru Arjan Dev (*Sree Gurū Granth Sāhib*, Gopal Singh, trans., p. XIX). See also Pashaura Singh, *The Guru Granth Sāhib*, pp. 125–50.

20. Harbans Singh, ed., *Encyclopedia of Sikhism*, vol. 2, p. 166.

21. For an elaboration on the role of the *rāg* and *kīrtan* in the Sikh tradition, see Mann, *The Making of Sikh Scripture*, pp. 87–99.

22. Mann, *The Making of Sikh Scripture*, p. 88.

23. Danielou, *The Rāgas of Northern Indian Music*, pp. 94–96.

24. Harbans Singh, ed., *Encyclopedia of Sikhism*, vol. 2, p. 170.

25. Harbans Singh, ed., *Encyclopedia of Sikhism*, vol. 2, p. 174. Mann, *The Making of Sikh Scripture*, p. 90.

26. Giani Sant Singh Maskeen, interview, January 22, 2003. Giani Maskeen acknowledges that the two different interpretations of "pañj" exist with reference to the *Pañj Granthī*.

27. For example, Bhāī Vīr Siṅgh (1872–1957 CE).

28. *Das-Granthī* literally "booklet of the tenth" is the counterpart to the *Pañj Granthī* in that it is an anthology of a selection of hymns taken from the *Dasam Granth* by the tenth guru—Guru Gobind Siṅgh.

29. *Srī Gurū Granth Sāhib-jī Vichon: Pañj Granthī* (Amritsar: Khalsa Brothers, n.d.).

## CHAPTER FIVE

1. Donald Lopez Jr., ed., *Religions of India in Practice* (Princeton: Princeton University Press, 1995), p. vii.

2. For a discussion concerning the Sikh *giānī*, see "Methodology" in chapter 1.

3. According to traditional scholars, the *mūl-mantar* consists of *EkOaṅkār* to the words *gur-prasād*, which was spoken by Guru Nānak, and believed by Sikhs to have been given by *EkOaṅkār*.

4. The *purātan* tradition argues that the *mūl-mantar* starts with *EkOaṅkār* to *gurprasād* and is followed by a verse (*salok*), which opens the *Jap-jī*. The *purātan* tradition defends their version of the *mūl-mantar* with two main arguments: (1) Bhāī Gurdās wrote a poetic verse (*Vārāṅ*, 39.1), in which he describes *EkOaṅkār* by providing a poetic commentary on each line of the *mūl-mantar* and the *salok*. Furthermore, the *purātan* tradition refers to *EkOaṅkār* to *gurprasād* as the *mahā* ("great") *mantar*, while it calls the *salok* portion as the *sach* ("true") *mantar*. The two *mantars* combined, *mahā* and *sach*, form the *mūl-mantar*. (2) A *cakra* believed to belong to Baba Dīp Siṅgh (a contemporary of Guru Gobind Siṅgh, who wrote copies of the *Gurū Granth Sāhib*) has both *EkOaṅkār* to *gurprasād* and the following *salok* inscribed on the *cakra*. Gurbachan Singh Khalsa Bhindranwale, audiotape, no date.

5. Giani Sant Singh Maskeen, lecture on audiotape, Khalsa Diwan Society, Vancouver, BC, 1994.

6. W. H. McLeod, *Gurū Nānak and the Sikh Religion* (New Delhi: Oxford University Press, 1979), pp. 37–38.

7. For a discussion on the evolution of the *mūl-mantar* in Sikh scripture, see Pashaura Singh, *The Guru Granth Sahib: Canon, Meaning and Authority* (Delhi: Oxford University Press, 2000), pp. 84–90; Gurinder Singh Mann, *The Making of Sikh Scripture* (New York: Oxford University Press, 2001), pp. 53–54.

8. We have chosen a more precise transliteration of the Sikh mantra, although readers may have or may in the future see it written as *EkOṅkār*, a familiar and accepted form used in the West.

9. Osho, *The True Name* (New Delhi: New Age International, 1994), pp. 4–5. Maskeen, lecture, 1994.

10. Parma Nand, "Ek Oṅkār," in Pritam Singh, ed., *Sikh Concept of the Divine* (Amritsar: Guru Nanak Dev University Press, 1985), p. 45.

11. Maskeen, lecture, 1994.

12. For a discussion on the monistic and monotheistic interpretations of *EkOaṅkār*, see M. P. Christanand Pillai, "Comparative Study of Monotheism in *Mūl Mantra* and the Bible," in Pritam Singh, ed., *The Sikh Concept of the Divine* (Amritsar: Guru Nanak Dev University, 1985), pp. 175–91. See also, Sher Singh, *Philosophy of Sikhism* (Jalandhar: Sterling Publishers, 1964).

13. Maskeen, lecture, 1994.

14. For a detailed discussion on the *mūl-mantar*, see Pritam Singh, ed., *Sikh Concept of the Divine* (Amritsar: Guru Nanak Dev University Press, 1985).

15. Jaswinder S. Sandhu, "Existential Themes in Eastern Spirituality: A Thematic Analysis of the Sikh Spiritual Tradition," in D. Sandhu, ed., *Alternative Approaches to Counseling and Psychotherapy* (New York: Nova Science Publishers, in press).

16. *GGS*, pp. 74–79.

17. *GGS*, pp. 74–79.

18. Jaswinder S. Sandhu, "The Sikh Model of the Person, Suffering, and Healing: Implications for Counselors," *International Journal for the Advancement of Counselling*, vol. 26, no. 1 (2004), p. 39.

19. Guru Amar Dās also makes reference to the five thieves: "Within this body are hid five thieves—lust, anger, greed, attachment and ego" (*GGS*, p. 600).

20. Sandhu, "The Sikh Model of the Person, Suffering, and Healing," p. 39.

21. *GGS*, p. 932.

22. *GGS*, p. 40.

23. *GGS*, p. 304.

24. Kamala Elizabeth Nayar, *The Sikh Diaspora in Vancouver: Three Generations amid Tradition, Modernity, and Multiculturalism* (Toronto: University of Toronto Press, 2004), pp. 86–88.

25. The "Four Watches of the Night" verses cited are taken from Srī Rāg M.1., *GGS*, pp. 75–76. The discussion of the phases of personal development according to the Sikh scripture is based on: *GGS*, pp. 74–78; 137–38. References to the "Four Watches of the Night" are also made by Guru Rām Dās, *GGS*, p. 76; and Guru Arjan Dev, *GGS*, p. 78.

26. Nayar, *The Sikh Diaspora in Vancouver*, p. 86.

27. Nayar, *The Sikh Diaspora in Vancouver*, pp. 86–87.

28. The discussion of the phases of spiritual development is based on: Guru Nānak, "Jap-jī," in *GGS*, pp. 7–8.

29. Dharam Singh, *Sikh Theology of Liberation* (New Delhi: Harman Publishing House, 1991), p. 81.

30. Dharam Singh, *Sikh Theology of Liberation*, p. 96.

31. Dharam Singh, *Sikh Theology of Liberation*, p. 81.

32. *GGS*, p. 943.

33. For a definition of the Hindu concept *śruti*, see footnote 7 in chapter 1.

34. For a discussion of the spiritual tune (or unstruck sound), see the following section on "Sikh Spiritual Practice."

35. McLeod, *Gurū Nānak and the Sikh Religion*, pp. 195–96.

36. Harbans Singh, ed., *Encyclopedia of Sikhism*, vol. 3, pp. 159–61.

37 *GGS*, pp. 1–8. Harbans Singh, ed., *Encyclopedia of Sikhism*, vol. 2, pp. 347–49.

38. *GGS*, pp. 7–8.

39. For a detailed discussion on the *khaṇḍs*, see Nirbhai Singh, *Philosophy of Sikhism* (New Delhi: Atlantic Publishers, 1990), pp. 196–209.

40. *GGS*, p. 3.
41. Sandhu, "The Sikh Model of the Person, Suffering, and Healing," p. 41.
42. Maskeen, lecture, 1994.
43. Maskeen, lecture, 1994.
44. Santokh Singh, *Fundamentals of Sikhism* (Princeton, Ontario: Institute of Spiritual Studies, 1994), p. 217.
45. There are contending interpretations of the term *karam* in the *khaṇḍs*. Many traditional scholars, such as Sher Singh, Kapur Singh, Sohan Singh, and others, interpret *karam* as being derived from a Persian word meaning grace. However, Nirbhai Singh argues that since the other four *khaṇḍs* (*dharam*, *giān*, *saram*, and *sach*) are derived from Sanskrit, it does not make sense to use a Persian term; instead, the Sanskrit definition of *karam* ("action") ought to be used. See Nirbhai Singh, *Philosophy of Sikhism*, p. 203.
46. Harbans Singh, ed., *Encyclopedia of Sikhism*, vol. 4, p. 84.
47. According to *Manusmṛti*, service is a dog's work that is meant for those belonging to the lowest of the four *varṇas*, the *śūdra* ("serving") class or even the outcastes of the *varṇa* system. See *Manusmṛti* 4.6 and 4.160.
48. Surinder S. Kohli, *Sikh Ethics* (New Delhi: Munshiram Manoharlal Publishers, 1994), p. 53.
49. Harbans Singh, ed., *Encyclopedia of Sikhism*, vol. 4, p. 85.
50. Harbans Singh, ed., *Encyclopedia of Sikhism*, vol. 4, p. 85.
51. Maskeen, lecture, 1994.
52. Harbans Singh, ed., *Encyclopedia of Sikhism*, vol. 3, p. 159.
53. Raghbir Singh Bir, *Bandgi Nama: Communion with the Divine* (Calcutta: Atam Science Trust, 1981), p. 58.
54. Maskeen, lecture, 1994.
55. Bir, *Bandgi Nama*, p. 56.
56. Bir, *Bandgi Nama*, p. 67.
57. Bir, *Bandgi Nama*, p. 67.
58. Giani Sant Singh Maskeen, *Prabhu Simran* (Amritsar: Bhai Chattar Singh/Jiwan Singh Publishers, 1992), p. 20.
59. Bir, *Bandgi Nama*, pp. 62–64.
60. Dharam Singh, *Sikh Theology of Liberation*, p. 96.
61. Dharam Singh, *Sikh Theology of Liberation*, p. 86.

## CHAPTER SIX

1. J. S. Grewal, *The Sikhs of the Punjab* (Cambridge: Cambridge University Press, 1991), pp. 40–41.
2. *Vārāṅ Bhāī Gurdās: Text, Transliteration and Translation*, vol. 1, Jodh Singh, transl. (New Delhi: Vision and Venture, 1998).
3. Similarly, it has been stated that Sant Kabīr was influenced by the Nāth tradition, but that he "redefined" Nāth terminology for the purpose of putting forward his own perspective on the world. Vinay Dharwadkar, *Kabīr: The Weaver's Songs* (New Delhi: Penguin Books, 2003), p. 212.

4. "As one might open a door by force with a key, so the Yogī may break open the door of release by means of Kundalinī." (*Gorakṣa Śataka* 51)

5. W. H. McLeod, *Gurū Nānak and the Sikh Religion* (Delhi: Oxford University Press, 1976), pp. 191–92.

6. McLeod, *Gurū Nānak and the Sikh Religion*, pp. 151–53.

7. Daljeet Singh, *The Sikh Ideology* (Amritsar: Singh Brothers, 1990), pp. 72–77; Jodh Singh, *The Religious Philosophy of Gurū Nānak: A Comparative Study with Special Reference to Siddha Goṣṭi* (Delhi: National Book, 1989), pp. 84–108.

8. See also *SG* 24, 25, 34, 46, 51, and 61.

9. For an elaboration on *gaṭkā* in the Sikh tradition, see Nanak Dev Singh, *Gatka: Dance of the Sword* (Phoenix, AZ: GT International, 1988).

10. Surinder Singh Kohli, *Yoga of the Sikhs* (Amritsar: Singh Brothers, 1991), p. 10. See also Daljeet Singh, *The Sikh Ideology*, pp. 74–77.

11. Jaswinder S. Sandhu, "The Sikh Model of the Person, Suffering, and Healing: Implications for Counselors," *International Journal for the Advancement of Counseling*, vol. 26, no. 1 (2004), pp. 33–46.

12. For a feminist perspective on the Sikh tradition, see Nikky-Guninder Kaur Singh, *The Birth of the Khalsa: A Feminist Re-memory of Sikh Identity* (Albany: State University of New York Press, 2005).

13. W. H. McLeod and Harjot S. Oberoi would be considered to be the most critical among modern scholars about the issue of establishing the *Sikh Rahit Maryādā*. For an elaboration on the dispute concerning the *Sikh Rahit Maryādā*, see W. H. McLeod, *Sikhs of the Khalsa: A History of the Rahit Maryada* (New Delhi: Oxford University Press, 2003) and Harjot S. Oberoi, *The Construction of Religious Boundaries: Culture, Identity, and Diversity in the Sikh Tradition* (Chicago: University of Chicago Press, 1994), pp. 305–417.

14. Louis E. Fenech. *Martyrdom on the Sikh Tradition: Playing the 'Game of Love'* (New Delhi: Oxford University Press, 2000), pp. 66–69; J. S. Grewal, *Sikhs of the Punjab* (Cambridge, Mass.: Cambridge University Press, 1991), p. 41.

15. The modern interpretations of the *Bhagavad Gītā* have been written specifically for the purpose of supporting social reform, the betterment of Indian society or nationalism. For a detailed analysis of such interpretations, see Robert Walter Stevenson, "Historical Change in Scriptural Interpretation: A Comparative Study of Classical and Contemporary Commentaries on the *Bhagavadgītā*" (Ph.D. dissertation, Harvard University, 1975). See also Satya P. Agarwal, *The Social Role of the Gita: How and Why* (Delhi: Motilal Banarsidass, 1993).

16. Wendy (Doniger) O'Flaherty, *Śiva: The Erotic Ascetic* (London: Oxford University Press, 1973), pp. 35–38.

## TRANSLATION

1. *Siddh* is an ascetic, one who has renounced the material world in pursuit of spiritual attainment. However, Guru Nānak uses the term interchangeably with the Nāth yogis.

2. The Sikh gurus are referred to as *mahalā*, which literally means majestic palace. The term *mahalā* is used to indicate the Sikh gurus who uttered the compositions contained in the *Gurū Granth Sāhib*. For example, the first guru—Guru Nānak—is referred to as M (*mahalā*) 1.

3. *Rāmkalī* meter is the musical measure that is meant to be sung in the morning after sunrise, in order to invoke a contemplative mood within the devotee. Harbans Singh, ed., *Encyclopedia of Sikhism*, vol. 2, pp. 156–79.

4. *EkOaṅkār* is the One Primordial Essence that is manifest in all.

5. "The grace of the True Guru" (*satgur-prasād*) refers to the grace of the Sacred Word (*śabad*) or *EkOaṅkār*.

6. *Sant* is a holy person or saint.

7. *Sahaj* is the yogic term for the ultimate goal; that is, the break away from duality and the experience of union.

8. *Śabad* literally means "word" (*śabda* in Sanskrit), and has the connotation of the Sacred Word that contains the essence of Ultimate Reality. In Sikhism, it refers to the sacred hymns contained in the *Gurū Granth Sāhib*. *Śabad* is believed to have been directly transmitted from *EkOaṅkār* in that it has the same essence.

9. *Mukti* refers to liberation from the cycle of rebirth (*saṅsār*).

10. *Siddhs* are very old and therefore see Nanak (in comparison) as relatively young (Bhāī Gurdās's *Vārāṅ* I). Indeed, the yogis consider Guru Nānak as a child, even if he is in actuality in the later part of his adult stage of life.

11. The One refers to *EkOaṅkār*.

12. *Hukam* literally means order, and refers to the natural order of the universe.

13. "Posture" (*āsan*; *āsana* in Sanskrit) refers to yogic posture. *Āsan* is one of the three primary physical exercises practiced in hath-yoga. The other two are *prāṇayam* (breath control) and *mudrā* (hand gesturing).

14. *Gurmukh* literally means the one "whose face [is to] the Guru," which refers to the one who is following the path or teachings of the Guru.

15. Charapaṭ (ca. eleventh to twelfth century) is regarded as one of the disciples of Gorakhnāth and is revered as one of the immortal Nāth teachers.

16. *Saṅsār* refers to the cycle of birth, death, and rebirth.

17. *Nām* literally means name, and refers to the ontological category denoting Divine presence of Ultimate Reality.

18. Loharipā (ca. tenth century) is regarded as one of the nine Nāth immortal teachers.

19. The dress of the Nāth yogis includes a patched coat, earrings, and begging bag.

20. The twelve branches of yoga are: *rāval, hetu, pāv, āī, gamaya, pāgal, gopāl, kaṅthaṛī, ban, ḍvaj, colī,* and *dās*. Professor Sahib Singh, *Srī Gurū Granth Sāhib Darpaṇ*, vol. 7 (Jalandhar: Raj Publishers, 1962), p. 37.

21. The "six philosophical schools" refers to the six orthodox Hindu philosophical systems: Pūrva Mīmāṃsā, Vedānta (Advaita, Viśiṣṭādvaita, Dvaita), Nyāya, Vaiśeṣika, Sāṃkhya, and Yoga.

22. The five elements are sky (symbolic of detachment), fire (burns impurities), air (neutrality), earth (patience), and water (purity). Sahib Singh, *Srī Gurū Granth Sāhib Darpaṇ*, vol. 7, p. 39.

23. The three worlds refers to the nether, the terrestrial, and the heavenly realms.

24. *Manmukh* literally means the one whose face [is turned to] the ego; that is, one who is not living according to the Guru's teachings, but whose actions are dictated by the ego or one's own desires.

25. The "snake of illusion" refers to a popular story about a blind man who is taught to identify a snake based on its qualities. However, the man misidentifies a rope for a snake. The story demonstrates how qualities and characteristics (*guṇs*) are deceptive in discerning the true nature of Reality. This story is told for the purpose of teaching the concept of *māyā*, which means illusion. *Māyā* refers to the transient material world (as opposed to Ultimate Reality, which is permanent).

26. *Sunn* (*śūnya* in Sanskrit) means emptiness and in Sikhism it refers to that which is to be filled with the resonance (*nād*). It is only in this state of *sunn* that one can experience the cosmic resonance of *EkOaṅkār*.

27. Although the Punjabi word *haṅs* (*haṃsa* in Sanskrit) is often translated as "swan," we have more precisely translated it here as goose. In his analysis of *haṃsa*, Vogel raises a pertinent question regarding translation; that is, do scholars have the right to translate a word that provides a connotation suitable for their own culture? Western scholars (followed by Indian scholars) have translated *haṃsa* as swan or flamingo, when it should be rendered "goose." The swan is a rare bird in India. And, unlike in the West (where the goose is regarded as an ugly domesticated bird), the goose in India is a strong and noble bird that migrates to the Himalayan Mountains. Interestingly, Lake Mansarovar on Mount Kailash (one of the areas Guru Nānak is considered to have met with the Nāth yogis) is an important migration place for Indian geese. Jean Phillipe Vogel, *The Goose in Indian Literature and Art* (Leiden: E. J. Brill, 1962), pp. 1–8.

28. *Udāsī* refers to the one who renounces the material world. However, in Sikhism, *udāsī* also specifically refers to Guru Nānak's four spiritual travels that he made in order to teach the Truth as he had realized it.

29. The home of the True Guru refers to the realization of the soul through the Guru's word or *śabad*.

30. "Unstruck sound" (*anahat-nād*) refers to the cosmic resonance that is experienced through the *dasam duār* (tenth gate), which is an intangible experience that connects the *gurmukh* and *EkOaṅkār*.

31. *Guṇ* means quality or attribute (in Sanskrit, *guṇa*), and refers to the three constituents that make up the material world: *sattva* ("being, true, pure"), *rajas* ("passion, excitement, activity") and *tamas* ("dark").

32. *Nirguṇ* (in Sanskrit, *nirguṇa*) means "without attributes or formless" and refers to the Guru or Ultimate Reality as formless, and *sarguṇ* (in Sanskrit, *saguṇa*) means "with attributes or form" and refers to God with form.

33. Vedas (ca. 1500–900 BCE) are the ancient Hindu scriptures referred to as *śruti* ("that which is heard"). The Vedas are regarded as sacred, authoritative,

and eternal. The four Vedas proper are *Ṛg*, *Sāma*, *Yajur*, and *Atharva*. The end portion of the Vedas is called the Upaniṣad.

34. The "inner secret" refers to the realization of the soul.

35. The eight occult powers are (1) to take on another physical form, (2) to enlarge the body, (3) to shrink the body, (4) to increase weight, (5) to attain anything, (6) to read the hearts or minds of others, (7) to influence others, and (8) to control others. Sahib Singh, *Srī Gurū Granth Sāhib Darpaṇ*, vol. 7, p. 51. The *gurmukh* does not literally attain these eight occult powers. Rather, the *gurmukh* is fulfilled through *nām*.

36. *Saṅiyāsī* (*saṃnyāsin* in Sanskrit) refers to an ascetic or one who has taken on the state of renunciation in pursuit of liberation. Śaṅkara is said to have established ten *saṅiyāsī* orders. They are said to be divided in six and four; the ten orders include: (1) *tīrath*, (2) *āśram*, (3) *ban*, (4) *āraṇaya*, (5) *giri*, (6) *parbat*, (7) *sāgar*, (8) *sarasvat*, (9) *bhāratī*, and (10) *purī*. Klaus Klostermaier, *A Survey of Hinduism* (Albany, NY: State of University of New York Press, 1989), p. 333.

37. Smṛtis and Śāstras are two categories of Hindu literature. While *smṛtis* "what has been remembered" refer to a certain class of scripture, including the two classic Hindu epics (*Mahābhārata* and *Rāmāyaṇa*), *śāstras* "doctrine or treatise" refer to texts like the Hindu socioreligious lawbooks (*Manusmṛti*). *Śāstras* can be viewed as a subcategory of *smṛti* literature.

38. In the popular and classic Hindu epic *Rāmayaṇ* (*Rāmāyaṇa* in Sanskrit) the island of Laṅka (present-day Sri Lanka) is the residing place of the evil king Rāvaṇ (Rāvaṇa in Sanskrit), where he kept Sītā as captive. King Rām Chand (Rāma in Sanskrit), along with his brother Lakṣmaṇ (Lakṣmaṇa in Sanskrit) and Hanumān and the monkey army, built a bridge of stones connecting South India and Laṅka in order to free Sītā and the slaves in Rāvaṇ's kingdom. Guru Nānak uses the demons in Laṅka symbolically to represent the five evils: (1) ego, (2) attachment, (3) greed, (4) anger, and (5) lust.

39. Rām Chand, Rāvaṇ, Babhikhen (Vibhiṣāna in Sanskrit) are characters in the *Rāmayaṇ*. Rām Chand is the son of the benevolent king Daśrath (Daśratha in Sanskrit) of the Kauśalyā dynasty who had been sent to the forest for fourteen years. Rāvaṇ is the malevolent king of Laṅka who kidnaps Rām Chand's wife Sītā. Babhikhen is the brother of Rāvaṇ who, after being dismissed by Rāvaṇ for having adhered to the ethical principles (*dharam*) for ruling, crosses over from Laṅka to South India and advises Rām Chand and his army on how to attack Laṅka and its King Rāvaṇ.

40. Just as light reflected from the sun enlightens the moon, wisdom can illuminate the mind. An awakened mind enables a person to cool or calm all desires.

41. The fourth state is the awareness of the soul (*turiyā avasthā*). The other three are: the awakened state (*jāgrat*), the dream state (*supan*), and the deep-sleep state (*suṣuptī*).

42. The nine gates refer to the openings of the human body: two eyes, two ears, two nostrils, the mouth, the anus, and the urethra. The tenth gate transcends the five senses (hearing, seeing, tasting, touching, and speaking).

It is regarded as an intangible experience that connects the *gurmukh* with *EkOaṅkār*.

43. According to yogic terminology, "the distance of three and seven fingers" refers to the inner heart (*hṛda*) from the navel point.

44. The three central pathways (*nāḍīs*) of the subtle body are (1) *suṣumanā-nāḍī* (*sukhmanā* in Punjabi) which runs along the axis of the body from the base of the spine to the top of the head, (2) *iḍā-nāḍī*, which originates at the base of the spine and twists around the central pathway and crosses over each of the seven major *cakras* that results in a calming effect, and (3) *piṅgalā-nāḍī*, which also originates at the base of the spine twisting around the central pathway and crossing over each of the seven central *cakras* that results in arousal of desires. See, L. Silburn, *Kundalinī: Energy of the Depths* (Albany, NY: State University of New York Press, 1988).

45. The "navel lotus" refers to the *manipura-cakra* ("jewel-city wheel"), which corresponds to the solar plexus and the fire element, the sense of sight, the digestive tract and anus. This *cakra* is significant in yoga because it is believed that, in any type of meditation or chanting, one has to channel energy from the navel and move it upward along the channel of *cakras*. Georg Feuerstein, *Yoga: An Essential Introduction of the Principles and Practice of an Ancient Tradition* (Boston: Shambhala Publications, 1996), p. 123.

46. Breath is *prāṇ*, the life force energy.

47. "The human tomb made from egg and sperm" refers to the human body (*sarīr*).

48. Unlike the Kartārpur and Damdamā versions of the *Siddh Goṣṭ* composition, the *Goindvāl Pothī* form of the hymn contains only seventy-two stanzas. While the basic text and meaning has remained the same, "the last stanza [of *Siddh Goṣṭ*] must have been added by Guru Arjan himself." Pashaura Singh, *The Guru Granth Sahib: Canon, Meaning and Authority* (Delhi: Oxford University Press, 2000), p. 102.

# Glossary of Punjabi Terms

| | |
|---|---|
| ahaṅkār | ego or the sense of being separate from others; ahaṃkāra in Sanskrit |
| Akāl | the Eternal or timelessness; epithet for God |
| amṛt | *"nectar"; sacred water; amṛta in Sanskrit* |
| anahat-nād | "unstruck sound"; a yogic term for the eternal sound; anāhata-nad in Sanskrit |
| ānand | bliss; *ānanda* in Sanskrit |
| arth | wealth and prosperity; one of the householder goals in Hinduism; *artha* in Sanskrit |
| āsan | "posture"; yogic physical postures; āsana in Sanskrit |
| āśram | the four Hindu stages in life; *āśrama* in Sanskrit |
| ātma | self or eternal soul; *ātman* in Sanskrit |
| bāṇī | "speech, utterances"; word or hymn |
| bhagat | devotee; *bhakta* in Sanskrit |
| bhakti | devotion |
| bhakti-yoga | "path of devotion"; one of the three paths described in the *Bhagavad Gītā* |
| cakra | psychospiritual centers of energy; according to yogic tradition, there are seven *cakras* located on the central pathway (*suṣumanā-nāḍī*) of the subtle body |
| cit | consciousness; sentient beings; memory according to Sikh theology |
| darśan | visual appearance of God to the devotee; *darśana* in Sanskrit |

| | |
|---|---|
| dharam | duty or righteousness; the performance of right action according to the moral and ethical regulations of nature and society; one of the five spheres in Sikhism; *dharma* in Sanskrit |
| dhyān | attention or concentration; meditation; *dhyāna* in Sanskrit |
| dvija | "twice-born"; males belonging to the three higher Hindu classes |
| EkOaṅkār | "One Primordial Essence manifest in all"; one of the primary Sikh mantras |
| giān | knowledge; wisdom; one of the five spheres in Sikhism; *jñāna* in Sanskrit |
| giānī | "learned one"; religious teacher or Sikh scholar; *jñānin* in Sanskrit |
| goṣṭ | "discourse or dialogue"; an Indian literary form |
| garisatī | a householder; one in the second Hindu stages in life; *gṛhasthin* in Sanskrit |
| guṇ | attribute or quality; *guṇa* in Sanskrit |
| gurbāṇī | "words or utterances of Guru"; the hymns of the Sikh historical gurus |
| gurdwārā | "the door to the Guru"; Sikh temple |
| gurmat mārg | the path of the gurmukh or spiritual one |
| gurmukh | "one whose face [is turned to] the Guru"; follower of the will or teachings of the Guru |
| Gurmukhī | "from the mouth of the Guru"; the Punjabi script |
| Guru | Ultimate Reality, Divine Name in Sikhism |
| guru | elder in general; spiritual master; teacher; one of the lineage of ten gurus in Sikhism |
| *Gurū Granth Sāhib* | "Revered Guru Scripture"; Sikh scripture |
| hath-yoga | "forced" or "aggressive" physical exercise; one form of yoga that emphasizes breath control; *haṭha-yoga* in Sanskrit |
| hukam | "order or command"; the cosmic order emanating from *Ek Oaṅkār* in Sikhism |

| | |
|---|---|
| iḍā-nāḍī | one of the two pathways that twist around the *suṣumanā-nāḍī*; cooling or calming effect when immaterial bio-energy flows through it |
| janam-sākhī | "stories of life"; the hagiographical accounts of Guru Nānak |
| jīv | life; individual being; psyche according to Sikh theology; *jīva* in Sanskrit |
| jīvan-mukti | one who has escaped the cycle of rebirth while still alive; one who has attained immortality |
| jñāna-yoga | "path of knowledge"; one of the three paths outlined in the *Bhagavad Gītā* |
| jogī | one who practices yoga; *yogin* in Sanskrit or yogi in Hindi/English |
| kal yug | dark age; *kali yuga* in Sanskrit |
| kām | sensual pleasures or desires; one of the householder goals in Hinduism; *kāma* in Sanskrit |
| karam | action; merit and demerit; *karma* in Sanskrit |
| karam | grace (Persian); one of the five spheres in Sikhism |
| karma-yoga | "path of action"; one of the three paths outlined in the *Bhagavad Gītā* |
| kathā | "story"; religious discourse; the sermons given by *giānīs* |
| kīrtan | hymn singing; the singing of scripture or religious literature |
| kundalinī | psychospiritual energy that moves through the *cakras* and is regarded as *śakti* consciousness, which inevitably merges with Śiva |
| laṅgar | the community dining hall in a Sikh temple |
| līlā | play or sport; usually used to refer to God's creation |
| manmat mārg | the path of *manmukh* or the path of ego reasoning |
| manmukh | "one whose face [is turned to] the mind"; one who is turned away from the Guru and follows one's own desires |
| mantar | word or formula; sacred syllable; *mantra* in Sanskrit |

| | |
|---|---|
| māyā | illusion; the transient material world |
| mudrā | yogic practice of hand gesture |
| mukti | liberation from the cycle of rebirth; *mukti* or *mokṣa* in Sanskrit |
| mūl-mantar | "root-mantra"; *mūla-mantra* in Sanskrit |
| nād | sound current; *nāda* in Sanskrit |
| nāḍī | pathway; according to the Indian yogic tradition, there are 72,000 arteries or pathways of the subtle body |
| nām | "name"; Divine Name; in Sikhism it is means to, but more often the goal of, liberation; *nāma* in Sanskrit |
| Nāth | "master"; name of a siddha or yogic tradition founded by Gorakhnāth; also called Kānphaṭa or Darṣinī; Nātha in Sanskrit |
| Nirguṇ | without attributes, or formless, usually used to describe Ultimate Reality; *nirguṇa* in Sanskrit |
| Pañj Granthī | "booklet of five"; Sikh book of hymns |
| pañj khand | "five spheres"; there are five spheres of spiritual development described in Guru Nānak's "Jap-jī" (*dharam*, *giān*, *saram*, *karam*, and *sach*) |
| pāṭh | reading of the scripture |
| pauṛī | a stanza of a *vār* |
| piṅgalā-nāḍī | one of the two pathways that twist around the *suṣumanā-nadi*; arousing or activating effect, when immaterial bio-energy flows through it |
| prāṇ | breath; life-breath; that which is life-giving; *prāṇa* in Sanskrit |
| prāṇayam | breath control; breathing exercises; *prāṇayama* in Sanskrit |
| pūjā | worship offering |
| rāg | tune, music; *rāga* in Sanskrit |
| rāj-yoga | "royal way"; name for classical yoga; *rāja-yoga* in Sanskrit |
| śabad | "word," "sound," or scripture; Sacred Word of the historical gurus or Guru; in Sikhism the means to liberation; *śabda* in Sanskrit |

| | |
|---|---|
| sach | Truth; one of the five spheres in Sikhism; *satya* in Sanskrit |
| sādh saṅgat | the community or company of other *gurmukhs* |
| sahaj | a yogic term for the ultimate goal of union, during which one transcends all duality |
| śakti | creative energy; feminine principle |
| salok | a verse in anuṣṭubh meter; *śloka* in Sanskrit |
| samādhi | transcendental state |
| saṅiyāsī | renunciate; one who is in the last of the four Hindu stages in life; *saṃnyāsin* in Sanskrit |
| saṅgat | "community"; often used to describe a community of devotees, renunciates or monks; *saṃgha* in Sanskrit |
| saṅsār | cycle of birth, death and rebirth; illusory world; *saṃsāra* in Sanskrit |
| sant | holy person or saint. The Sant tradition (ca. fifteenth to seventeenth century CE) comprises a group of Hindi-speaking poet-saints in northern India (such as Rajasthan and the Punjab) who taught a more "radical" path to liberation in which the realization of a *nirguṇ* is to be attained through devotional meditation on the Divine Name. |
| saram | effort; one of the five spheres in Sikhism |
| sarguṇ | with attributes or form; usually used to describe Ultimate Reality; *saguṇa* in Sanskrit |
| sarīr | physical body; *śarīra* in Sanskrit |
| sat | true; pure; truth; *satya* in Sanskrit |
| sevā | selfless service for one's community, society or humanity |
| siddh | an ascetic; an accomplished one; *siddha* in Sanskrit |
| siddhi | supernatural or occult powers; attained with meditation or yoga |
| simraṇ | remembrance or recitation; in Sikhism it is a practice of reciting the Divine Name |
| sukhmanā-nāḍī | central pathway that runs from the base of the spine toward the head, in which the cakras are located; *suṣumanā-nāḍī* in Sanskrit |

| | |
|---|---|
| tantra | refers to the body of esoteric theory and practice viewed as heterodox and unsystematic; took shape ca. first century CE and flourished from the eighth century to the fourteenth century |
| tapas | "heat"; energy accumulated through practices of meditation |
| tīrath | pilgrimage place; *tīrtha* in Sanskrit |
| udāsī | one who renounces the material world; in Sikhism, also refers to Guru Nānak's four spiritual travels and hence means a prolonged absence from the home |
| vār | a narrative poem suitable for singing; found in Sikh scripture |
| varṇa | "color"; the four Hindu social divisions or classes (Brahmin, *kṣatriya*, *vaiśya*, and *śūdra*) |
| vichār | "thought, thinking"; religious discourse |
| yoga | "union" also refers to the "path, discipline, way"; path of mental and physical discipline; philosophical system formulated by Patañjali |

# Bibliography

## PRIMARY SOURCES


*Ādi Srī Gurū Granth Sāhib* (Sri Damdami Bir). Amritsar: Sri Gurmat Press, standard pagination.

*Bhagavadgītā*, F. Edgerton, trans. Cambridge, Mass.: Harvard University Press, 1944.

*Buddhist Mahāyāna Texts Part II*, Max Müller, ed. and trans. Delhi: Motilal Banarsidass, reprint [1849] 1968.

*Dhammapada*, John Ross Carter and Mahinda Palihawadana, trans. Oxford: Oxford University Press, 2000.

*Haṭha-yoga Pradīpikā*, Pancham Singh, trans. Reprint [1915]; New York: AMS, 1974.

*Jaina Sūtras*, Hermena Jacobi, trans. Oxford: Clarendon Press, 1884.

*Janam-sākhī Paramparā*. Kirpal Singh. Patiala 1969.

*Bījak of Kabir*, Linda Hess and Sukhdev Singh, trans. Delhi: Motilal Banarsidass, 1983.

*Manusmṛti*, M. N. Dutt, trans. Varanasi: Chowkhamba Press, 1979.

*Patañjali's Yoga Sūtras with the commentary of Vyāsa and the Gloss of Vācaspāti Miśra*, Rama Prasada, trans. Reprint [1912]; New York: AMS, 1974.

*Purātan Janam-sākhī*, Bhai Vir Singh, ed. Amritsar 1982.

*The Bhagavad Gītā*, W. H. Johnson, trans. Oxford: Oxford University Press, 1994.

*The Hymns of the Ṛg Veda, translated with a popular commentary*, J. L. Shastri, ed. Delhi: Motilal Banarsidass, 1973.

*The Middle Length Sayings (Majjhima-Nikāya)*, vol. 1: *The First 50 Discourses*, I. B. Horner, trans. London: Luzac and Company, 1948.

*Upaniṣat-Saṃgrahaḥ*, J. L. Shastri, ed. Delhi: Motilal Banarsidass, 1984.

*The Thirteen Principal Upanishads*. Robert Ernest Hume, trans. Reprinted; Delhi: Oxford University Press, 2nd ed., 1989.

*Vārāṅ Bhāī Gurdās: Text, Transliteration and Translation*, 2 vols., Jodh Singh, trans. New Delhi: Vision and Venture, 1998.


## SECONDARY SOURCES


Benard, Elizabeth Ann. *Chinnamastā: The Aweful Buddhist and Hindu Tantric Goddess*. Delhi: Motilal Banarsidass, 1994.

Bir, Raghbir Singh. *Bandgi Nama: Communion with the Divine*. Calcutta: Atam Science Trust, 1981.

Briggs, George Weston. *Gorakhnāth and the Kānphaṭa Yogīs*. Reprint [1938]; Delhi: Motilal Banarsidass, 2001.

Brooks, Douglas Renfrew. *The Secret of the Three Cities: An Introduction to Hindu Śākta Tantrism*. Chicago: University of Chicago Press, 1990.

Conze, Edward. *Buddhist Thought in India: Three Phases of Buddhist Philosophy*. Ann Arbor: University of Michigan Press, 1967.

Cort, John E. *Jains in the World: Religious Values and Ideology in India*. New York: Oxford University Press, 2001.

Danielou, Alain. *The Rāgas of Northern Indian Music*. London: Barrie and Rockliff, 1968.

Dasgupta, Surendranath. *History of Indian Philosophy*. Cambridge: Cambridge University Press, 1951.

———. *Yoga as Philosophy and Religion*. New York: Krishna Press, 1974.

Dharwadkar, Vinay. *Kabīr: The Weaver's Songs*. New Delhi: Penguin Books, 2003.

Dwivedi, Hazari Prasad. *Nātha Sampradāya*. Varanasi, 1966.

Dyczkowski, Mark S. G. *The Doctrine of Vibration: An Analysis of the Doctrines and Practices of Kashmir Śaivism*. Albany: State University of New York Press, 1987.

Eliade, Mircea. *Yoga: Immortality and Freedom* (Bollingen series 41). Princeton: Princeton University Press, 1969.

Fenech, Louis E. *Martyrdom on the Sikh Tradition: Playing the 'Game of Love.'* Delhi: Oxford University Press, 2000.

Feuerstein, Georg. *Yoga: An Essential Introduction of the Principles and Practice of an Ancient Tradition*. Boston: Shambhala Publications, 1996.

Goudriaan, Tuen. "Introduction, History, and Philosophy," in *Hindu Tantrism*. Leiden: E. J. Brill, 1979.

Grewal, D. S. *Guru Nanak's Travel to Himalayan and East Asian Region, A New Light*. Delhi: National Book Shop, 1995.

Grewal, J. S. *Sikhs of the Punjab*. Cambridge: Cambridge University Press, 1991.

———. *Contesting Interpretations of the Sikh Tradition*. Delhi: Manohar, 1998.

Halbfass, Wilhelm. *Tradition and Reflection: Exploration in Indian Thought*. Albany: State University of New York Press, 1991.

Hardy, Friedhelm. *Viraha-Bhakti: The Early History of Kṛṣṇa Devotion in South India*. Delhi: Oxford University Press, 1983.

Hawley, John Stratton and Mark Juergensmeyer, *Songs of the Saints of India*. New York: Oxford University Press, 1988.

Iyenger, B. K. S. *The Tree of Yoga*. Boston: Shambhala Publications, 1989.

Klostermaier, Klaus. *A Survey of Hinduism*. Albany: State University of New York Press, 1989.

Kohli, Surindar Singh. *The Sikh Philosophy*. Amritsar: Singh Brothers, 1992.

———. *Yoga of the Sikhs*. Amritsar: Singh Brothers, 1991.

———. *Sikh Ethics*. New Delhi: Munshiram Manoharlal Publishers, 1994.

Laidlaw, James. *Riches and Renunciation: Religion, Economy and Society Among the Jains*. Oxford: Clarendon Press, 1995.

Lopez Jr., Donald, ed. *Religions of India in Practice*. Princeton: Princeton University Press, 1995.

Macauliffe, Max Arthur. *The Sikh Religion: Its Gurus, Sacred Writings and Authors*, 6 vols. in 3 books. Reprint [1909]; Delhi: DK Publishers, 1998.

Mann, Gurinder Singh. *The Making of Sikh Scripture*. New York: Oxford University Press, 2001.

McLeod, W. H. *Sikhs of the Khalsa: A History of the Rahit Maryada*. New Delhi: Oxford University Press, 2003.

———. *Exploring Sikhism: Aspects of Sikh Identity, Culture and Thought*. Delhi: Oxford University Press, 2000.

———. *Gurū Nānak and the Sikh Religion*. Delhi: Oxford University Press, 1976.

———. *The Evolution of the Sikh Community*. New Delhi: Oxford University Press, 1975.

——— and Karine Schomer, eds. *The Sants: Studies in the Devotional Tradition of India*. Delhi: Motilal Banarsidass, 1987.

———. *The B40 Janam Sākhī*. Amritsar: Guru Nanak Dev University, 1980.

Merry, Karen L. "The Hindu Festival Calendar," in *Religious Festivals in South India and Sri Lanka*. Edited by Guy R. Welbon and Glenn E. Yocum. New Delhi: Manohar Publishers, 1982.

Müller, F. Max. *The Hymns of the Rig Veda in the Saṃhitā and Pada Texts*. London: Trubner, 1877.

Nand, Parma. "Ek Oṅkār," in *Sikh Concept of the Divine*. Edited by Pritam Singh. Amritsar: Guru Nanak Dev University Press, 1985.

Nayar, Kamala Elizabeth. *Hayagrīva in South India: Complexity and Selectivity of a Pan-Indian Hindu Deity*. Leiden: Brill, 2004.

———. *The Sikh Diaspora in Vancouver: Three Generations amid Tradition, Modernity and Multiculturalism*. Toronto: University of Toronto Press, 2004.

Nayar, Nancy Ann. *Poetry as Theology: The Śrīvaiṣṇava Stotra in the Age of Rāmānuja*. Wiesbaden: Otto Harrassowitz, 1992.

Oberoi, Harjot S. *The Construction of Religious Boundaries: Culture, Identity, and Diversity in the Sikh Tradition*. Chicago: University of Chicago Press, 1994.

O'Flaherty, Wendy (Doniger). *Śiva: The Erotic Ascetic*. London: Oxford University Press, 1973.

Oliville, Patrick. *The Early Upaniṣads: Annotated Text and Translation*. New York: Oxford University Press, 1998.

Osho. *The True Name*. New Delhi: New Age International, 1994.

Pillai, M. P. Christanand. "Comparative Study of Monotheism in *Mūl Mantra* and the Bible." In *The Sikh Concept of the Divine*, Pritam Singh, ed. Amritsar: Guru Nanak Dev University, 1985.

Renou, Louis. *Le Déstin du Veda dans l'Inde*. Paris: Adrien Maisouneuve, 1960.

Sandhu, Jaswinder Singh. "The Sikh Model of the Person, Suffering, and Healing: Implications for Counselors," *International Journal for the Advancement of Counselling* 26, no. 1 (2004): 33-46.

———."Existential Themes in Eastern Spirituality: A Thematic Analysis of the Sikh Spiritual Tradition." In *Alternative Approaches to Counseling and Psychotherapy*, D. Sandhu, ed. New York: Nova Science Publishers, in press.

Silburn, L. *Kundalinī: Energy of the Depths*. Albany: State University of New York Press, 1988.

Singh, Daljeet. *The Sikh Ideology*. Amritsar: Singh Brothers, 1990.

Singh, Dharam. *Sikh Theology of Liberation*. New Delhi: Harman Publishing House, 1991.

Singh, Harbans, chief ed. *The Encyclopedia of Sikhism*, vols. 1-4. Patiala: Punjabi University, 1998.

Singh, Jodh. *The Religious Philosophy of Gurū Nānak: A Comparative Study with a Special Reference to Siddha Goṣṭi*. Varanasi: Sikh Philosophy Society, 1983.

Singh, Nirbhai. *Philosophy of Sikhism*. New Delhi: Atlantic Publishers, 1990.

Singh, Pashaura. *The Guru Granth Sahib: Canon, Meaning and Authority*. Delhi: Oxford University Press, 2000.

Singh, Pritam (ed.). *Sikh Concept of the Divine*. Amritsar: Guru Nanak Dev University Press, 1985.

Singh, Ranbir. *Glimpses of the Divine Masters*. New Delhi: International Traders Corporation, 1965.

Singh, Sahib. *Srī Gurū Granth Sāhib Darpaṇ*, 10 vols. Jalandhar: Raj Publishers, 1962–1964.

Singh, Santokh. *Fundamentals of Sikhism*. Princeton, Ontario: Institute of Spiritual Studies, 1994.

Singh, Sher. *Philosophy of Sikhism*. Jalandhar: Sterling Publishers, 1964.

Smith, Brian K. *Reflections on Resemblance, Ritual and Religion*. New York: Oxford University Press, 1989.

Sontheimer, Günther D. and Hermann Kulke, eds. *Hinduism Reconsidered*. New Delhi: Manohar Publishers, 1989.

White, David Gordon. *The Alchemical Body: Siddh Traditions in Medieval India*. Chicago: University of Chicago Press, 1996.

## OTHER SOURCES

Gurbachan Singh Khalsa Bhindranwale. Audiotape. No title. No date.

Giani Sant Singh Maskeen. Lecture on audiotape. Vancouver, BC: Khalsa Diwan Society, 1994.

———. Interview with authors. Surrey, BC, 22 January 2003.

Giani Kishan Singh Parwana. *Gurdwārā* lecture. Toronto: Sri Guru Singh Sabha, 1991.

# Index

ALSO IN SPEAKING TIGER

# INVOCATIONS AND PRAYERS of Khwaja Abdullah Ansari of Herat

*Translated by*

Sardar Sir Jogendra Singh *and* Arthur John Arberry

*Introduction by* Syeda Saiyidain Hameed

Khwaja Abdullah Ansari—Pir-i-Herat, or 'Sage of Herat'—who lived in the eleventh century, is revered as one of the world's great and earliest Sufis. He turned to tasawwuf (Islamic mysticism) at a very young age, and came to be regarded as an extraordinary teacher and mystic, and an authority on Islam. Thousands were drawn to him and became his followers, and to this day his poetry and prose—collected in Persian and Arabic texts that are widely regarded as masterpieces—inspire and instruct scholars, seekers and the pious faithful alike. Abdullah Ansari's tomb in Herat, in modern-day Afghanistan—a country ravaged in recent decades by discord and violence—remains a place of pilgrimage and peace for millions. In that beautiful sanctuary and elsewhere—including Panipat in India, where his descendants settled in the thirteenth century—his legacy and teachings continue to give solace to humanity, guiding us towards humility and compassion.

This compilation of Abdullah Ansari's invocations, prayers and counsels, selected from translations by two celebrated scholars, is a book of wisdom for all times. It is of particular relevance today, over a millennium after these words were spoken and recorded. As Syeda Hameed writes in her introduction, for our highly troubled and deeply hurt world, this is the healing hand of a wise Sufi Pir. It is a text for the ages.